# Turkey Today

# Turkey Today

*A Nation Divided
over Islam's Revival*

## MARVINE HOWE

**Westview Press**
A Member of the Perseus Books Group

*Some material in chapter seven first appeared in:* "As General's Seek Military Solution, Kurdish Problem Poisons Turkish Life," *Washington Report on Middle East Affairs,* October 1996, pp. 8, 107–108.

*Some material in chapter nine first appeared in:* "Turkey's Dilemma: What's on Women's Heads," *Ms. Magazine,* April/March 1999, pp. 14–20.

Published in 2000 in the United States of America by Westview Press, 5500 Central Avenue, Boulder, Colorado 80301-2877, and in the United Kingdom by Westview Press, 12 Hid's Copse Road, Cumnor Hill, Oxford OX2 9JJ

Find us on the World Wide Web at www.westviewpress.com

Library of Congress Cataloging-in-Publication Data
Howe, Marvine.
    Turkey today : a nation divided over Islam's revival/Marvine Howe.
        p.  cm.
    Includes bibliographical references and index.
    ISBN 0-8133-3764-x (hc)
    1. Islam and secularism—Turkey.   2. Islam and state—Turkey.   I. Title

BP190.5.S35 H69   2000
322'.1'09561—dc21

00-024978

The paper used in this publication meets the requirements of the American National Standard for Permanence of Paper for Printed Library Materials Z39.48-1984.

10   9   8   7   6   5   4   3   2   1

*For Mary West*
*who has cheered, coddled,*
*criticized when needed . . .*

# Contents

# Illustrations

# *Preface*

Rarely is anyone indifferent about Turks and Turkey.

There are those who hate the country and its people out of hand. They are often ethnic Greeks or Armenians held hostage to their view of historical events. Or they are persons who have never visited Turkey but have been indelibly impressed by stereotypes of the *ferocious Turk*, starting with Attila the Hun and Tamerlane and culminating with the *tortionnaires* of the film *Midnight Express*.

Generally those foreign diplomats, students and scholars, businesspersons, journalists, and ordinary tourists who have traveled around the country and gotten to know present-day Turks fall in love with the place and its inhabitants. I am admittedly in the second category. For this reason, I am concerned about the divisions that are tearing the country apart.

Turkey today is nothing like it was in 1979, when I was first sent there to open the Ankara bureau for the *New York Times*. I had come from years of working in the Arab world and was surprised at the extent that Turkey had turned its back on the Middle East and placed its sights on Europe and the United States. At that time, the country was engulfed in violence, instigated by a minority of left-wing and right-wing extremists. When the military intervened in September 1980, many Turks breathed a sigh of relief, although their democratic freedoms were drastically curtailed and have not been fully restored even now.

After a long absence, I returned to Turkey in 1995 to see old friends— and have gone back every year since for lengthy visits. I was astonished at the transformations. The economy had blossomed, with new industries, highways, offices, and high-rise apartments everywhere and consumerism (and inflation) soaring. A vigorous press, radio, and television had multiplied and seemed to know no bounds. There'd been an explosion in education, with new universities opening all over. Democratic political life was in full swing, and new nongovernmental organizations flourished. The long-simmering Kurdish problem had become a costly but seemingly contained insurgency.

The most spectacular development was the Islamic revival. The Islamist-led party, which had not been taken seriously in the past, suddenly emerged as the main force in local elections, even winning in the capital, Ankara, and the economic center, İstanbul. Devout Muslim men in beards and cloaks and women wearing headscarves and *chadors* appeared even in the most fashionable neighborhoods. Islamic publications and all sorts of Islamic cultural and professional organizations, including an Islamic human rights group, proliferated. It seemed as though they were setting up a whole new parallel society.

Only when the Islamists came in first in national elections at the end of 1995 did secularists perceive an "Islamic threat." Under Islamist prime minister Necmettin Erbakan's coalition government, Turkish society appeared dangerously split, with the generals heading the opposition.

This book is first of all an attempt to understand the role of Islam in Turkey, three-quarters of a century after Atatürk's Western, secular revolution. Likewise, I have tried to depict the secular society and its concerns. There is also a look at the Kurdish drama and its impact on the life of the country. In the end, I hope to present an accurate picture of Turkish democracy, its strengths and weaknesses.

My aim is to give the general reader a better idea as to who Turks are and where they're going. At the same time, I hope to get policymakers to listen to the broad spectrum of Turkish opinion presented here.

This is my personal album of some of the interesting people I have met in Turkey over the years—of course there are many more. Although I am not always in agreement with what they have to say, I have tried to represent their opinions fairly. This is an extended reportage about today's Turkey for readers who want to know more about this strategic country than the usual sound-bites on violence. It is an attempt to understand the resurgence of Islam in a country that for more than three-quarters of a century has been fixated with Western civilization.

Always, I have kept in mind that Turks are very much like the French; they will complain about corruption in public life, abuses by state security forces, threats to democracy. But it's not the business of a foreigner to criticize. The voices here are mainly Turkish. And just maybe this book will help Turks listen to one another in this divided society.

*Marvine Howe*

# Acknowledgments

In these pages, I have named many of the people who have helped me on my journey through the maze of contemporary Turkey. Many others necessarily remain anonymous.

Here I make special mention of those colleagues, academics, diplomats, and friends whose insights have been particularly valuable over the years. The short list includes: Emel Anil, Sirma Evcan, Metin Munir, Mehmet Ali Kışlalı, İlnur Çevik, Sedat Ergin, Özgen Acar, Fehmi Koru, James Wilde, Dr. Nilüfer Narlı, Dr. Feride Acar, Nur Mardin, Ceylan Orhun, Aişe Zadil, Serpil Gogen, Gülter Kolankaya, Jale Ersoy, İnci and Fatih Pirinçcioğlu, Professor Talat Halman, the late Professor Ahmet Taner Kışlalı, Korkut Özal, Ambassador Ahmet Banguoğlu and Nilgün Banguoğlu, Counsellor Metin Kiliç, former American ambassadors to Turkey Ronald Spiers, Morton Abramowitz, and Marc Grossman and embassy officials Robert Pistana, Helena Kane Finn, and Mary Ann Whitten, the American Research Institute in Turkey's İstanbul Branch director Dr. Antony Greenwood and Ankara Branch director Dr. Toni Cross and her husband İhsan Çetin. And my particular appreciation of Stephen Kinzer, İstanbul bureau chief of the *New York Times,* for his informed, lively, and prolific coverage of Turkey at the close of the twentieth century.

Also many thanks to the *News-Gazette* and Mountain Copy Graphics of Lexington, Virginia, and Ali Burçak Soydan, Turkish student at Washington and Lee University, for their technical help. Finally, a word of gratitude to my editor, Jennifer Chen, for her interest and patience.

*M.H.*

# A Brief Guide to Turkish Pronunciation

Thanks to Atatürk's Language Reform, Turkish letters sound the way they look for the most part. It's a phonetic language, pronounced the way it is written.

Keep in mind the following exceptions:

â like a in car
c like j in January
ç like ch in cheer
e like e in hen
g like g in God
ğ like g in sleigh
ı like i in edible
İ like i in hit
j like z in azure
ö like oe in Goethe
ş like sh of shore
û like oo of cool
ü like eau in beauty

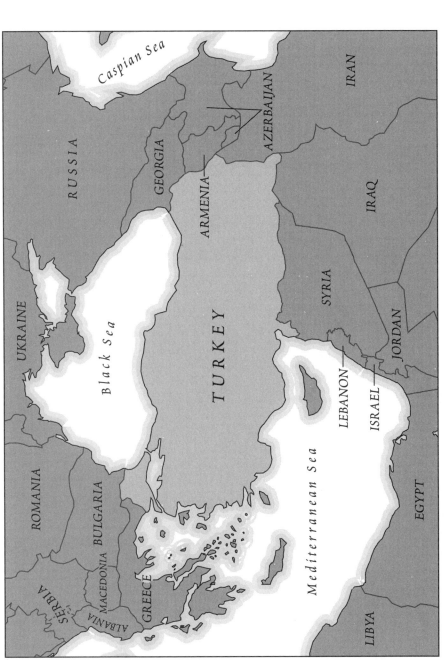

Turkey

# 1 ~

---

## Between Two Worlds

---

Every time I approach The City, a current of excitement flows through me, as if I were being drawn into the pages of history still in the making. From the dark restive waters of the Bosphorus, I feel a raw vibrancy on both sides of the strait linking Europe and Asia. As soon as I step ashore, I am enveloped by a magnetic energy—they say İstanbul is built on quartz. This force, along with its unique geography, has made İstanbul the capital of two great empires and one of the most strategic centers in the world.

In many ways, İstanbul—which comes from the Greek phrase "to the City"—has not changed since I lived in Turkey in the late 1970s and early 1980s. That unforgettable profile of towers and domes and minarets still casts a magical spell. The Golden Horn still turns to gold in a certain light. And you can still lose all sense of time and place in the endless labyrinth of the old quarters. Even now the city exudes that special air of exotic mystery, shabby grandeur, and raucous marketplace.

But wooded hills along the Bosphorus and surrounding fields have been consumed by concrete. Hastily built squatter settlements called *gecekondu* (literally "built overnight" in Turkish) have solidified and been transformed into stark, overcrowded neighborhoods. Ultramodern shopping malls, hotels, gourmet restaurants, and fitness centers have multiplied in a pell-mell race with a profusion of new mosques and religious schools.

The main difference is the Turks. İstanbul is still a great multicultural meeting place but is increasingly divided into two worlds. This is not a classic schism between East and West, rich and poor, or traditional and progressive. It is not even the kind of religious factionalism that wracks other countries, because about 98 percent of Turkey's 65 million inhabitants are Muslim. More and more evident is the great divide between two

*Timeless İstanbul; view from the Golden Horn with Topkapı Palace in the background and the busy Bosphorus Strait traffic between Europe and Asia.*

concepts of life: a secular lifestyle with its inherent freedoms and insecurities and a religious way with its certainties and strict controls.

This polarization is especially noticeable among women. More active women have appeared in public life in business, the arts, academia, and even politics, including a political novice with an engaging smile who became the country's first woman prime minister. At the same time, an increasing number of young girls and women have taken refuge behind headscarves, long raincoats, even black shrouds, and view woman's role essentially as wife, mother, and homemaker.

In fact, the duality in Turkish society has existed since Mustafa Kemal Atatürk laid the foundations of a modern secular republic three-quarters of a century ago. The early years of the Republic were shaken by violent uprisings of religious leaders and stern repression by the secular state. After World War II, the authoritarian regime relaxed and gave way to a more democratic, multiparty system. The new breed of politicians remained true to Atatürk's project of Westernization but was more tolerant of Islamic practices and actually courted the Islamic vote.

When I first arrived on the scene, Turkey's problems were essentially political, not religious. Society seemed to have achieved a manageable modus vivendi on the religion issue, with the dichotomy defined largely as an urban-rural matter. The urban elite generally held that, with the spread of education and material well-being, the religious-minded countryside would be gradually won over to the ideal of secularism. The hinterland had very little to say about this, or at least the cities didn't listen.

But by the mid-1980s, the countryside was moving massively to the cities. An active Islamic community appeared, citizens still imbued with strong spiritual values and religious traditions, who had not been absorbed by the long period of secular rule.

İstanbul, with its foothold in Europe and promise of jobs, became the main destination for the rural rush, the population doubling in two decades to around 12 million. This is a microcosm of Turkish society where the contest between two vastly different models of Islamic life is being played out.

No new walls have been put up to demarcate the two sides. In fact, the geographics are increasingly blurred. The old city around the awe-inspiring mosques of Sultanahmet, Süleymaniye, Fatih, and Eyüp is still a magnet for the faithful and the center for Islamic demonstrations. But in recent years, large numbers of tourists have eroded the religious atmosphere of the area.

Across town, Istiklâl Boulevard, once the cosmopolitan heart of the city with its churches, theaters, and boutiques, has become the favorite promenade of traditionally clad families. Even Bağdat Boulevard, İstanbul's smartest and fastest-developing neighborhood on the Asian side of the Bosphorus, has begun to attract veiled shoppers, keen to discover the latest line of underwear at Marks and Spencer.

There are to be sure glaring economy-based divisions that have always existed: sumptuous palaces and mansions along the Bosphorus inhabited mainly by the secular elite and the *gecekondu* ringing the city and teeming with traditional migrants. The difference is that more luxury villas are being built in the equivalent of gated communities. Likewise, the squatter settlements are expanding and now look to Islamic organizations for help rather than to left-wing groups as they used to do.

These two worlds are juxtaposed in striking fashion near the Bay of Beykoz, on the Asian side of the Bosphorus. On a wooded hill overlooking the bay, an exclusive new development has been built around a former sultan's hunting lodge. Flowering California-style, million-dollar villas provide the last word in comfort, secluded privacy, and spectacular views of İstanbul across the way.

Sprawling over neighboring hills, Sultanbeyli is a grim treeless settlement whose streets are named for heroes like Iran's Khomeini and Rafsanjani. The most prominent buildings are the mosque, a huge *İmam Hatip* (religious secondary school), and a Koranic school, surrounded by barbed wire and looking like a concentration camp. Few men are visible during the day. Women can be seen getting water from the public fountain or sitting along the muddy streets, crocheting and minding young children. In the main square stands a gilt statue of Atatürk, which the settlement tried unsuccessfully to reject. The people of Sultanbeyli (population 300,000 and growing) used to vote Socialist but now vote heavily for the pro-Islamic party.

The deepest divisions run along invisible lines. The secular establishment—most big businesses, banking and tourism, academia, much of the media and the arts, traditional political parties, and new civic groups, with the protective guidance of the armed forces—has unswervingly pursued the Western-oriented project set down by Atatürk. But in the 1990s, this entrenched elite has been rocked by the Islamists' sudden rise to the halls of power. Hard-core secularists, led by the military, are convinced that Islamists have been plotting to restore a Muslim theocratic state and must be stopped. Even the most enlightened circles are troubled that a significant part of the population does not think the way they do and have begun to question the Islamist agenda.

On the other side of the ideological chasm, Islamic groups are staking out a position for themselves. Little by little, Islamists are in the process of creating what amounts to a parallel society. Leading this movement are Islamist politicians who, after their brief stint in government, are still an important force in Parliament and have carved out spheres of influence in over 600 municipalities around the country, including Ankara and İstanbul. The Islamic network includes professional and business associations, women's organizations, academic groups, Muslim human rights associations, cultural societies, two television channels, and a flock of periodicals. The common complaint was that Islamic concerns were not given a fair hearing by secular counterparts, and so the Islamic movement decided to do its own thing.

As I moved around these circles, I looked for markers to indicate where this pivotal country is headed. Is violent struggle inevitable between defenders of the secular state and militant believers? Or will one side simply subdue the other, as we have seen since the days of Atatürk?

Or is it just possible that through a dynamic dialogue, some kind of accommodation can be reached and Turkey can become the first true Muslim democracy?

Turkey's Islamic society is hardly monolithic, ranging from mystics who oppose involvement in politics to politicians determined to restore *Sharia* (Islamic law), by violence if necessary. The Islamist-led Refah (Welfare) Party, which was recently banned and has regrouped its forces, often speaks with contradictory voices. Some radical politicians regularly denounce secular oppressors and Western policies in Bosnia and the Middle East and tend to blame the United States and Israel for all Turkey's woes. Others from the same political family sound like Pat Robertson Republicans with reassuring talk of tolerance and family values.

Mehmet Ali Şahin (SHAH-in), Refah's former leader in İstanbul and now a parliamentarian, is of the latter breed. We met at Refah's İstanbul headquarters in the working-class Topkapı district (not to be confused with the Ottoman palace of the same name), which looked like an exclusive men's club with wall-to-wall carpeting, comfortable leather chairs, potted plants, and not a woman—not even secretaries—in sight.[1]

Wearing smart rimless glasses, a sporty houndstooth jacket, striped shirt, and flowery tie, Şahin apologized for not speaking English. He is a graduate of the University of Theology and a teacher of theology; his wife teaches French and Arabic, and they speak Arabic at home.

Firmly denying allegations that Refah received major support from Iran and Saudi Arabia, he said most funds came from party members (limited to the equivalent of about $1,200 a year), including Turkish workers in Germany, and from religious and social foundations. Under Turkish law, he stressed, political parties cannot receive foreign aid.

What were the Islamist party's long-term aims? I asked. If it came to power on its own, without the constraints of a coalition, would it seek to impose *Sharia?* (The Islamic code regulates everything from hairstyle and dress to divorce and polygamy, providing brutal punishment for crimes of adultery and theft and death for apostasy.)

Şahin said it was necessary first of all to change the constitution to eliminate the ban on religious parties: "Going into the twenty-first century, nobody can block beliefs and ideas," he insisted. Without mentioning *Sharia*, he indicated that his party would seek to do away with the Swiss legal code, adopted by Atatürk in 1926. "We defend our local views and believe we should make our own laws, according to our own circumstances and way of life; why go to Switzerland?"

Emphasizing that Refah was an inclusive and tolerant party, Şahin pointed out that on taking office, Refah's mayors visited churches and synagogues as well as mosques to say: "I am your mayor." He added that Refah's mayor of İstanbul's Beyoğlu district even won the endorsement of the American consulate general, which canceled its decision to move to the suburb of Sarıyer because Beyoğlu's streets are so much cleaner now and the area looks so much better. His account was later confirmed by the U.S. consulate general.

Islamists tend to form a closed society and are not yet skilled in public relations. They were astonished that I wanted to meet an Islamist family outside the political leadership. Friends suggested Abdurrahman Dilipak, a prominent Islamic writer, television debater, and businessman. When I called for an appointment, I was told to contact "the copyright agency." Tuğba Albayrak, who heads Telif Hakları Ajansı Proje Danışmanlığı (Copyright Agency Project Association, or TEHA), offered to introduce me to Islamic writers, teachers, actresses, and businesspeople, for a price.

"Our members' time is valuable and they are so much in demand by television and the press; this way they can be paid for their time," she explained. I objected that this was not the way American journalists worked but agreed to pay an exorbitant "interpreter's fee" for an interview with Dilipak.

The Dilipaks live across the street from a new mosque (he is a member of the board) in a middle-class community of four- and five-story buildings in the Kadıköy district on the Asian side of the city. A gaunt man in his mid-forties with a trim Islamic beard, Dilipak greeted me affably but did not extend his hand. Later he confessed proudly he has been married twenty years and "never touched another woman."[2] In fact, his wife handles the makeup for his frequent television appearances so that he will not be sullied by the hands of another woman. Besides TV, he writes regularly for two magazines and two newspapers and is author of forty-three books (in Turkish), including: *Terrorism, Islamic Fighters, A Child in Palestine, The Gulf War, Kemalism from a Different Angle,* and *Secularism.* He is actively involved in sixteen businesses, including TEHA, and belongs to the Independent Industrialists and Businessmen's Association (Müstakil Sanayici ve İşadamları Derneği, or MÜSİAD).

His wife, Ayşe, wearing a blue jean jacket, a floral headscarf, and a long black skirt, was introduced as the head of a university students' association, but remained quietly in the background with her two-year-old child.

Ali Osman, their nineteen-year-old son, said he is studying English, has some non-Muslim friends, enjoys Beethoven and Mozart, and hopes to be a writer "just like my father." His brother Ahmet Taha, age thirteen, is studying German, and their sister, Fatima Zehra, eleven, is working on French and Arabic.

For Dilipak, the most important change in Turkey in the past decade is "the river coming back to its own bed," his description of the Islamic revival. He attributes this phenomenon to certain "environmental factors," new national structures in the wake of World War II, the Iranian revolution, the anti-Soviet movement culminating in the Afghan War, the American defeat in Lebanon, and Islam's loss of its holy places in Jerusalem.

"The Islamic movement in Turkey has strong historical references; unfortunately we have been separated from our own culture," Dilipak said. For the past seventy years, he continued, Turks have learned about Western culture, specifically American. Turkish intellectuals have had contacts with all the neighboring communist movements and their cultures. European classics have been translated into Turkish. But Turks don't know their own classics. Stressing that he does not reject Western civilization per se, he said he is "selective." He likes American computer programs (I saw an IBM Notebook and a Mackintosh Desktop in his office) but prefers alternative medicine to Western therapy.

Dilipak surprised me with a bitter indictment of the popular *İmam Hatip* or religious schools, of which he was a graduate. Calling them "prisons," he said it is not the business of government to teach Islam, and these government-controlled schools should be closed.

He made it clear that he favors changing the constitution to allow the establishment of Islamic law. "Yes, of course I want *Sharia*," he said, adding that there were seven court cases against him for saying just that.

What about Turkish women? I asked. Would they voluntarily give up their rights and retire to a life of seclusion under *Sharia*? Would they accept the Koranic precept that a good wife must be obedient to her husband?

"Islamic women can work and study—in fact all the elementary teachers are women," Dilipak retorted. Then distancing himself from strict Islamic regimes like Saudi Arabia where women are jailed for driving automobiles, he said his own wife drives the car because he doesn't have a license.

"My wife can motivate my acts. We are not enemies. We try to understand each other." Under *Sharia*, he claimed, there would be no pressure on women. They would be free to choose their lifestyle. He specified that any Turks who did not want to live by Islamic rules would have their rights. It would be like the old Ottoman system of *millets* or nation-states, where Jews and Christians lived by their own codes.

When I suggested that this was not so in the Iranian or Sudanese theocracies, the soft-voiced Dilipak exploded in a diatribe against the United States and the Western press: "Why do American journalists only talk about Sudan! Why not ask about Bosnia, Chechnya, Ngorno Karabagh!"

This was obviously the end of the meeting, but I pressed on. Was he afraid of a military intervention if the Islamists won the next elections? Could Algeria happen here?

His response had an ominous ring: "We don't want the Algerian situation here. If the military act, we are waiting."

The lay society is just as divided in its response to the Islamist challenge. Some open-minded circles in business, banking, and the media suggest that the trouble lies with flaws in Turkish democracy and have called for a more democratic constitution with guarantees of freedom of religion, thought, and expression. A leading journalist, Nuri Çolakoğlu, who heads NTV (Turkey's CNN), criticizes the secular parties for failing to come up with a credible leader and an alternative agenda to the Islamists. He and others hold that the main cause behind the growth of Islamism is the wide disparity in the distribution of wealth.

Historian Binnaz Toprak equates the Islamic surge with the rise of the Moral Majority in the Reagan years. After the 1980 coup, she notes, the Turkish military tried to get rid of politics and create a new sense of community, based on "family, barracks and mosque."[3] Over high tea in a friend's home, Professor Toprak listed other factors behind the return to Islam: the painful shift to a free market economy, support prices withdrawn from agriculture, rapid urbanization, and the collapse of the left. In her opinion, Refah was "a party of the system" with hardworking, committed members and a populist message for a Just Order. But she acknowledges that many people feel threatened in the belief that the Islamists will seek to impose another way of life.

Dr. Turkan Saylan,[4] who was born in 1935, says proudly she belongs to "the Republican Generation," that is, born with equal rights and all the free social and educational facilities established by Atatürk. She firmly believes the Republican regime is under attack by antisecularists and must be protected.

I first met Dr. Saylan at İstanbul's Leprosy Hospital, where she spends three days a week on the rehabilitation of lepers and the treatment of people with other skin diseases. The rest of her time is divided between her work as professor of dermatology at İstanbul University Hospital and as president of the Association in Support of Contemporary Living (ÇYDD).

Dr. Saylan and a group of friends founded ÇYDD (pronounced CHID) in 1989 to defend Atatürk's principles, Republican laws, modern education, and human rights against Islamic extremists. She had traveled all over Turkey to study the leprosy situation and at the same time had noted the rise of the Islamist movement.

There had been problems with an Islamic backlash from the beginning of the Republic, said Dr. Saylan. After the *medrese*—Islamic schools—were closed in 1934, Islamists went underground and formed a counterrevolutionary movement. When multiparty democracy was introduced in 1950, Islamists surfaced and openly attacked the system. They would tell poor people they were poor because they didn't pray or their womenfolk wore short skirts, which made God angry. Politicians used religion to get votes.

Dr. Saylan, who appears much younger than her age, with short-cropped red hair, interrupted our conversation from time to time to receive patients. With no sign of embarrassment, a young woman lifted a voluminous veil to show the doctor skin problems on her upper arms. Another woman in a headscarf pulled down the pants of her teenage son to reveal the rash on his leg.

Resuming her story, Dr. Saylan said ironically it was the Americans, with their Green Belt theory of Islam as an effective arm against communism, who were largely responsible for the major boost given to the Islamist movement in the 1980s. Turkey's generals were so afraid of communism that they made religion compulsory in public schools and substantially increased the number of *İmam Hatip* schools. The last straw was admitting *İmam Hatip* graduates into universities.

Many *İmam Hatip* graduates came to medicine, and the difference in their education was obvious, Dr. Saylan stressed. The Islamic students learned dogma but forgot science. Men were taught that to touch a woman was a sin. Women insisted on wearing veils because they had been told their hair would turn to snakes if it showed.

Striking a theme common among secularists, Dr. Saylan asserted that Islamists wanted to brainwash young people, turn them into obedient herds. That's why they were so opposed to the new law for eight years' compulsory education in state schools. It was ÇYDD that had started the campaign for eight years' public schooling and got the Higher Education Council to approve the ruling.

"There is no doubt that the Islamists want to go backward, that they want to return to *Sharia*," she insisted. "This would be negating a whole line of reform, which began with the Tanzimat (period of Westernization in the mid-nineteenth century) and continued through Atatürk until today. We're not going to let them weaken the system."

As I made my rounds of the secular world, I found women much more alarmed than men over the Islamic specter. These are the educated, emancipated women, the disciples of Atatürk who cannot forget the Islamic revolution in neighboring Iran. Women like my friend Yasemin Pirinçcioğlu, who watched with bewildered fascination the disintegration of the worldly, progressive society under the Shah, so like her own. A Muslim, Yasemin leads a thoroughly Western life. She was taught Muslim prayers by her grandmother and introduced to the Bible, the Koran, and the Talmud by her mother. Sophisticated in manner and dress, Yasemin is mother of two teenagers, used to run her own catering business, and now manages the family V.I.P. travel agency. Her pleasures are the latest art exhibits at the new galleries, fashion and interior decoration shows at the luxury hotels, moonlight cruises on the Bosphorus, and concerts and opera galas at the Atatürk Cultural Center with the kind of audience you'd see in New York, London, or Paris.

Yasemin is troubled by the proliferation of veiled women in public buildings, parks, and along the streets of what was once the European part of town. She is even more concerned about the growing number of fully covered girls going to religious schools.

"Some of them are only seven years old and won't ever get the chance to have a broader vision of life," Yasemin remarked over coffee in her secluded home in the woods of Tarabya, one of the rare green suburbs of İstanbul.[5] She then told me stories of Islamic cults preying on young people and vast sums of money spent to recruit Islamic activists.

"I can cohabit with Islamists but will they respect my rights?" Yasemin asked, voicing a concern heard more and more in the scintillating salons of İstanbul.

It is this divided universe, so different from the Turkey I used to know, that I now set out to explore. In these pages, I have chronicled my journey to better understand the Islamic challenge as well as the secular renewal and what it means for Turkey and the rest of us on the threshold of the twenty-first century.

# 2 ～

## Whatever Happened to Atatürk's Revolution?

Ankara is Atatürk's dream capital, an orderly, modern city in the center of the Anatolian heartland. Broad shady avenues are lined with sober public buildings, comfortable villas, spreading high-rises, genteel clubs, cosmopolitan shops, and restaurants. Ample green spaces are embellished with a feast of fountains. The ancient citadel area with lively markets and all manner of artisans is being refurbished for tourists. The *gecekondu* (shantytowns built overnight), which have mushroomed on surrounding hills since the 1970s, are progressively being replaced by high-rise apartments, lacking in picturesque charm but probably more livable.

On a hillock in the heart of the city rises the local acropolis, the austere mausoleum of Anıtkabir, honoring Mustafa Kemal Atatürk, founder of the Turkish Republic. When I covered Turkey for the *New York Times* from 1979 to 1984, the name Atatürk was sacred. People in those days did not openly question this twentieth-century prophet and his ideal of creating a new Turkish citizen and a secular, Westernized Turkey from the ruins of the Ottoman Empire.

Ankara has changed radically since I lived there. It is no longer a staid, bureaucratic town, choking on pollution and suffering from shortages of almost everything. The city has come of age and is a lively capital with a growing industrial base.

But the most striking change is the new Islamic presence. A powerful rival to Anıtkabir now towers on the Ankara skyline: the vast Kocatepe Mosque with four soaring minarets, which draws large crowds for Friday prayers. On the hill above the Presidential Palace, the Atakule shopping mall is usually thronged with women, many wearing headscarves. An elected Islamist mayor keeps the streets clean and speaks disparagingly of Western culture, particularly sculpture. Even Atatürk has come under attack. Islamists, liberals, and Kurds criticize him for being an authoritarian leader who imposed his reforms from the top and tried to obliterate the people's cultural identity.

Which leads to the basic question. Whatever happened to Atatürk's revolution? For another look at Atatürk and his myth, I returned to Anıtkabir, past the parade of Hittite lions guarding the monument and the bas-reliefs celebrating Turkey's 1919–1922 War of Independence to the Hall of Honor. Anıtkabir has always been the place of choice for any kind of public ceremony. Now it has become a popular pilgrimage site, and the number of visitors has increased visibly.

A hot wind passed through the columns as Turks of all ages and condition, from hip teenagers to solemn bureaucrats and soldiers, country folk and a sprinkling of headscarved women, gathered reverently at the marble tomb.

It was the fateful summer of 1997, when the secular elite, led by the military, drew the line against the spread of Islamic fundamentalism. Convinced that Atatürk's revolution was in danger, secularists united against the Islamist-led coalition.

I was accompanied by Gülter Kolankaya, a Turkish-American friend. Gülter lives in California with her husband and two children but goes back to Turkey every year because her roots run very deep.[1] Slender and blond and very Californian in her ways, Gülter is a dedicated Kemalist, as Atatürk's followers are known. Hers is an Atatürk-generation family. Her husband, Savaş, is a construction engineer who respects her independence. Her mother is a former member of Parliament and a pioneer in special education. Her deceased father was an air force officer. One sister is the director of an orphanage, the other sister is a business administrator, and their brother is an architect.

For Gülter and many of her compatriots, Atatürk is a combination of George Washington, Abraham Lincoln, and John F. Kennedy: defender of the land against foreign domination, liberator of women from subservience, charismatic leader who restored national pride.

With obvious admiration, Gülter translated Atatürk's words inscribed in gilt on the monument: "Power belongs to the people. . . . If people can't find their power in themselves as a nation, they will become slaves of another nation." On another wall is one of Atatürk's best-known phrases

*Atatürk, wearing his favorite Panama hat, surrounded by the first group of Turkish women parliamentarians. The poster was put out by KA-DER, a women's organization (patterned after Emily's List), which aims to get more women into Parliament.*

that sums up his nationalistic creed: "How fortunate is he who can say 'I am a Turk'."

The exhibit records highlights of Atatürk's remarkable career. Born in Salonika (then Macedonia, part of the Ottoman Empire; now Greece) in 1881, Mustafa Kemal came from a modest family; his father was a minor customs official, his mother a strong-willed, pious peasant woman. A graduate of the Staff College in 1905, he had a brilliant military career, serving with the Ottoman Army and later leading Turkey's War for Independence. On display are memorabilia of his victorious campaigns against the Italians in Tripoli in 1911, in defense of the Dardanelles from the Allied fleet in World War I (1915), and against Greek forces in 1922.

Most of the space, however, is devoted to Atatürk the statesman and educator, who became president of the new Turkish Republic in 1923, abolishing the Ottoman institutions of sultan (temporal ruler) and caliph (spiritual ruler). This is a memorial to his driving ambition to create a contemporary, European society whose dominant religion happens to be Islam. Here are symbols of the sweeping changes he imposed on everything from the laws of the state and the role of religion to the language, dress, habits, and outlook of the people.

On display are the icons of Kemalism, unlike those of any other creed. There is Turkey's Latin alphabet of 1928, which replaced Arabic script, and Atatürk's language book, purged of Arabic and Persian influences. Also his favorite books in French, English, German, and Turkish; his modern (for the times) telephone, typewriter, and physical fitness equipment. There are his European silver and crystal dining sets, cigarette holders, and a collection of brass ashtrays. And his proudly Western wardrobe, including tweed jacket and golf pants, tuxedo, top hat, cufflinks, walking stick, cape, and marshal's uniform. Oddly out of place is a miniature Koran that can be read only with a magnifying glass, the symbolism of which is open to interpretation. Only someone familiar with other Muslim countries or the Ottoman lifestyle can fully appreciate the radical connotations of these everyday objects.

Naturally there is little evidence of the more controversial aspects of the leader's character: his choleric moods, autocratic temperament, obsessive womanizing, and penchant for tobacco and alcohol (he died of cirrhosis of the liver).[2] Nevertheless, various personal artifacts suggest an unorthodox personal life. Pictures show the wife he divorced after two and a half years of marriage and his seven adopted children. A congratulatory telegram is addressed to his favorite adopted daughter Sabiha Gökçen, Turkey's first woman pilot. There is his will, in which he left almost everything to his ruling Republican People's Party at his death in 1938.

After our visit to Anıtkabir, Gülter appeared exhilarated and disturbed. The exhibit reminded her of the broad scope of Atatürk's reforms and what is at stake should Islamists seek to restore Islamic rule. She confided that she has watched with alarm how Islamic groups were getting more organized and powerful since the early 1990s and feels that the secular community must stop the movement. Now that her son and daughter are grown, Gülter said she was seriously considering returning to Turkey to follow her mother's footsteps into politics. She believes there is a very real danger that Turkey could share the fate of Iran and blames secular politicians from both the left and right for being so slow to react to the Islamic threat.

Gülter's mother Zekiye Gülsen was an MP for the conservative Justice Party from 1969 to 1979 and is still deeply involved in politics. We met over garden lunch at a friend's home in Umitköy, a new suburb west of Ankara. With her sandy hair and fair complexion, Mrs. Gülsen looks Irish. The talk naturally turned to Atatürk, as conversations do in Turkey.

How would Atatürk view the Islamic revival? I asked.

"He would think the country is in danger and do something about it,"[3] Mrs. Gülsen responded soberly. "Step by step Refah has penetrated the administration and acquired enormous money and power. There are too many other political parties and they are too divided. When there is such tremendous danger, the mainstream parties must come closer together and the left can support the right."

I had heard this argument when I first came to Ankara. Why couldn't the warring politicians put aside their differences for the good of the nation? Only then, the country was engulfed in violence, and the danger came from the left and right extremes.

The 1980 military coup, which I lived through, was aimed at doing away with the old order of partisan politics and renewing Atatürk's program with a team of dedicated Kemalists. Restoring order by draconian measures, the military leaders dissolved all the political organizations and bundled the leading politicians off to intended oblivion. Once armed with a strict new constitution, the generals were ready to return to their version of democratic rule with new elections and new faces.

Emerging from this carefully supervised process was Turgut Özal, the man who had restored the country's economic credibility. Özal was no Atatürk but like Atatürk, a man of vision who attracted a broad political following. A devout Muslim, Özal once defined himself[4] to me as "a political conservative, economic liberal, and left-of-center on social questions." While I was still covering the area, Özal opened up the country's economy, relaxed political restrictions, and lifted the ban on the old politicians, who promptly bounced back, more fractious than ever.

Feride Acar (AJ-jar), professor of political sociology at the Middle East Technical University (METU), who took her Ph.D. at Bryn Mawr, dates the start of the Islamic revitalization to the early 1980s, after the military takeover. "The military didn't realize the political nature of Islam at the time," Dr. Acar pointed out, as we sipped lemonade in the walled garden of her villa.[5] The armed forces had a Kemalist view of religion as a personal moral force, she said. For that reason they tolerated the revival of religious orders and the construction of religious schools and made religious courses obligatory in public schools. It was still Cold War times and the generals, like other Western leaders, saw religion as a barrier to the greater evil of communism.

Islamists also benefited from the democratizing trend under Turgut Özal, who believed everybody's voice should be heard, emphasized Dr. Acar. In the mid-1980s, religious orders and cults and the Refah Party began actively to recruit supporters among the migrant communities, disenchanted with a Western development model in which they had no share.

"It is clear that Atatürk's reforms have not reached so far as many people had hoped," noted Dr. Acar, an avowed secularist, who has kept her analytical cool on the Islamic revival. "Those people flocking to the mosque are not fanatics. There is an increasing return to religious practices in people's daily lives that we did not see ten years ago. This is a sociological fact. Many young people simply want personal freedom. The average Refah Party voter does not call for return to a theocratic state but favors the democratic system."

On the METU campus, the Islamist movement rose from 1988 to 1994, but since then, the momentum has declined sharply, according to Dr. Acar. The secular opposition has gotten organized and is doing what the Islamists have been doing for years, giving out scholarships to poor students. "We're creating an alternative lifestyle to the Islamic way," Dr. Acar concluded.

Since the city's main campuses have always been the backbone of the Kemalist movement, I decided to revisit them. METU is an immense bucolic island on the edge of town, known in the 1970s as a hotbed of leftist protest. Now it looks very much like an American campus. The only signs of rebellion were a few girls in headscarves and long raincoats.

Ayşen Ergin, assistant to the president of METU and an assistant professor of coastal engineering, said there were only nine headscarves out of 250 students in her department. "But raising barriers only stirs hostile reaction," Dr. Ergin said over lunch in the faculty dining room. "We have to talk to these young people, win them over, reach out to them through education."[6]

Bilkent is a shiny new university suburb, ten miles west of Ankara, with a first-class hotel and restaurant, spectacular fitness center and sports complex, and the finest concert hall in the country. On campus, not a headscarf is in sight, but young women scurried about in revealing T-shirts, fitted jeans, and miniskirts that might make Atatürk's head turn. The two main clubs were vying in student elections: Ata (means Father in Turkish), a Kemalist-nationalist group; and Yankı (Echo), made up mostly of ex-Ata people who stand for much the same thing but differ on budget priorities.

A very secular friend, İhsan Çetin, who teaches economics at Bilkent, recalls defending the right of one of his students to attend class with her head covered at the peak of the Headscarf War in the early 1990s. "After-

ward, she came up to thank me, thinking I was one of them (Islamists),"
İhsan recounts. "Confessing that I enjoy a glass of *rakı* (spirits locally
called 'lion's milk') from time to time, I asked if her friends came to
power, would she defend my right to *rakı*? Without blinking an eyelid,
she replied: 'You will change'."[7]

At downtown Gazi University, on the other hand, the Islamic presence
was strongly visible, making up about half the student body and coming
mostly from rural Anatolia. Cennet Köse, a recent graduate of Gazi
dressed in a loose sweater, jeans, and boots, says that five out of twelve
people in her class were religion-minded."There are advantages in going
with the Islamists," Cennet admitted. "If you go to a *hoca* group (cult), they
give you headscarves and a long coat, housing money, an allowance and
even find a job for you. Refah also pays everything for students who join,
even though it's against the law. The other political parties don't do this."[8]

The new Islamic fervor among the Western-educated young people obviously cannot be explained solely by material incentives. Şerif Mardin, a
professor of sociology at American University and author of *Religion and
Social Change in Modern Turkey,* is one of the earliest critics of the Atatürk
paradigm. In a recent publication, he commends the young republic for
its conceptualization of the democratic ideal "as government of the people and by the people."[9] Then he describes what he calls the negative side
of Atatürk's revolution. "The new republican ideology, by denying the
place of Islam as a discourse and its role as a 'cement' of society, increased
the distance between the educated and the uneducated. . . . Islam established bridges between social groups because it functioned as a common
language shared by upper and lower classes."

Andrew Mango, a British authority on Turkey, has just published a
comprehensive life story of the Turkish leader. Speaking of the Atatürk
legend not long ago, Mango told Stephen Kinzer of the *New York Times:*
"You could say very cynically that the cult is a way in which a particular
class or caste maintains itself in power. Whenever the members of this
caste are challenged, they pick up a bust of Atatürk and throw it at the of-
fender."[10]

Mango does not deny the importance of Atatürk-worship. "It's a way
to bring Turks into the march of humanity, to open the country out to the
world," he said in the interview. "To young people in Turkey today, Kemalism means equality of the sexes, dancing, music, travel abroad, and
the feeling that nothing essential separates them from European or American culture. It is what keeps Turkey within modern civilization."

But it is Turkish women who are most thankful to Atatürk for granting them legal equality with men and who make up a powerful lobby to keep the Atatürk flame alive. On the Republic's seventieth anniversary, the Association in Support of Contemporary Living (ÇYDD) published a book, *Atatürk: From the Past to the Future.* In one essay, Necla Arat, who heads the women's studies program at İstanbul University, wrote that Atatürk's reforms in family law, the Turkish Civil Code, and women's suffrage were "breakthroughs not only within the Islamic world but also in the Western world."[11]

Professor Arat cites a 1925 declaration by Atatürk for which most modern Turkish women venerate him: "A society, a nation is made up of both sexes, male and female. Is it ever possible that we only improve one part of this mass and leave the other part aside if we expect the whole nation to improve? Is it ever possible for a society to be divided in two and to raise up to the skies while half of it is chained to the ground? Thus the steps towards progress must be taken jointly by men and women on a friendly basis."

It was a male and usually acerbic columnist, Emin Çölaşan, who best captured the essence of Atatürk in this ÇYDD memorial. Recalling the total disintegration and defeat of the Ottoman Empire after the Balkan War and World War I, Çölaşan wrote that only a great man could establish a new and contemporary state out of such a dark picture. "Atatürk is the symbol of modernism. He is light, brightness, civilization, modernism, interests of the state, science," he wrote.[12] "Atatürkism is not a static concept: It is being oriented to new things. It is the unity of the country and the people. It is a rationalism. It is not lacking belief but staying away from fanaticism. Therefore it is valid even today."

Many scholars attempting to define Atatürk's ideology start with the Six Arrows, the basis of his Republican People's Party: Republicanism, Nationalism, Populism, Revolutionism, Secularism, and Etatism. Others prefer to define Kemalism as a dynamic force for the transformation of society or simply the modernization of society. A readable, serious discussion of the issue is found in *Atatürk and the Modernization of Turkey,* edited by Jacob M. Landau.

The government organ charged with propagating Kemalism among the new generations is the Atatürk Supreme Council for Culture, Language, and History. This agency, established in 1983 under the prime ministry, groups Atatürk's old Research Center, Language Institute, and other organizations, which had been set up to give form to the new Secular Culture. I suppose that by the 1980s, it was assumed that the Secular Culture was sufficiently consolidated to downsize the effort.

After some difficulty, I finally located the council's Atatürk Cultural Center and Bookstore at an outlying site, where it moved from its central location at Kavaklıdere several months before. Other people must have the same problem finding the place, as I was the only visitor. I was curious how this government department had fared under the Islamist prime minister.

"The Atatürk Cultural Center continues its work regardless of who's in control of the government," a nervous official told me, emphasizing that only the council president was authorized to give me any information about the center. He explained that the center had moved because of "space considerations," although the new building appears much smaller.

From what I learned unofficially, it seems the center's work consisted mainly of organizing conferences, which have little relation to Atatürk. Recent symposia dealt with Ottoman architect Mimar Sinan and folk hero Nasreddin Hoca. A major event being planned was the celebration in 1999 of the 700th anniversary of the establishment of the Ottoman Empire. The current edition of *Aris*, a glossy magazine published by the center, featured reports on weaving arts, an interesting topic but again the relevance escaped me.

In the bookstore, I found various books on Atatürk: Atatürk and the military, Atatürk and the emancipation of women, the Atatürk revolution, the Atatürk era. I wondered who reads these books. A few volumes are in English, obviously for the occasional tourist who might get lost in the area. Most books in Turkish are priced at more than most students or *gecekondu* people can afford. Nor are these publications being sent out to schools or other institutions for distribution to the public. In fact, there are no other branches of the center and no mailing lists.

Perhaps the center's low-key approach to the Atatürk legend was the result of nearly a year under the direction of an Islamist prime minister. Or maybe it reflected the complacency of the Kemalist elite, at least until the 1995 elections. But it seemed to me if this was the way the Atatürk Cultural Center has waged the propaganda war with the Islamists, no wonder Atatürk's capital elected an Islamist mayor.

Yet there are clear signs of an Atatürk awakening. How else to explain the massive national backing for the founder of the Turkish Republic in *Time* magazine's Persons of the Century campaign?[13] In what *Time* calls

*Downtown Ankara Chamber of Commerce building decked out with giant painting of Atatürk for Children's Day celebration.*

"an electronic maelstrom," votes for Atatürk largely surpassed Churchill and everybody else in the category of Warriors and Statesmen. There are also lively debates over this Turkish hero/villain on the Internet.

The Father of the Turks, as his name signifies, would probably have been amused by the controversy over plans for a film on his life. Laurence Olivier's son, Tarquin Olivier, a financier, was prepared to finance the film and had signed on screen star Antonio Banderas to play the Turkish hero. But news of the project rocked Greek Americans, who flooded Banderas with protest letters in the summer of 1998, causing the actor to pull out of the film. Most Greeks cannot forget that it was Atatürk who drove the Greek forces out of Anatolia in Turkey's War of Independence.

*Atatürk*, an eighty-minute documentary by a young Turkish director, Tolga Ornek, did appear at the end of 1998. This comprehensive portrait of the Turkish leader describes his personal strengths and weaknesses as well as his military, political, and social achievements. It includes a number of glowing testimonials like that of William J. Crowe Jr., former  chairman of the U.S. Joint Chiefs of Staff, who is quoted as saying: "In my opinion, he was the best military man of this century."

At home, Atatürk's portrait gazes sternly from walls everywhere. His statue and bust adorn even the most obscure village. Middle-class men and women proudly wear small gold Atatürk buttons on their lapels. Every Atatürk anniversary is celebrated with pomp and patriotism.

Exuberant crowds turn out for classical concerts and ballets as if they were taking part in a plebiscite on Atatürk's vision of a secular European life.

Ahmet Taner Kışlalı, an old friend and a professor at Ankara University's Faculty of Political Sciences, talked enthusiastically of "an Atatürk revival" and cited his own case as evidence.[14] A Social Democrat and former minister of culture, he recounted that after the 1980 coup, his name was on a military blacklist; he couldn't sign his articles and was constantly afraid of arrest. Now his book, *Atatürk, Democracy and Secularity*, was in its eleventh edition; people lined up for hours at his book signings; he was invited to lecture in military schools, even the War Academy.

Kışlalı linked the renewed interest in Atatürk to the 1993 murder of Uğur Mumcu, a human rights activist, who had been investigating Islamic undercover groups for the leading secular newspaper *Cumhuriyet*. The crime was one of a series of attacks on secular personalities, generally believed to be inspired by Iranian or Saudi secret services.

"Mumcu's death shocked the nation, it was a kind of mass awakening, with people everywhere saying: What can I do to save democracy and Kemalism?" Kışlalı recalls. Thus the Atatürk Thought Association was born, and has now become one of the largest civic movements in the country with over 400 branches and 70,000 members, uniting the political left and the right.

"People have come to realize that Kemalism is relevant today because it is nationalism based on shared culture, not religion or ethnicity, and can be adapted to present conditions." Kışlalı said. Disputing the Islamist contention that the Kemalist era was a repressive one, Kışlalı argued: "Atatürk was not against religion; I am fifty-seven years old and never saw state pressure on the personal practice of religion, though there may have been some excesses."

It's not an either/or situation, Kışlalı stressed, pointing to a recent poll that shows that 84 percent of Turks respect and love Atatürk, and equally, 84 percent attach importance to religion.

Kışlalı was convinced that Atatürk could not have accomplished his revolution in a country like Iran. He cited historical factors to demonstrate that Turkey is "different" from other Muslim countries. For one thing, women played an important role in pre-Islamic Shamanist society in Anatolia. Even in the Islamic period, the Turks from Central Asia had women leaders, and men and women took part in religious ceremonies together. The Ottoman sultans generally did not apply Islamic law. They charged interest and did not observe the ban on alcohol or Islamic punishments like cutting off hands of thieves or stoning women adulterers.

Secularists have taken their gains for granted, Kışlalı contended. "Only now that people risk losing Kemalism are they ready to fight for it," he said, adding that it was a good thing that Refah was given its chance in power "because now Erbakan and his followers have revealed their true aim is to establish an Islamic state."

# 3 ~

---

## *Welfare's Society*

---

With swirls of dust, flashing daggers, and fireworks, turbaned soldiers reenact the conquest of İstanbul from Byzantine rule in 1453. Gathered at the base of the medieval fortress of Rumeli Hisarı, the crowd exults: Allah! Allah!—as if the victory were only yesterday.

A popular Sufi singer, wearing sleek black silk pants and shirt and clasping roses, warbles the Ninety-nine Names of Allah like a love song. In the background, a chorus chants the *Shehade:* "There is only one God and Mohamed is his Prophet."

This spectacular of militant faith was part of a five-day tribute to Sultan Mehmet II, who transformed the old Constantinople into İstanbul, capital of the Ottoman Empire. Ottoman rule lasted six centuries and at its height (the sixteenth century) reached from Mesopotamia to the gates of Vienna. In the past, this historic event had been celebrated like a tourist attraction. In recent years, under the Islamist mayor of İstanbul, it has become a major annual celebration, superbly organized by the pro-Islamic party, with the participation of tens of thousands of supporters.

The rallies and seminars honoring Mehmet the Conqueror as a champion of Islam appeared to be in open contradiction with the tenets of the Turkish Republic. I found it quite extraordinary that an Islamic-oriented party would be permitted to co-opt this national hero, after three-quarters of a century of strict secularization. This is a dramatic illustration of the ambivalence of Turkish life today. It is clear that despite severe restraints on religion in public life, the roots of Islam are still widespread and will flower when given the chance.

*Necmettin Erbakan, father of the modern Islamic movement in Turkey and the Republic's first Islamist prime minister.*

Until its controversial closure in early 1998, the pro-Islamic Refah (Welfare) Party enjoyed phenomenal success to become the strongest party in the country in just twelve years. Refah's leaders generally tried to remain within the law, arguing that Refah was not an Islamic party but was inspired by Islamic principles. More radical militants, however, did not hesitate to call for the restoration of Islamic law, sending tremors through the Kemalist establishment.

The man behind Refah's tour de force was Necmettin Erbakan, a smiling grandfatherly figure who became this secular nation's first Islamist prime minister. It was Erbakan who fashioned Refah into the largest grassroots political organization in the country with a base of 4 million members, which came to be seen by the military and others as a threat to the secular Republic.

When I first met Erbakan in 1980, he was head of an earlier incarnation of Refah called the National Salvation Party. The Islamist boss was regarded as a shrewd politician but not a national leader—nor a menace to national security. This was no stereotype ayatollah but rather a kind of Islamic evangelist, impeccably dressed in the latest European styles, with a predilection for five-star hotels. Committed to his cause, he did not marry until age forty-two and now has three children. In private interviews, he sounds like a cross between a Christian Democrat and a Social Democrat, preaching high moral values, order and progress, social justice and social welfare, happiness and salvation. But on the stump, he was the consummate Third World radical, crusading against Turkey's Western ties and ubiquitous Zionist plots and in favor of a new Islamic Order.

Erbakan was born in 1926 in the conservative Black Sea town of Sinop, the son of an Ottoman judge. It was the same year that the young Republic's National Assembly repealed the Islamic *Sharia* and replaced it with a new Turkish civil code, based on Swiss law. A clever, pious young man, Erbakan studied mechanical engineering at İstanbul Technical University. It was there that he fell under the influence of Hoca Zahit Kotku, a respected sage of the Nakşibendi Brotherhood, known for his anti-Western, pan-Islamic view of the world. Experts say it was Kotku who instilled in Erbakan the ambition to form an Islamic political party. (There must have been an intense political atmosphere at İstanbul Tech at that time because two of Erbakan's classmates, Süleyman Demirel and Turgut Özal, went on to form political parties and become president, and a third classmate, Recai Kutan, was to succeed him as head of the new pro-Islamic Fazilet Party after Refah was banned.)

Graduating with honors, Erbakan pursued his studies, receiving a Ph.D. at Aachen University in Germany. When he returned home, he taught engineering, set up Turkey's first diesel engine factory, and became the head of the influential Union of Chambers of Commerce. In 1969, Erbakan tried to join Demirel's conservative Justice Party but was refused. After this rebuff by his old colleague, Erbakan won a parliamentary seat as an independent from the religious city of Konya. He then proceeded to set up the first clearly pro-Islamist party in modern Turkey, the National Order Party. Supported by most of the Islamic communities, the new party openly campaigned for the restoration of religious values and was closed down for violating secular principles shortly after the military coup of 1971.

Escaping to Lugano, Switzerland, Erbakan remained in self-exile for about a year, then returned to found a new political organization, the National Salvation Party. In accordance with Turkish law, none of the founders of the banned National Order Party were registered as founders of the new group. But the political message was the same: in favor of spiritual and material development within the framework of the democratic order.

To the surprise of the political establishment, the fledgling National Salvation Party won 11.8 percent in the 1973 general elections. Soon Erbakan was allowed to assume his place at the head of the pro-Islamic party, which now held the balance of power and was wooed by the major parties on the left and right.[1] In fact, the Islamist leader served as deputy prime minister in three government coalitions in the 1970s, first with the Republican People's Party, led by Bülent Ecevit (and founded by Atatürk), then twice with Demirel's Justice Party.

These coalitions were riven with ideological differences and didn't get much done, but Erbakan demonstrated his willingness to work within the secular republican system. At the same time, he consolidated his support by allocating large sums to the Religious Affairs department and state-controlled industrial enterprises. He also placed his cadres in the key ministries of Interior, Justice, Trade, Agriculture, and Industry, establishing a strong base in the bureaucracy for the future Refah Party.

Although the main aim of the September 12, 1980, military coup was to end the rampant, extreme left-wing–right-wing violence, an immediate pretext for the intervention was the National Salvation Party's rally in the religious city of Konya on September 6. With Erbakan at their head, party militants turned out in strength to protest against Israel's move to declare Jerusalem its capital. Green Islamic banners waving, the frenzied crowd called for the return to *Sharia* in Turkey. As Mehmet Ali Birand, a prominent Turkish journalist, writes, "it was difficult to imagine any other action so guaranteed to infuriate the staunchly secular and Kemalist army commanders."[2]

Aiming to eliminate politics as usual and start afresh, the generals abolished all parties and confiscated their property. The Islamists received special treatment. Erbakan was held for over 200 days (Ecevit and Demirel were detained under a month), and he and his colleagues were tried by Ankara's Martial Law court on charges of attempting to set up an Islamic state. They were finally acquitted in 1985.

Meanwhile, after the ruling National Security Council ended the ban on political activities in 1983, all the old parties trickled back onto the scene with new names, including the Islamist party, now called Refah. By 1987, restrictions were lifted on the former political leaders, and they all returned to their respective parties. In the first free general election of November 1987, Refah Party, under Erbakan's leadership, received 7.2 percent of the vote—not enough votes to meet the required 10 percent threshold to get into Parliament.

The best account I have read on the rise of the Islamic movement is *Islam in Modern Turkey,* written by a group of experts. Editor Richard Tapper writes:

> Indeed, after the military intervention of 1980, government attitudes changed. Without abandoning the basic principle of secularism, the generals, as well as the powerful intellectual élite of judges, professors and administrators who controlled the media, adopted a new approach to protecting it. A tacit admission of the failure of the ideology and forms of Kemalist republicanism led to a reassessment of its elements and a perception of the need for reinforcing an unchanging national culture and eliminating foreign influences. A departure from strict traditional secularism was supported by the newly active tarikats and substantial Islamic funding from abroad, channelled into educational facilities and huge budget increases for the Directorate of Religious Affairs.[3]

Tapper notes that in the late 1980s, however, the idea of the Turkish-Islam Synthesis (religion as an element of culture and social control but not politicized) "was intellectually discredited, and there was evidence of a backlash from strict secularists, while the Islamic 'threat' was defused by the integration of religious ideals into the programmes of most political parties." Once again, the role of religion in the Turkish state had to be redefined, he concludes.

Turkey now settled back to enjoy a new democratic era, and most people paid little heed to the diligent efforts by Erbakan and his supporters to put Refah on the national map. The first wake-up call came with local elections of March 1994, when Refah won the mayorships of Ankara, İstanbul, and twenty-eight other cities, 327 smaller municipalities, and 19 percent of the vote nationwide.

In the wake of this electoral triumph, Erbakan joined his mayors and thousands of supporters at Eyüp Sultan Mosque in İstanbul to give "thanks to God." His words sent an electric shock through cosmopolitan secular circles. "This is a present to us from God. Refah Party will soon be in power. There is no solution to the present crises but the Just Order. Our victory will not end here. Our next aim is the World Islamic Unity. İstanbul is the political capital of the Muslim world."[4]

When I visited Turkey in the spring of 1995, the secular establishment was full of foreboding over the prospect of national elections scheduled for the end of the year. Moderating his discourse, Erbakan targeted the disenchanted with his denunciation of oppression and corruption at home and the arrogance of Europeans who refused to accept Turks as equals. Political analysts predicted Refah would continue to rise as long as the secular parties remained splintered and unable to provide solutions to the country's serious economic problems.

The pundits were on mark. In legislative elections on Christmas Eve 1995, Refah won first place with 21.4 percent, followed by the main liberal and conservative parties, Motherland and True Path, each with just over 19 percent, trailed by the Democratic Left with 14.7 percent and the left-of-center Republican People's Party with only 10.7 percent.

Although the election results came as a blow to the secular camp, they could hardly be taken as an Islamist landslide aimed at altering Turkey's political direction. In fact, secular optimists, including most foreign diplomats, saw the vote as 79 percent of the country upholding democratic secular republican values by voting for secular parties. Only a small core of Islamists (maybe 10 percent) had voted for Refah, secularists contended; the remainder was a protest against the failure of mainstream parties to resolve major problems.

Nevertheless, Refah's showing was sufficiently strong to put it at the head of the line to lead a coalition government and play a significant role in Parliament. Even hardened Kemalists recognized that Islamists have become a fact of life, their life.

How did it happen? Analysts who followed Refah's advances closely say the party's growing popularity was due first of all to the splintered state of the secular parties rather than any sudden religious revival. Other factors were Refah's hard work, old-fashioned ward politicking, and advanced technology.

Using techniques resembling those of the Chinese communists, the Islamists have built a formidable grassroots organization, based in the *gecekondu* (squatter settlements) around the main cities. Each neighborhood was organized into cells, with committees at the street and district level. Refah cadres distributed bread and other foodstuffs, clothing, and heating fuel to the needy on a regular basis, and at election time, canvassed the neighborhoods for support. The other parties admit they could not compete in zeal or dedication.

Refah's secret weapon turned out to be its women, who worked the poor neighborhoods from door to door, offering health, education, and welfare services as well as politics. One of Refah's stars was Sibel Eraslan, an active Islamic feminist whose father was a Kemalist military officer.

Although she has a law degree, she cannot appear before the bar because she insists on wearing a headscarf. Almost single-handedly, Ms. Eraslan organized Refah's Women's Branch, composed of 18,000 volunteers, who in turn reached out to 200,000 women a month.[5] Despite her efficiency and zeal, she lost her post at Refah in 1995, after criticizing the party's failure to name any women candidates for national elections. Now she has returned to the party to work at the local level and tries to keep out of the public eye.

After Erbakan, the best-known face of Refah was İstanbul's mayor, Recep Tayyip Erdoğan (AIR-do-an), often referred to as probable successor to the party chief. Early on, Erdoğan succeeded in riling many of his secular constituents by a series of "Islamic" gestures. First there was a ban on alcohol at all municipal functions and tea gardens; then closure of shelters for abused women; introduction of Islamic techniques in the city's slaughterhouses; permission for members of the fire department to wear beards; defiance of international conventions by painting yellow road signs in Islamic green; stuffing municipal services with Islamists; and plans to build a grand mosque at Taksim Square, the secular heart of the city.

Envisioning a Turkish Qadhafi, I requested an interview with Mayor Erdoğan. But there was nothing aggressively Islamic about this forty-one-year-old Marmara University graduate in economics and political science and amateur soccer player. He was the picture of an urbane Western gentleman, sporting a trim mustache, dapper tweed jacket, and dark green shirt. He cordially shook hands with me (unlike many Islamists I know) and produced a Refah Party deputy as interpreter to make sure he was understood.

"Before we came to office, there was widespread corruption and bribery; now many people are in jail and we have a clean administration," Mayor Erdoğan boasted.[6] Then he spoke at length of other accomplishments: the removal of "hills of garbage"; additional sea jets and sea buses to ease traffic congestion and works nearly completed on the light rail; refurbishment of the city's water supply; easing pollution problems by increased use of natural gas; and stopping trucks from bringing poor coal into the city.

"Next winter," he promised, "İstanbul's air will also be clean." (It wasn't, but there was some improvement and at least he deserves credit for trying.)

Asked why he had closed the women's shelters, the mayor said: "Shelters are not good for women; we have alternative places called *huzur—*

relief and support facilities—where they can learn handicraft courses. In our culture, if a woman is badly treated she goes to her family."

As for the mosque at Taksim, the Vakıf (Islamic foundation) wanted it, and the City Council has voted in favor, he said. Then cutting short my questions, he excused himself for another appointment. It was a pro's interviewing technique: Say what you want to say, then leave.

In parting pleasantry, I told him how impressed I was with all the *No Smoking* signs around City Hall and suggested if he could get the Turks to stop smoking he could do anything.

"We've removed all the ashtrays and banned smoking because it's important for our health; we don't allow cigarettes or alcohol in municipal buildings," Erdoğan said firmly.

But when an aide took me upstairs to his office to get the mayor's biography, I noticed three ashtrays on his desk. "Oh, I can smoke," he said confidently, giving me a glimpse of laxity behind the facade at City Hall.

Abdullah Gül, formerly deputy chairman of Refah and another heir apparent to Erbakan, gave me a closer look at Refah and its position on key issues and direction. The personable, forty-six-year-old Gül speaks excellent English, is not afraid of tough questions, and often appeared as Refah Party spokesman, particularly in Western circles.

It was the spring of 1996 on the eve of the formation of the first Islamist-led government in modern Turkey. Receiving me in Refah's parliamentary chambers, MP Gül came across more like a reasonable, soft-spoken academic than a fiery Islamic militant. Refah, he indicated, is fully aware of democratic constraints—the need to compromise with its coalition partners and the secular majority in Parliament.

"Our main priority is the economy," said Gül, who has a Ph.D. in economics. "People are suffering a lot from the economy. All economic indicators are negative: inflation, unemployment. Everyone is asking for a job. Out of ten people who come to me, nine are asking for a job. Nine percent of the budget is going to investment. They (the previous government) did not create jobs. We promise we will really concentrate investments in production and job creation.[7]

"Distribution of income is also very bad. Over the last year, real wages have been going down. Housing, education, health pose really serious problems. Corruption is very widespread; I feel ashamed. But there are no corruption charges against Refah's municipalities. Refah has shown what it can do at the municipal level in the past two and a half years, paying off most of the enormous debts and investing in services for the people. Nobody denies this. The country has enormous resources; some are untouched but it needs good organization, efficient management, dedicated people."

What changes would Refah make in foreign policy? I asked, recalling Erbakan's earlier criticism of NATO (North Atlantic Treaty Organization) and the European Union.

"The main elements of foreign policy will remain as they are now but we want a more open Turkey," Gül said. Refah aims to develop relations with the United States and Europe but also with Asian and Pacific countries as well as the Islamic lands that were once Turkish provinces and share a common culture. He hoped NATO would continue, recalling Turkey's important role for peace when communism was a force to be reckoned with. "But when we see wrong policies, we criticize them, particularly in Bosnia, where 300,000 people were massacred in the heart of Europe."

As for the European Customs Union, Gül said Turkey had signed the agreement and a Refah government would be bound by it but would call for new negotiations to "correct mistakes." The terms, he pointed out, are not good for Turkey, which is expected to implement decisions without being a full member in the decision-making body. He was also critical of the secrecy around the signing of the recent defense treaty with Israel, but did not suggest its abrogation.

Commenting on the Kurdish conflict, which had taken some 30,000 lives since 1984 and drained the economy, the Refah spokesman said: "We believe we can solve it. Kurds have confidence in us; in the last general elections and also two years ago in local elections, the Kurdish people voted for us—not for HADEP [the Kurdish nationalist People's Democracy Party]. The official approach was wrong from the beginning. You don't invade an area that you are trying to integrate; it's your area, has been for thousands of years. . . . No, you cannot solve this militarily. We always said no to martial law; we said we should have civilian administration out there. If they want to speak Kurdish, let them speak."

In response to secularists' concerns for their personal freedoms in an Islamic society, Gül said: "We are a democratic party. We will get legitimacy from the people's support. Of course we give democratic guarantees; you cannot go back; you cannot force people [to practice Islam] against their will. We are not going to impose limitations; we are going to give wider freedom."

On the contrary, he said, it is necessary to end official restrictions on religious practice and expression. Islamic journalists are jailed on charges of being "antisecular." Women suffer discrimination for wearing headscarves. Turkish military officers are forbidden to go to the mosque in uniform and are sacked for going on the pilgrimage to Mecca or allowing their wives to wear headscarves. Yet, he pointed out, there is a mosque in the Pentagon, where officers can pray in uniform.

"Refah wants the same secularism they have in America," Gül emphasized, noting that the party has suggested the Turkish constitution be amended to include a translation of the American Bill of Rights.

Did he fear military intervention? I asked. (On three earlier occasions in 1960, 1971, and 1980, the Turkish armed forces, as guardians of Atatürk's legacy, seized power to restore law and order.)

"The military don't want to intervene and they cannot. Turkey is not the Turkey of the 1960s nor the 1980s. . . . People don't like military intervention. Of course the military are our military, our army, but if the generals intervene people won't like it."

All eminently reasonable. From everything Gül said, it seemed that Refah aimed at a corrective action, not a revolution. I felt that as long as "system" men like Gül, Erdoğan, and even Erbakan remained in charge of the Islamic-oriented party, there would be room for accommodation between the two worlds.

The trouble is that Refah speaks with different voices. Party hardliners, some of them in positions of influence, have scared the secular public with their intemperate words. A leading firebrand, Refah parliamentarian Hasan Mezarçı, made headlines some time ago with a clear threat: "Even if only five million of us remain, a *Sharia* government will be established." Refah MP Şevki Yılmaz incurred the wrath of his colleagues when he insulted Parliament in foul terms. Another Refah deputy, İbrahim Halil Çelik, directly challenged the military, saying if the army couldn't control 3,500 PKK (the Kurdish guerrilla movement), how will they control 6 million Islamists?

When charges were brought against these hot-tempered politicians, they were ousted from the party. But even the new, more conciliatory Erbakan has been widely reported making incendiary statements, such as that the transition to the Just Order would be made "with or without bloodshed."

This kind of talk was viewed as tantamount to sedition by archsecularists, particularly those in the military and the public prosecutor's office. Even more tolerant laypeople could not trace with any degree of certainty the border between rhetoric and reality. Nor could they predict who would inherit Erbakan's mantle once he leaves the scene. Like the country, the experts were deeply divided over Refah and its role.

A leading Islamic columnist, Fehmi Koru argued forcefully in favor of secular Turkey's democratic experiment with an Islamic-oriented party holding the reins of power.[8] "The Welfare Party, contrary to many people's preconceived notions, is not a religious party," Koru wrote in the *Muslim Politics Report* of the Council on Foreign Relations. "Party leaders are not clerics. The party program is not based on the *Sharia*. Campaign issues can easily be called secular. It might be a bit misleading but not totally wrong to claim that Welfare is the Turkish equivalent of Christian Democratic parties in the West."

Alan Makovsky, an influential Turkey expert and senior fellow at The Washington Institute for Near East Policy, made this insightful assessment shortly after Erbakan came to power:

> Turkey's first-ever Islamist Prime Minister, Erbakan is tactically a pragmatist, but strategically an ideologue. To stay in power, he is willing to compromise in the short run. Notwithstanding three decades of consistently anti-Western and anti-Zionist (and anti-Semitic) pronouncements, Erbakan initially will not challenge fundamental Turkish policies affecting relations with the U.S., NATO, and even Israel, because he lacks the leverage to do so. The powerful National Security Council (NSC), whose foreign policy recommendations are rarely over-ridden by Turkish governments, is dominated by secularists from the military and from Çiller's secularist True Path Party. (Of the NSC's ten members, Erbakan is the only representative of the Refah Party.) In the meantime, Erbakan will try to do what he can— through use of the budget, government appointments, the bully pulpit— further to Islamize Turkish society and add an Islamic tone to its foreign policy.[9]

In a thoughtful analysis of "Turkey's Islamist Challenge," Sabri Sayarı, head of the Institute of Turkish Studies at Georgetown University, concludes that Erbakan's main aim in leading a coalition government was not to make major policy changes but to gain greater legitimacy.[10]

"Turkey's Islamists believe that time is on their side and that they need to be patient," Professor Sayarı writes. "They also believe that once the secular foundations of the Republic are sufficiently weakened, Islamists can proceed with their ultimate goal of creating an Islamic state in the region's only predominantly Muslim and democratic country."

But no one could say for sure what is the ultimate intent of Turkey's Islamists.

# 4 —

## Other Islamic Faces

Every Monday night, members of the 300-year-old Halveti Cerrahi religious order gather at the lodge in the Fatih quarter of İstanbul to come closer to Allah through music and dance. They are doctors, businessmen, lawyers, and civil servants, sometimes accompanied by their families. Little boys are allowed to wander about freely, but women and girls are hidden on the balcony behind a wooden screen.

"This is a place of prayers; we are here to serve Allah," a worshiper, who is a senior airport official, told me as we waited for the dervishes to begin their ritual. "Many things happen in Turkey. You have violence all around. Everything is messed up. The Halveti believe we will have peace, *inch Allah.*"

The word *dervish* comes from the Persian *darwish*, meaning doorsill, and refers to a person on the threshold of enlightenment. I had seen dervishes dance in Konya to commemorate the death of the Sufi poet, Mevlâna Celaleddin Rumi. There the dance was presented as a major cultural event in a gymnasium before a thousand spectators, including diplomats, tourists, leaders of society, and of course Mevlevi (followers of Celaleddin).

The ceremony in the Halveti lodge is a religious happening, like the Brazilian Macumba dance, African chants, adult Sunday school, and a session of spiritualism, all rolled into one.

Before the ritual began, the *Sheik* or master of the order, an affable man with a white mustache and beard and wearing a black shirt and cloak, welcomed visitors, responded to their questions, and graciously accepted any gifts (not obligatory). He tried an offering of cigarillos but admitted his preference for Turkish cigarettes. Swiss chocolates were shared with visitors and worshipers.

*Anatolian Islam is strongly influenced by mystics like the thirteenth-century poet Celaleddin Rumi, known as Mevlâna, or Our Master. Some of his followers become dervishes who chant, sing, and whirl to reach a state of ecstasy.*

Through a rug merchant as interpreter, the *Sheik* told us of the order's tenets: "We live in predestination. We believe in resurrection and a day of justice."

Noting that Islam reveres Christ and Moses as major prophets, the *Sheik* asserted: "Truth is one only seen from different lightbulbs. If Jews or Christians do something wrong it is not the fault of Christ or Moses. Muslims can also make mistakes. Man can differentiate right from wrong."

His train of thought was interrupted by a German woman who asked the *Sheik* to interpret her complex dreams, which he obligingly did at great length.

The worship service started shortly before 11:00 P.M. in the main hall. More than a hundred men in business suits, jeans, and working clothes, many with white caps, bowed and kneeled, bobbed up and down again, reciting their prayers. After a half hour, the rugs were removed and the music began, a haunting call led by the *ney* (reed flute) and followed by the *kudum* (small double drum) and *bağlama* (a kind of mandolin). Women could be heard chatting on the balcony, which irritated some older men.

Then as the worshipers chanted *La illah illa'llah*, sixteen dervishes filed in, wearing tall tan stovepipe hats representing the tombstone, black cloaks symbolizing the grave, white shirts and long skirts for a shroud, and soft leather boots. The dervishes, mostly in their twenties, bowed to the musicians and the *Sheik* and the ballet commenced. First they bowed deeply and kissed the floor. Then bowing to the next person in line, they slowly went round and round in a kind of pirouette. As the chanting intensified, all the dervishes, except the two lead dancers, shed their cloaks in a sign of abandonment of all worldly attachments and started to whirl. They danced with head tilted and arms outstretched, the right hand face upward and the left down, which means: What we take from Allah, we give to the people, keeping nothing for ourselves.

The crowd swayed and chanted *Ya Hi Ya Allah Ya Hi!* while the dervishes whirled faster and faster. Then on a sign from the leader, the dancers stopped short and the chorus cried *Hu! Hu!*—that is, all the names of God in one. This routine was repeated three times, and each time the whirling became more frenetic until the dervishes and the singers appeared to reach a state of ecstasy. In closing, the dancers bowed and put on their cloaks. The lead singer recited verses of the Koran, and the assembly raised their hands, chanting *Allah! Salam Aleikum!* It was almost one A.M.; all the worshipers rose and many went to the next room for fruit and tea and conversation with the *Sheik* late into the night.

Religious brotherhoods like the Halveti have long played an important role behind the scenes in Turkey. Under the sultans, the various orders came to dominate town and village life and reach deep into the ranks of the governing elite. During the revolution, the brotherhoods generally supported the nationalists, and ten *sheikhs* took part in the first Grand National Assembly.

But in early 1925, *Sheik* Said, chief dervish of the Nakşibendi led a Kurdish insurrection against the new Republic. Atatürk reacted firmly, crushing the rebellion and setting up "independence tribunals," which convicted and executed *Sheik* Said and forty-six of his followers. After this direct challenge, Atatürk shut down the Kurdish orders, banning their ceremonies and dress, and later dissolved all the brotherhoods, seizing their assets and closing their sanctuaries.[1] The religious orders were literally driven underground—they used to hold meetings in caves. Since the democratic era beginning in 1950, religious orders called *tarikatlar* have been tolerated and very soon demonstrated they still had a strong grassroots following.

The return of the *tarikatlar* has been just as important as the rise of Refah in the Islamic revival. The brotherhoods have regained much of their influence in rural society and among shopkeepers and artisans in the towns and even in government. Their support is courted by the main political parties. Some *tarikatlar* have become actively involved in politics, education, publishing, TV and radio, and job networking.

The most influential religious leader in Turkey today is the ascetic Fethullah Gülen, follower of the Sufi mystic Mevlâna Celaleddin Rumi. Dr. Nilüfer Narlı, an expert on Islam, writes that Gülen was at one time a disciple of Said-i Nursi, a religious leader associated with radicalism and the Kurdish cause, who died in 1960. Now Gülen avoids being identified with the Nursi and has founded his own religious society, the Fethullahis, until recently known for their moderation and loyalty to the secular state. Narlı describes Gülen as a flexible, pious man who speaks with passionate fervor on a personal rather than an institutional level.[2]

Gülen, in his early sixties, comes from a well-to-do family in İzmir, never married, and has a large following including university students and professors and wealthy Anatolian businessmen as well as workers. It is said he spends his time raising money to build schools and has founded over 100 schools and a university in Turkey and some 200 schools in Central Asia.

Angered by secular allegations that religious schools are "hotbeds of criminal fundamentalism," Gülen recently offered to turn over nearly 300 of his schools to the Ministry of Education. Caught off guard by the proposal, the minister merely responded that he had not yet received a concrete application on the matter. Education experts have described Gülen's establishments, however, as model private schools.

According to his followers, Gülen believes that Islam is compatible with a modern democratic state. He has personally shunned politics up to now but has encouraged his followers to support one or another of the conservative political parties. Although he has not said so, Gülen seems to be building a moderate alternative to Refah, with his own religious foundation, charity organizations, businesses, and media empire—newspapers and magazines, book publishing, television network, and video companies.

Gülen appears on Turkish television quite often but rarely meets with Western journalists. In his first interview with an American publication, he told my friend James Wilde, İstanbul correspondent for *Time* magazine, that Turkey was "freer to live in an Islamic way than any other Muslim country."[3]

Commenting on the religious revival, Gülen said: "Because of the collapse of the iron wall, people throughout the world are returning to traditional values and religion. The same is true in Turkey. We have been Muslims for ten centuries. We are rediscovering our religious values. This cannot be labeled as fundamentalism. There are fundamentalist movements, Muslim, Christian, and Jewish, but Islam is a middle way and condemns extremist movements. The great majority of Muslims in Turkey want a moderate religious way of life and they are against extremism of any kind."

In conclusion, Gülen said: "To prevent the rise of extremism and fundamentalism, sufficient importance must be given to people's democratic and basic freedoms as well as economic problems."

Gülen has been carrying out a personal campaign for interreligious dialogue. In February 1998, he discussed the issue with Pope John Paul II in the Vatican. Later Gülen met in İstanbul with Eliyahu Baksi Doron, Israel's Chief Rabbi of Sephardic Jews, for interfaith talks.

Despite his conciliatory gestures and words, Gülen has not been exempt from the military crackdown on Islamic radicals. In one of their periodical briefings on fundamentalism in February 1998, a group of generals reportedly conveyed to then Deputy Prime Minister Ecevit their concerns about Gülen.

Although expressing comprehension for the military's sensitivity on the exploitation of religion, Ecevit strongly defended Gülen as a respectable figure and stressed that had it not been for Gülen and his schools, Central Asia and Azerbaijan would have fallen under the influence of Iranian fundamentalism.

Nevertheless, in June 1998, a record 167 officers and noncommissioned officers were expelled from the army, most of them reportedly "fundamentalists" and members of Gülen's community.[4] There had been press reports in the past that Gülen encouraged his followers to infiltrate police schools and military high schools.

The most serious crisis erupted a year later during an investigation into a wire-tapping scandal, when senior officers of the Ankara police department were accused of eavesdropping on calls of prominent businessmen and political personalities, even the prime minister. The police responded that they were monitoring calls of Islamist activists in the police and identified them as followers of Fethullah Gülen. Press reports said intelligence services had uncovered a plot by Fethullahis to infiltrate the state bureaucracy with the aim of establishing a system based on *Sharia*.[5] Officials expressed skepticism over these allegations, calling it a smokescreen to hide illegal activities by police elements, but the damage was done.[6]

Some secular intellectuals are deeply mistrustful of this apparently moderate Islamic leader, who criticized Refah, supports right-wing secular parties, and calls for "dialogue and tolerance." Many others see Gülen as the main hope for some kind of accommodation between the secular and Islamist worlds.

Whether Gülen is a positive or negative influence, it is not at all sure how active a role he can play in Turkey's future. He is said to suffer from diabetes and heart problems and recently spent some time in the United States getting medical treatment.

The Department of Religious Affairs provides a very different perspective on Turkish Islam. This little-publicized agency has been considered something of an anomaly in the secular state's hierarchy and has been deeply resented by Islamists as an official watchdog. Probably that's what Atatürk intended it to be when he established it under the prime minister's office in 1924.

But over the years, it has become a powerful bureaucracy, with a generous budget and 88,500 employees. Inadvertently, it is partly responsible for the growth of the Islamic movement. The department provides religious personnel for all the mosques, organizes religious training, and is charged with religious publications. An Overseas Division sends religious personnel to countries with a substantial Turkish population, such as Germany. And ever since the collapse of the former Soviet Union, the state agency has been actively engaged in Islamic politics.

Of late, Mehmet Nuri Yılmaz, president of the Religious Affairs Department, has been complaining that his office is understaffed—with serious consequences. Yılmaz has informed the National Security Council (the supreme military-dominated, policymaking agency) that because of the shortage of religious personnel, mosques are being misused for propaganda by religious sects and the banned Kurdistan Workers Party.[7] He noted that there are a total of 72,418 mosques in Turkey, presumably under the control of his department, but he stressed that he did not have the staff for 11,000 of them. Where there is no official İmam (preacher), the local worshipers elect their own, he said, adding that in the southeast, these elected İmams have been disseminating Kurdish nationalist propaganda.

Obviously the huge bureaucracy has let things get out of hand.

When I visited the Religious Affairs leader in his office next to Kocatepe Mosque a year earlier, he made no mention of personnel shortages but on the contrary talked of expansion. He said the government agency was involved in the construction of thirty-six mosques in the new Muslim republics of Central Asia and the Caucasus, with financing from private Turkish religious foundations. The department has also opened three faculties of divinity and six secondary schools in the former Soviet Union, staffing them with Koranic teachers and supplying Korans in Arabic.

"Russia didn't provide enough mosques or religious schools and so when the Central Asian countries won their independence, they came to us for assistance because of old cultural ties," Mr. Yılmaz explained.[8] "Iran wanted to help in the beginning but failed; the public wanted Turkey."

What, I wondered, would Atatürk think of his secular state's new missionary zeal?

As if he were reading my mind, Mr. Yılmaz added, "There was no problem between Atatürk and religion. He was not against Islam, but some of his statements were distorted. He believed in secularism or freedom of religion, not *no* religion. On his order, the Koran and the commentaries were translated into Turkish."

Coexisting with the state's Islamic hierarchy are a number of unofficial authorities on Islam, professors of theology and authors who have gained the respect of Islamic thinkers around the world.

Among these sages is Professor Hayrettin Karaman of Maramara University's Faculty of Theology. We met in his cubbyhole lined with books at the Islamic Encyclopedia office, near the faculty on the Asian side of the Bosphorus. Professor Karaman said there are now twenty faculties of theology in Turkey, most of them opened in the past decade, with about 8,000 students. Graduates work mostly in the Department of Religious Affairs.

I asked Professor Karaman my basic question: Is Turkish Islam different?

The majority of Turks belong to the Sunni or orthodox branch of Islam, which means as far as doctrine, ritual, social activity, and theory, there is no difference, Professor Karaman began.[9] In practice there are variations. In dress, for example, Turkey and Egypt are similar in the belief that both men and women should be covered but leaving the face and hands open.

The question of religious authority also differs, he pointed out. In Iran, no one can oppose the judgment of the religious authorities. In Egypt, the public listens to the learned authorities of El Ahzar University, but scholars are free to obey or issue conflicting *fetwas* (religious decrees).

In Turkey, Professor Karaman noted, there is the Religious Affairs High Council (an official body), whose decisions are considered the norm for muftis and other religious cadres. On a parallel informal track, there are a number of academic men who can make *fetwas*, or religious edicts.

Without false modesty, Professor Karaman explained that some people who know him from his books, articles, and lectures "consider my knowledge better than that of the muftis and ask me for counsel." He receives calls from believers night and day to pronounce *fetwas* on a wide range of everyday issues. For example, not long ago he ruled that abortion was acceptable in the case of a woman with a brain-dead child in her womb.

His views tend to be liberal even on such delicate issues as Salman Rushdie. Dr. Karaman said he has publicly criticized both *The Satanic Verses* and the late Ayatollah Khomeini's implacable response. The Turkish scholar holds that one may criticize doctrine but it is not acceptable to abuse the sacred quality of religion. If Rushdie lived in a Muslim country, he should be taken to court and given the right to defense. But since the British writer does not live in a Muslim country, Muslims do not have the right to judge and punish him. All that can be done is take him to an international human rights court or sue him under British law.

Expressing high esteem for the Sufi orders like the Mevlevi and the Nakşibendi, the religious scholar said, "I take their interpretation of the Koran seriously. I believe they are more successful at religious education than the teachers in the state schools."

Questioned about the ideological fathers of Turkish Islam, Professor Karaman named the Muslim scholar Sait Halim Paşa from the Ottoman era. This *grand vizier* (prime minister) during World War I was a scholar on social issues and a significant figure in the Islamic revival movement. Other sources of religious inspiration are the nineteenth-century Islamic reformists from Cairo, Jamal al-Din al-Afghani and Muhammad Abduh. Professor Karaman said he preferred the latter's focus on education to politics.

In the past, Konya used to be Anatolia's center for religious scholarship, but today there is no one center, according to Professor Karaman. Because of competing official and unofficial religious authorities, there are various centers: İstanbul, Ankara, Van, İzmir.

What did he think of the movement of some Islamists to restore the caliphate that the Islamic spiritual leadership abolished by Atatürk in 1924? Professor Karaman was adamant: "A new caliphate is out of the question. The idea of a single authority in the Muslim world, with all its divisions, is implausible. No nation would give up its authority. We may, however, build a Muslim Union, along the lines of the European Union."

A prominent Islamic scholar who has caught the attention of the secular public is Dr. Yaşar Nuri Öztürk, dean of İstanbul University's Faculty of Religion. Wherever I went the summer of 1998, secularists were talking about him and saying he made sense to them. His could be described as the Turkish nationalist interpretation of Islam.

Author of several books on Islam who frequently appears on television, Professor Öztürk describes himself as "a modern Islamic follower of Atatürk."[10] Receiving me in his office in the old city, the graying Islamic educator wore a bright yellow sport shirt. Many of his opinions seem to be the basis of official thinking on Islam (particularly among the military).

Declaring that he "loves and respects" Atatürk's progressive revolution, Dr. Öztürk said it was necessary to separate the force of government from the rules of heaven. Emphasizing that there was no need to change the secular constitution, he said *Sharia* is a set of rules from the Koran, whose interpretation is "relative," related to geography and time.

He described Islam as "a path of universal standards" and insisted that it was not at all incompatible with democracy. Reiterating that Islam is one, he made a distinction between "the religion of the Koran and religion of tradition," between "Islamization and Arabization."

Unlike most Islamic scholars, he favors using Turkish for prayers. Since Islam is a universal religion, people can say their prayers in their own language, he said, making the same arguments as Roman Catholics who prefer the vernacular to Latin.

Although expressing respect for the mystic dimension of Sufism, he argued that the activities of brotherhoods should be "halted or circumscribed" because they caused many problems, specifically the abuse of human rights.

According to his understanding of the Koran, a woman is not obliged to cover her head. But he disagrees with the ban on headscarves in universities because he says "it will only benefit political Islam."

"The danger today is political Islam," Dr. Öztürk said. He contends that there is a collusion of outside powers pushing political Islam in Turkey "to weaken the country." He openly accused Muslim neighbors, whose systems are failing, and non-Muslim countries like Greece and Russia, for their own motives.

"I hope Turkey's future will be a Koranization, embracing modernity and the essence of religion," he concluded. "But what I see on the scene and the streets is an Arabization of the masses, using political arguments and money. The situation is not good."

A more conciliatory, more cosmopolitan Islamic outlook can be found at İstanbul's Research Center for Islamic History, Art and Culture. This little-publicized center of learning is located in the recently restored nineteenth-century Yıldız Palace surrounded by romantic Yıldız Park with its gardens and tea houses.

Islamic scholar Ekmeleddin İhsanoğlu has directed the center since its creation in 1980 by the Organization of the Islamic Conference, which aims to improve cooperation among Muslim states and provide an Islamic voice in world affairs. Its basic mission has been to keep Turkey's foot in the Islamic world, despite its secular stance and despite often strained relations with its Muslim neighbors like Syria, Iraq, and Iran.[11]

"Our center is above politics," Dr. İhsanoğlu told me, emphasizing that occasional political tensions among the fifty-five members did not affect the center's activities. The main objective of the center is to preserve the Islamic heritage through publications, restoration work, seminars, and other cultural exchanges.

A major project that is under way is The History and Culture of Bosnia and Herzegovina, undertaken in cooperation with the Bosnian government and aimed at the restoration and preservation of that war-torn country's cultural and architectural heritage. The center has organized a series of workshops to coordinate the international academic effort in assisting Bosnia's reconstruction and urban preservation action.

Other regional research projects undertaken by the center include a history of Islamic Civilization in Southeast Asia and new research on Islamic Civilization in West Africa. The center also sponsors calligraphy classes, art exhibits, and lectures on a wide range of topics from Human Rights in Islam to Islamic poets, musicians, and architects.

In an effort to promote better understanding of Islam, Dr. İhsanoğlu frequently takes part in interreligious conferences. He even organized a gathering of faiths for Hillary Rodham Clinton during her visit to Turkey in March 1996. Among those present were the Grand Mufti of İstanbul, the Greek Orthodox Patriarch, the Syrian Orthodox Archbishop, the Armenian Patriarch, the Chief Rabbi, and the General Secretary of the Bishops' Conference. After an exchange of views, the American First Lady wrote in the center's visitors' book: "Thank you for your work on behalf of understanding, coexistence, and peace."

Summing up the center's goal, Dr. İhsanoğlu told me, "We want to build a network of minds, souls, and hearts to work for the future."

A significant and little-known Islamic minority in Turkey is the Alevi community, a heterodox Muslim group, who claims to constitute 25 percent of Turkey's population. Because of harsh repression by the orthodox Sunni majority, the Alevis tend to keep their religious practices private. Their main mystic center was founded by a thirteenth-century holy man, Hacı Bektaş, based in the Anatolian heartland and also revered by the Bektaşi sect.

From the outset, the Alevis supported Atatürk's modernization program, and some people believe the revolution might not have happened without them. Until recently the Alevis were identified with left-wing secular parties. In modern times, they have rarely made headlines except when they were victims of some fanatic Islamic attack.

But things are changing. In a bid for Alevi support, Prime Minister Yılmaz included assistance for Alevi associations and foundations in the 1998 budget, for the first time ever. Also in an attempt to court the Alevi vote, the ruling liberal Motherland Party and left-wing politicians have given increased importance to the annual Hacı Bektaş Festival.

The Alevis increasingly define themselves as Alevis, rather than socialists or progressives, and can no longer be taken for granted. Reha Çamuroğlu, an Alevi historian and a leader of the Barış (Peace) Party, told me why.

Over cappuccinos in İstanbul's popular Marmara Café, Çamuroğlu (CHOM-u-roll-oo) said there was a combination of factors behind the Alevi return to their roots: the collapse of the Socialist bloc, the appearance of the Kurdish problem, the development of radical Islam, and the Iranian revolution. "All this affected Alevis and we suddenly discovered we had religion."[12]

The thirty-nine-year-old Alevi academic, with grizzled mustache and gold-rimmed glasses, gave me some insights into this secretive religion, dismissing the common belief that Alevis follow the Shiite branch of Islam without going into detail. Alevis' religious thinking is "wholly different" from mainstream Sunni Islam, he emphasized. First of all, Alevis believe that women and men are equal. Monogamy is favored and marriage with four women forbidden. In their traditional rituals, men and women dance together. Also Alevis hold their worship services in a large house and do not need to pray in a mosque.

Çamuroğlu said that the Alevis set up Barış because the left-wing parties had not given them much of a political role. Out of the 550-member

Parliament, there were fewer than 25 Alevis. When the Socialists were in government, Alevis were given a few ministerial posts "but it was not satisfactory," he said. "Our cadres demand more of a voice."

Another complaint is the apparent complacency, even connivance, of the authorities (including Socialists) in two serious assaults on Alevis. In the summer of 1993, a group of well-known liberal Alevi writers and singers met for a summer arts festival in the conservative city of Sivas. One of the guests, the left-wing author Aziz Nesin, antagonized the local population by an antireligion speech. An angry mob of Sunni fundamentalists lay siege to the group of intellectuals for eight hours. Their hotel was set on fire, and thirty-seven people were killed, including thirty-three Alevis, but Nesin escaped. Çamuroğlu said the military platoon in Sivas had failed to help the Alevis, and later the Socialist Party did nothing to punish the attackers.

Then in the spring of 1995, unknown assailants threw a bomb in an Alevi café in the Gazi district of İstanbul, provoking widespread street protests. Thirty Alevi teenagers were killed in clashes with the police. "Twenty policemen were identified from films shot of the melee and have been brought to trial, but the legal proceedings are continuing and the policemen are still on duty," the Alevi leader protested.

Since this conversation, the Ankara State Security Court has handed down death sentences to thirty-three fundamentalists found guilty in the Sivas case, stirring widespread denunciations from the Islamist press and accusations of a "revenge" verdict. The case will now go to the Supreme Appeals Court, but whatever the final decision, the Sunni-Alevi animosities continue.

Alevis suffer from official discrimination in various ways, according to Çamuroğlu. "The hidden ideology of the state is that only a Turk and Sunni Muslim can be a real citizen," he complained. "Compulsory religious instruction in public schools is Sunni Islam and makes no allowances for Alevis' beliefs. The Religious Affairs Directorate does not employ Alevi religious leaders and makes Sunni propaganda with government funds."

In reaction to what was seen as bias and injustice, a group of Alevis led by a wealthy businessman, Ali Haydar Veziroğlu, founded the Democratic Peace Movement in November 1995. But they were accused of being "against the constitution" because they called for the elimination of the Department of Religious Affairs.

What began as an Alevi movement has now become "a peace project for all Turks and people of all origins are welcome," Çamuroğlu emphasized. He said Barış aims to

- eliminate illegal groups in the state system (covert security organization and underground economy)
- decentralize the government structure
- privatize key sectors of the economy like state banks
- achieve integration with the European Union
- resolve the Kurdish problem with the recognition of cultural rights, free press, and free education

He acknowledged that the formation of the new Alevi-led Peace Party could hurt the traditional left-wing parties. But Çamuroğlu insisted on the need for a group to promote "the Alevi way."

"The right-wing parties always give importance to liberal economic policies; the left to liberal political ideas," the Alevi leader said. "Our party defends liberalism in both politics and economics."

# 5 ⬿

## On the Dark Side

As I came to understand the diversity of Islamic groups in Turkey, it seemed that some kind of accommodation with modern secular democracy was not only possible but essential.

There are radicals, to be sure, and fundamentalists, but so there are in any society that permits free expression. Most Turks are just as opposed to the extremes as are Spaniards or Americans.

Then invariably something happens to shatter my vision. Abruptly, some unpredictable violent words or actions evoke the long-standing stereotypes of militant Islam, the Islamic threat, Islamic *jihad* (holy war).

Religious violence in Turkey cannot begin to compare with the vicious orgy of killings in Algeria or the deadly mass assaults in Egypt or the sectarian strife in Lebanon. But it is there, around the corner—ready to erupt without warning, and often going without retribution.

One problem is the multiple sources of violence. In the troubled spring of 1997, a string of assassinations, shootouts, and bomb attacks was attributed variously to state gangs, Kurdish terrorists, leftists, rightists, and Islamist radicals. Some arrests were made but the truth remained elusive.

An important factor is the dangerous neighborhood. In fact, it is remarkable the spillover of violence has not been greater in view of traditionally unfriendly neighbors like Iran, Iraq, Syria, Greece, Russia, and Armenia and until the end of the Cold War, the former Soviet Union and other communist states. On any number of occasions, Turkish Military Intelligence has detected the presence of a foreign hand in local acts of violence. In the past, communists were generally blamed, and more recently Greeks and Greek Cypriots.

There is said to be evidence of Iranian and Libyan involvement in some of the Islamic violence. But until lately, Turkish authorities generally considered Islamist undercover activities did not warrant poisoning already tense relations with Islamic states. Besides, this kind of intelligence made good bargaining chips in diplomatic negotiations for higher stakes. For a long time Ankara turned a blind eye to Iranian support of local Islamist groups in hopes of winning Iranian cooperation in curbing PKK guerrillas on its soil. But when Turkey's Islamic-led government initiated a rapprochement with Iran in 1997, the Turkish military drew the line. A senior army commander publicly denounced Iran for supporting the PKK and terrorism. At the instigation of the military, several Iranian diplomats were expelled for interfering in local affairs.

Another reason for the impunity enjoyed by some right-wing militants is the fact that the police have been heavily infiltrated by Islamists and the extreme right. Supporting this theory are recent incidents in which police and Islamist demonstrators joined forces to attack journalists.

Undoubtedly the most sensational single violent action was the assassination attempt against Pope John Paul II in 1981. A young Turk, Mehmet Ali Ağca, was convicted of the shooting, but controversy swirled for months over who was behind the deed. Ağca's early statements indicated that he was involved with Islamic extremists. But several highly regarded political analysts presented a convincing scenario, alleging that he was the tool of Eastern European communists, namely Bulgarians.

Previously, Ağca had gained national notoriety when he was tried and convicted for the murder of a prominent liberal newspaperman, Abdi İpekçi, in İstanbul in 1979. There had been rumors at the time that his escape from prison and flight abroad had been arranged by the extreme right-wing Nationalist Action Party.

After the botched attempt on the pope, the *Times* sent me out to Ağca's hometown of Malatya in eastern Turkey. There I talked to family and friends in the bleak slum district of Boztepe, where he grew up. People who knew him insisted that he was not particularly religious, and his brother confirmed that he did not keep the Islamic fast or go regularly to the mosque. However, Ağca did graduate from the local Teachers Training High School, which was known to be strongly influenced by the Nationalist Action Party. And in conversations with neighbors and local journalists, I learned that Ağca was often seen in the company of Idealists—a militant youth group inspired by the Nationalist Action Party.

"Mehmet Ali Ağca was a psychopath used by international terror," a senior official told me. Several schoolmates argued that he had no strong political views and "did it for money."

Like so many incidents of violence in Turkey, much of the Ağca story remains a mystery, even after all these years.

Although it is not acknowledged officially, governments have found it expedient to blame some of the more horrible political killings on "Islamist extremists." For example, the authorities charged that the 1993 assassination of Kurdish parliamentarian Mehmet Sincar was the work of the illegal Islamist group Hizbullah. Yet human rights organizations have listed this as a "mystery killing," with the complicity of the security forces.

Islamist-inspired violence became a problem in the late 1980s, with the assassination of a number of secular intellectuals. In 1990, the establishment was shocked by the murder of Muammer Aksoy, president of the Turkish Law Society, and Bahriye Uçok, a secular scholar on Islam, allegedly by religious fanatics. These deeds were followed by arrests in the fundamentalist community. But it was widely believed that the real authors of these crimes had escaped unpunished.

The case that attracted a good deal of public attention was the 1993 carbomb murder of investigative reporter Uğur Mumcu. In the early 1980s, I met often with the modest, scholarly Mumcu (MUM-jew) at the secular newspaper *Cumhuriyet*, located across the street from the *New York Times* office in Ankara. Mumcu kept detailed files on human rights violations and was the best source I knew in those difficult times before and after the military coup. Colleagues tell me that at the time of his death, Mumcu was investigating activities of undercover Islamic groups from Iran and Saudi Arabia and probably fell victim to one of them. But officially the murder remains unsolved.

The majority of Turkey's Islamists categorically condemn these acts of violence. On the contrary, Islamists like Erbakan have persistently demonstrated that they favor the restoration of an Islamic state through democratic means.

There are undeniably radical individuals and groups who seek the violent overthrow of the secular state. These extremists sometimes express their revolutionary views publicly. Most of the time, they operate in shadowy groups and have resorted to terrorist tactics, including bomb attacks and assassinations.

Metin Heper, dean of Bilkent's School of Economic, Administrative and Social Sciences, says thus far the influence of these groups has been only marginal, probably because they are so dispersed and have not established links among themselves and because they lack any real leader.[1]

The best-known militant Islamic groups—which is not to say much is known about them—are three clandestine Turkish-based organizations: Hizbullah, IBDA-C (the Islamic Front of Fighters of the Great East), and the Islamist Activists Organization (IHO). Another radical group, the Anatolia Federated Islamic State, better known as Kara Ses (Black Voice), is located in Germany.

In her report on Moderate and Radical Islamism in Turkey,[2] Nilüfer Narlı, associate professor of international relations at Marmara University, provides a good deal of information on these shadowy groups. Hizbullah (Party of God) was formed in southeast Turkey after the Iranian Islamic revolution in 1979, but split into two groups after the 1980 military coup. Narlı explains that the Menzil group, taking its name from the bookstore in Diyarbakır where the militants met, viewed the Kurdish struggle to be as important as the Islamist struggle. On the other hand, the İlim group—also named for a bookstore—favored armed *jihad* and was not interested in the Kurdish cause. In fact Narlı writes that the İlims reportedly collaborated with fundamentalist police officers against the Menzils and the Kurdistan Workers Party (PKK) in 1991 and 1992.

According to press reports, the "Hizbullah threat" is growing.[3] The Turkish group subscribes to the Iranian model and receives funds from foreign-based Islamist organizations. This banned terrorist group was tolerated as long as it fought against separatists of the PKK. But by 1994, Hizbullah's acts were considered counterproductive, and there were widespread arrests.

Since then, Hizbullah is said to be actively spreading radical Islamist propaganda in student hostels and through private Koranic courses, which are not controlled by the state. As part of the clampdown on militant Islamists in the spring of 1998, police announced several major operations against Hizbullah in the southeast around Diyarbakır and Batman. According to documents seized at the time, Hizbullah counted an estimated 20,000 militants and sympathizers in the region.

During a seminar at Ankara University in celebration of the seventy-fifth anniversary of the Republic, the Security General Directorate announced that major progress had been made in the fight against "fundamentalist organizations." İhsan Yılmaztürk, chief of antiterrorist operations, said investigations revealed Hizbullah's involvement in 400 murder cases and stated that some 3,000 Hizbullah militants had been arrested.[4]

At the same time, the security official claimed that "almost all" of the activists of IBDA-C and IHO had been apprehended and were in jail. He charged that these two organizations and Hizbullah had taken up arms with the aim of destroying the existing democratic, secular constitutional system and establishing Islamic rule.[5]

Over the past decade, IBDA-C has emerged as one of the most violent groups, taking responsibility for several bomb attacks against Christian targets, like the Greek Orthodox Patriarchate and a couple of churches. They also claimed bomb attacks against Aya Sofya, some banks, and a failed car-bomb attempt against a Jewish community leader in Ankara. Usually the attacks were aimed to terrorize and have caused damage but no victims.

The public got some insight into the kind of people who belong to this dark world in early 1995, when a bomb went off in the hands of a terrorist at the Atatürk Thought Association in Ankara. The bomber, who died from his injuries, was identified as an IBDA-C militant. He was said to be a bright twenty-four-year-old graduate of prestigious Bosphorus University, employed at the State Institute of Statistics.

IBDA-C claimed credit a couple of years ago for the time bomb that exploded at a downtown İstanbul café, killing two people. They declared their act was to protest against the New Year's Eve celebrations, which they called "a Christian habit imposed on Muslims."

Occasionally, the Turkish press will produce incendiary statements by "a captured leader" of IBDA-C, claiming that the Islamists were arming themselves. Such reports appear intended to pave the way for repressive measures against Islamists.

In her report on the Islamist radicals,[6] Narlı writes that unlike many radical groups, IBDA-C was not inspired by the Iranian revolution but by Said-i-Nursi and other Kurdish figures of southeastern Turkey. Its publications openly call for armed struggle to restore the *Sharia* in Turkey.

Dr. Narlı mentions another radical group: Muslim Youth, founded in the early 1980s by Mehmet Güney, a militant of Erbakan's old National Salvation Party. This group, also influenced by Said-i-Nursi and the Palestinian HAMAS, advocates armed warfare against the state. The Muslim Youth is said to be well organized in certain universities and *İmam Hatip* high schools. Many of the student protests and street demonstrations held after Friday prayers at some İstanbul mosques were said to be organized by the Muslim Youth.

The head of the İstanbul branch of the Muslim Youth and a score of militants were arrested in June 1994, according to Dr. Narlı. They reportedly had organized various fund-raising events to buy arms and pay for military training for their members.

Besides these organizations, Dr. Narlı says there are around 300 smaller radical Islamic groups in Turkey, with some 15,000 guerrillas who received military training in Afghanistan, Iran, Pakistan, and Lebanon in the period from 1980 to 1990.

Kara Ses, led by a self-proclaimed caliph, Metin Kaplan, is active among Turkish immigrants in Europe. In November 1998, Turkish authorities arrested twenty-seven Kara Ses militants, suspected of plans to make "kamikaze attacks" on Atatürk's mausoleum, Aya Sofia, and other important sites in Ankara and İstanbul.[7]

Some Islamist organizations are so clandestine that it is not clear they really exist. One of these is called "Mohammed's Army." Secularists have obtained letters trying to recruit young people for this secret military group. But I have seen no evidence that this army has ever done anything or is preparing to do anything. And I'm certain the Turkish authorities would step in forcefully if any kind of armed movement ever appeared.

But other ominous aspects of resurgent Islam are definitely a matter of concern. Some incidents have received broad exposure in the secular media, particularly those involving cult leaders who have been denounced for sexual abuse. For instance, there was the case of a beautiful, pious girl named Fadimeh, who appeared on television to recount how she had been deceived by the leader of an Islamic sect.

"With the increasing visibility of Islamists, we secularists have learned a lot about religion, how it can be used and abused," says my friend Sirma Evcan, a former political analyst with the *Turkish Daily News*. "Most people have no idea that the concept of sex appears so frequently in the Koran."

Generally, scandals involving Islamic cults who prey on young people never make the news. Yet everybody knows about them. For example, there's the case of the three teenage sisters who were kidnapped by followers of a *hoca* (Islamic teacher) in İstanbul and held against their will for a week. Finally, after the family hired a private detective, the three girls were found in a religious school in the Fatih district. The kidnappers were handsome, well-dressed young men who offered the girls jobs and apartments if they agreed to join the sect.

In what sounds very much like religious scams in the United States, some *hocas* (HO-jas) have lured rich students away from home, getting them to sign contracts to take up "an Islamic lifestyle."

Then one hears complaints of violence by religious zealots, particularly in the holy month of Ramadan. Some gangs will beat up students who dare to snack or smoke during Ramadan's daytime fast or who just look religiously incorrect. Not long ago, an art student I know was beaten up by a gang of militant Islamists on a street in İstanbul's fashionable Ortaköy district, because he wears long hair and an earring.

In a much-publicized case not long ago, an İstanbul barman appeared on television with the word *Allah* tattooed on his arm. Considering this an act of blasphemy, a fanatic Islamist murdered the barman in cold blood.

Certain verbal threats, when repeated often enough, can create a state of anxiety. A foreign journalist who has made İstanbul his home has been warned several times by Islamic militants that "when the Islamists take over, all foreigners will have to leave."

There are also countless wild, menacing statements made by mayors, deputies, and other prominent Islamists. Some militants like Hasan Mezarçı, former Refah deputy for İstanbul, have appeared in court for their fiery declarations. Mezarçı, already in jail for insulting Atatürk, faced a new trial for reportedly declaring during the 1994 election campaign that an agreement had been reached between Refah and the banned Kurdish nationalist PKK to establish two states: an Islamic *Sharia*-based state and a Kurdish state.[8] Refah's leadership has never openly stated such aims, which would be subject to criminal prosecution.

Another firebrand and former Refah deputy, Şevki Yılmaz gained national notoriety over a speech he made at a pro-Islamic rally in Germany in 1990. Mayor of the Black Sea town of Rize at the time, Yılmaz insulted certain members of Parliament and the Parliament itself, as well as other prominent politicians. He also called for the implementation of *Sharia* in Turkey.[9] Such statements were said to be against the integrity of the state, and the deputy's parliamentary immunity was lifted at the end of 1997.

During the heated discussions over the *İmam Hatip* schools in the spring of 1997, İbrahim Çelik, a former Refah deputy from the southeastern town of Şanlıurfa, warned that if these religious training schools were closed, "the people would rise up and the country would be a sea of blood."[10]

Military intelligence has failed to provide any concrete evidence of links between the Islamist political leadership and the clandestine Islamist groups. But they have successfully collected a number of rash statements over the years by Refah militants, which are highly damaging to the democratic image the Islamists have tried to project.

When confronted with official charges that some of Refah's leadership was involved in radical movements like Hizbullah, Erbakan told the Constitutional Court: "It is not possible for us to keep an eye on all four million members."[11]

Mezarçı and other loose cannons have been disavowed by Refah's leadership and expelled from the party. But it is not easy to forget their words.

The authorities have also clamped down on radical brotherhoods like the Aczmendi. In the spring of 1997, more than 100 members of this sect were sentenced to three years' prison for challenging the secular order. The indictment cited a declaration by Aczmendi leader Müslüm Gündüz, who told the İstanbul daily *Milliyet* that if those in power did not prefer the *Sharia*, the public would bring it and a lot of blood would be shed. Expressing the hope that God would prevent the bloodshed, he stressed that they did not want to shed blood—but if they were forced to act in the name of religion, no one could stop them.

It is never easy to distinguish between Islamic rhetoric and intent. Even if such threatening declarations are merely exercises in hyperbole to appeal to young zealots, they sour the atmosphere. The modus vivendi between secularists and Islamists is so fragile that almost any outrageous remark by any Islamist public figure—or any radical secularist for that matter—can permanently damage those attempts to establish trust between the two communities.

# 6 ～

---

## A Glance Backward

---

Before Islamic roots, Christian roots, and before that Shamanist roots. To understand Turkey today, a brief reminder of the historical context might be useful. Other people have chronicled Turkey's long and eventful past and described its notable monuments. I will merely provide a glimpse into the many layers of civilization that have occupied this land known as Asia Minor or Anatolia since Paleolithic times more than 10,000 years ago.

During my five years in the area and numerous visits, I have seen much of this breathtakingly beautiful country, larger than France and Germany put together. Sometimes I was accompanied by my able Turkish assistant or colleagues, but I also traveled a good deal alone or with my niece. I covered earthquakes, leftist rebellions, Islamic protests, and the Kurdish insurgency. I drove the entire length of the land when there were few gas stations and virtually no highways (unlike today). I also used public buses—a good way to get to know people—unbelievably slow trains, even the old Orient Express from Baghdad to İstanbul, and some very small planes flown by ex–fighter pilots. Never did I feel personally threatened as an American or a woman, although once in a fifth-class hotel (my rating) near Aphrodisias, my panic-stricken niece took refuge in my room because a local admirer had broken into her room. (My lovely niece was stalked in Greece as well.)

The overriding impression that I retain of Anatolia is that this is indeed holy land. Some believe this was the birthplace and rebirth of the Judeo-Christian civilization, the garden of Eden, and the resting place of Noah's Ark. This, it is said, was home of the great mother goddesses Cybele and Artemis. Here too are many spiritual centers of Islam, some shared by other religions.

Even to the newcomer, it's like coming home again. Although many place names have changed, there are guidebooks, like the invaluable *Biblical Sites in Turkey*, which give the historical names and the modern Turkish equivalent.[1] The Turkish authorities now publish maps, which include ancient names, familiar to readers of the Bible or the classics (see Map 6.1.).

Many antiquities may also appear familiar because similar pieces are found in leading museums of the world, many of them illegally smuggled out of the country. Under Turkish law, all antiquities found in Turkey belong to the state.

An old friend, Özgen Acar, is Turkey's leading investigative journalist in antiquities. His revelations in *Archaeology* and *Connoisseur* magazines have helped Turkey recover important treasures.

Among Acar's most celebrated cases is the recovery of the Lydian Hoard from the Metropolitan Museum of Art in October 1993. The 363 pieces of gold and silver, marble sphinxes, and wall paintings had been stolen in 1966 from sixth-century B.C. mounds near Manisa and Uşak in western Turkey. After prolonged investigations, the looters were arrested and the art dealers involved identified, but it took a six-year legal battle to persuade the Met to repatriate its acquisition.[2]

Then there was the three-ton, second-century marble sarcophagus, somehow secreted out of Turkey in 1986 and purchased by Damon Mezzacappa, a New York investment banker. He loaned the Garland Sarcophagus, as it is called, to the Brooklyn Museum, which proudly put it on display. Subsequently Mezzacappa offered to donate the magnificent piece, but the museum refused, apparently wary of how the sarcophagus was acquired. Such donations are tax deductible at the full market value of the gift, in this case $11 million. The collector finally donated it to the American-Turkish Society, which duly returned it to Turkey.[3]

The latest legal battle ended in March 1999, with the restitution to Turkey of what is known as the Elmalı Hoard, some 2,000 Greek and Lycian coins smuggled out of Turkey in the early 1980s and later purchased by investor William I. Koch, then a trustee of the Boston Museum of Fine Arts.[4]

Acar says that with the high prices paid for antiquities—the Elmalı coins were said to be worth $10 million—the looting of Turkey's historic sites is likely to continue. Today's looters are not archaeologists, who work under close government supervision. Generally amateurs and petty thieves work for professional smugglers, some of whom are sophisticated art dealers, usually based in Munich.

"But Turkey has shown it is determined to recover its stolen heritage and so maybe museums and collectors will exercise more caution in purchasing antiquities," Acar said.[5] He noted that Turkey is now negotiating the return of the Zeus Temple from the Pergamon Museum in Berlin and what is known as King Priam's treasure from Troy in the Pushkin Museum in Moscow.

My mentor on Turkey's archaeological wonders is Toni Cross, director of the Ankara branch of the American Research Institute in Turkey. ARIT is an umbrella group for some forty American and Canadian universities, research centers, and museums with archaeological or other scholarly programs in Turkey.

"In no other country can you find vestiges of so many great civilizations—Hittite, Phrygian, Urartian, Greek and Roman, Byzantine, Seljuk, Ottoman—and archaeologists have just scratched the surface," Toni emphasizes.[6]

Toni fell in love with her Turkish husband when they were both students at West Virginia University in the mid-1960s, and then she fell in love with his country. Possessing a degree in archaeology from Chapel Hill, she has visited the major archaeological sites around the country. At ARIT, she is involved with teams from American universities currently working at a score of sites. She spends her summer vacations digging at Kinet, which is almost certainly ancient Issos where Alexander the Great triumphed over Darius and the Persian army in 333 B.C.

Now with Toni's help, I have reassembled my memories to give them a chronological sequence, although in many cases the civilizations overlap. Here then is my personal Time Chart, a rapid tour of historic sites that have left an indelible memory.

My journey into this multilevel melting pot begins in Ankara at the Anatolian Civilizations Museum, housed in an Ottoman covered bazaar and certainly the best introduction to this country's absorbing history. The dynamic museum director, İlhan Temuzoy, has assembled an extraordinary collection of Anatolian treasures dating back to Paleolithic times. The best of the Old Stone Age artifacts—stone tools, teeth and bone fragments—were found in the Karain cave north of Antalya and are displayed at the Anatolian museum.

Also on display is wonderful Neolithic wall art, discovered in the big double mound at Çatalhöyük, located on the central Anatolian Plain about thirty miles southeast of Konya. Çatalhöyük is the oldest Neolithic settlement in Turkey, dating back 9,000 years. It was first excavated in the

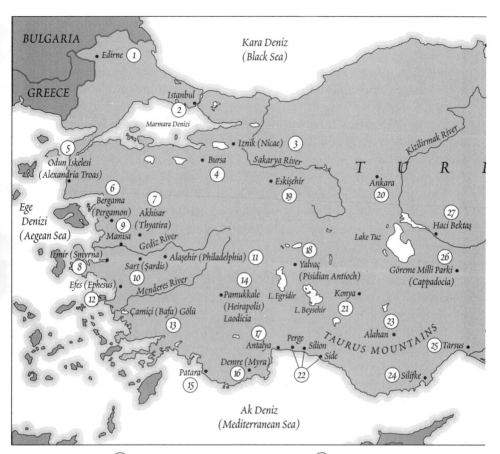

Sites of faith in Turkey

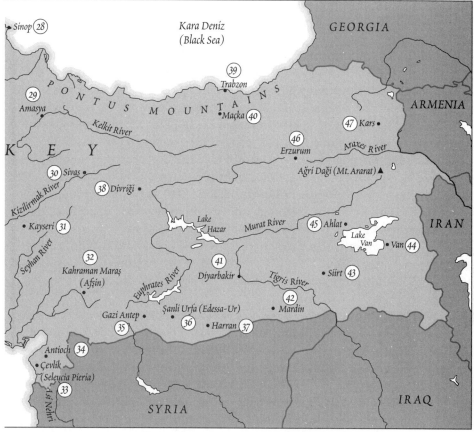

Sinop ㉘

Kara Deniz
(Black Sea)

GEORGIA

㊴
Trabzon

PONTUS MOUNTAINS

㉙
Amasya

Maçka ㊵

ARMENIA

Kelkit River

㊻ Kars •

㊼

K E Y

㊺
Erzurum

Araxes River

㉚ Sivas •

Ağrı Dağı (Mt. Ararat) ▲

Kızılırmak River

㊳ Divriği •

• Kayseri ㉛

Lake
Hazar

Murat River

㊺ Ahlat •

Lake
Van

IRAN

• Van ㊹

Seyhan River

㉜
Kahraman Maraş
(Afşin)

㊶

Diyarbakir •

Tigris River

• Siirt ㊸

Euphrates River

㊷
• Mardin

Gazi Antep •

Şanlı Urfa (Edessa-Ur) •

㉟

㊱

• Harran ㊲

Antioch ㉞

• Çevlik
(Seleucia Pieria)

㉝

Asi Nehri

SYRIA

IRAQ

early 1960s by British archaeologist James Mellaart, who believed he had uncovered a cluster of houses with shrines probably dedicated to a fertility cult because of the wall paintings and figurines. Mellaart's work was cut short after allegations that he had smuggled artifacts from another site out of the country. Excavations were stopped for three decades and only recently resumed. In the reconstituted sanctuary in the Anatolian museum, there are murals of giant bulls, hunting scenes, religious rites, and voluptuous mother-goddess figurines of terra-cotta and stone.

"This is the first time in human history that such wall paintings have been found in family dwellings rather than in shrines," İlhan Bey, as the director is known in the world of archaeology, told me.[7]

That tireless and sensitive travel writer, Freya Stark, who traveled throughout Turkey in the late 1950s and 1960s, has this to say of Çatalhöyük in her book *Turkey: A Sketch of Turkish History:*

> What has been excavated shows a prosperous Stone Age commercial culture, with metal beginning with wooden utensils varied and sophisticated, and woollen textiles developed (the sheep appears to have been the first domesticated animal). The houses were sun-dried mud, set into wooden moulds as they are in Saudi Arabia. The flat roofs were reed under mud, as in Mesopotamia; light could penetrate through little windows under the eaves. The staircase was a ladder and an opening in the roof (which also served as chimney and is still to be found in the north). . . . Every third room would be a shrine, decorated with paint that often imitated weaving; a place with no trace of sacrifice, but some evident holiness in plaster reliefs and sculptured female breasts or bulls heads endlessly repeated, and figures of riders, or of women giving birth—sacred symbols that develop through the 7th millenium.[8]

For me, one of the main charms of historic sites in Turkey was that very often I had them to myself, except in summer when archaeologists might be on duty. Aside from the big-name places like Ephesus and Sardis, very little has been done to commercialize historic ruins, although that may be changing with the influx of tourists.

It was a wondrous experience to visit the site where the Judeo-Christian civilization may have been born: the Garden of Eden. Bound by the Tigris and the Euphrates Rivers and once a land of green pastures, most of the Harran Plain today is a barren copper-colored desert and a far cry from the traditional images of the Garden of Eden. (Some scholars locate Eden farther south near the mouth of the two rivers in southern Iraq, but that marshy site looks even less like paradise lost.) At any rate, according to local legend, Adam farmed on the Harran Plain and Moses herded his sheep on the TekTek Mountains nearby. Turkish engineers today insist, however, that the fertility of ancient Mesopotamia, the Land Between the Rivers, will be restored with the completion of the Southeastern Anatolia Project's irrigation scheme.

Harran itself dates from the fifth millennium B.C. and was an important cult center with its temple to Sin, the Hittite God of the Moon. There is an alien atmosphere about the clusters of cone-shaped mud-brick houses. Still visible are remnants of the city wall, once three miles long, and an inner fortress from the Hittite period. Locals readily point to the site of "Aran's House" where Abraham and his family are said to have lived before undertaking their journey to the Promised Land of Canaan. The Grand Mosque of Harran, built around A.D. 750, is the oldest mosque in Anatolia, and its thirty-three-meter-high minaret remains largely intact. This is the site of the first Islamic university, famous for its scientific scholars.

Slightly to the north, the city of Şanlıurfa (known variously as Orrhoe, Ursu, Edessa, Ruha, and Urfa) dates from the second millennium B.C. and is called the City of Prophets. Abraham, Job, Jethro, and Elijah are said to have lived here and are revered by Muslims and Christians alike.

Present-day Şanlıurfa exudes all the exotic charm of a traditional Middle Eastern city: bustling covered markets, caravanserais, arcaded mosques, walled castle, secluded mansions with separate male and female quarters, and above all, wonderful legends.

The natives point out the cave where they say Abraham was born and hid until he was ten because the despot Nimrod had ordered all children killed. They tell how Abraham demolished the idols in the temple, angering Nimrod, who had him thrown from the castle wall into a great fire. Then, the story goes, God told the fire to be gentle to Abraham and keep him safe and cool. The fire turned into water and the burning logs into fish and Abraham found himself in a bed of roses. Today Muslim pilgrims come from all over to see the lake filled with sacred carp at the foot of the castle wall.

You will also be shown The Place of Job, the cave where it is said Job underwent his trials and tribulations for seven years without abandoning his faith. Another story has it that the King of Osroane, Abgar Ukomo, was the first ruler to proclaim Christianity as the official religion of the kingdom. When the king urged Jesus to come to Urfa to preach his religion, Jesus is supposed to have sent him a piece of cloth with the image of his face on it and a letter blessing the city.

In eastern Turkey, mystical Mount Ararat is revered by many Christians and Muslims as the final resting place of Noah's Ark after the Great Flood. The Bible refers to "the mountains of Ararat," and the Koran recounts that Noah's vessel finally landed on El Jedi, as Ararat is called in Arabic. Even that worldly traveler, Marco Polo, mentioned that the ark had come to rest on Mount Ararat.

No one in modern times has produced tangible proof of the ark's presence, although there have been many sightings and books written about these claims. For one thing, access to the area was strictly limited for many years because the Soviets suspected all ark seekers were really spies monitoring their installations on the other side of the mountain. Then, despite its benign beauty, Ararat with its perpetually snow-covered peaks rising up to 16,945 feet can be a threatening place. Climbers must face ferocious sheepdogs, marauding nomads, bottomless snow-covered pits, and above all serious weather—gales that reach 150 miles an hour, sudden snow and ice storms, and generally smothering cloud cover.

Nevertheless, when Turkish authorities eased restrictions in the summer of 1983, scientists, alpinists, adventurers, and all kinds of Christians flocked to the mountain. No mountaineer and ill-equipped for the challenge, I joined the rush to get a feel for the quest and was glad to turn back at the first camp at 10,500 feet.

My unofficial guide was Ahmet Ağa, a Kurdish tribal chief who claimed to own the deed to the southern side of the legendary mountain and was firmly convinced that the ark is on Ararat, "as the Koran says."[9] He noted that an American professor had sighted a wooden outcrop in the glacier at the Ahora gorge on the other side of the mountain. "I believe with the proper technology, the ark can be found," the Kurdish chief said.

The most prominent climber that year was the late American astronaut James B. Irwin, who told me after two failed attempts: "It's easier to walk on the moon. I've done all I possibly can, but the ark continues to elude us."[10]

As far as anybody knows, the first great empire on Anatolian soil was that of the Hittites, an Indo-European people who flourished from the beginning of the second millennium B.C. until their downfall about 1200 B.C.. The Hittite capital Hattuşaş (now called Boğazkale) was located in a rugged region 120 miles east of Ankara. German archaeologists have been working on digs in the area for almost a century, but there's much more to find.

Toni Cross compares Boğazkale to Mycenae—its contemporary—in the style of fortifications and the monumental stone. "Only Mycenae is relatively small and Boğazkale is huge!" she points out.

Hattuşaş's four-mile-long fortifications were once guarded by larger-than-life gods with almond eyes and ferocious lions to keep evildoers away. Three great gates remain in the massive wall and the ruins of the palace and foundations of close to thirty temples. The original relief of the Warrior God on the Royal Gate has been carted off to the Anatolian museum. Time has covered most of the sanctuary of Yazılıkaya, on the outskirts of the ancient city. But still visible is the natural shrine with all the deities of the Hittite pantheon and a spectacular parade of Hittite soldiers carved onto the rocky outcrop. One comes away from Hattuşaş with a new respect for the grandeur of what was once the Hittite civilization.

Only when I visited the excavations at Gordion, just sixty miles west of Ankara, did I understand that virtually all of Anatolian history had passed through here. The modest village of Yassıhöyük, the present name of Gordion, is located on the fertile plain along the Sakarya River (Sangarius in ancient times), an area of rolling wheat and sugar beet fields, grazing cattle, and mounds as far as one can see.

Gordion for me, and I guess most people, is a place where Alexander the Great encountered an inscrutable knot, mastered it, and went on to conquer the Persian Empire in the fourth century B.C. In modern times, the area is remembered for the decisive battle of Sakarya in the summer of 1921, when Atatürk's troops halted the Greek advance.

Eighty tumuli have been located in the district and thirty-five of them excavated, according to Kenneth Sams, director of the excavations, who first came to Gordion in 1967 as a graduate student.[11] It was the German brothers Gustav and Alfred Korte who discovered the conical burial mounds in 1900 and opened five tombs. Most of the excavations, including the tomb believed to be that of King Midas, have been done under the auspices of the University of Pennsylvania Museum since 1950. Their finds reveal that the area was inhabited since the Bronze Age and occupied successively by Hittites, Phrygians, Persians, Lydians, and Galatians before the Romans, Byzantines, and Seljuk Turks.

Sams has concentrated on the little-known Phrygians, who were believed to have come from the Balkans and "were very much here from the eleventh century B.C. to the late fourth century." A good deal can still be seen of the Phrygian capital including a well-preserved monumental gate and the foundations of an eighth-century B.C. royal palace complex, with *megarons*, administrative buildings, and rows of shops and workshops.

But it is the great tomb attributed to the Phrygian King Midas that astonishes lay visitors. Even if it is proved one day this was not Midas's last resting place, some important ruler must have been buried in the grandiose structure. Like other Phrygian tombs, there is no door, and excavators had to dig a tunnel through the mound to gain access to the burial chamber. This is like a log cabin made of huge petrified juniper logs, formerly sealed off with layers of pebbles and clay. Surrounded by pine-lined walls, the pine bed where the body lay stands in one corner of the chamber. The tomb also contained three grand bronze cauldrons, bronze vessels, ceramic bowls, and a number of sophisticated three-legged wood inlay tables and two fine wood inlay screens. The main wooden objects have been carefully studied, conserved, and put on display in the Anatolian Museum. To my surprise, no gold or silver was found within this hermetically sealed vault. Not wishing to add to the controversy, I can only wonder if in the end, Midas of the Golden Touch had somehow had enough of all that gold.

King Midas is also associated with another famous site of antiquity, Sardis, now called Sart, located fifty-five miles east of İzmir. According to Greek mythology, every time Midas bathed in the Pactolus River nearby, it was filled with flakes of gold. Another king whose name has become synonymous with great wealth is Croesus, ruler of the Lydian Empire, which succeeded the Phrygians in the eighth century B.C. King Croesus was the last of his dynasty to rule from Sardis, and is credited with establishing the first state mint there.

Local citizens still lament that the riches of Midas and Croesus were plundered by Persian armies. In recent years, however, this prosperous farm village has begun to capitalize on its history to become a popular tourist destination.

Archaeologists from Harvard and Cornell, working at Sart, have made important discoveries from the Lydian and Roman Ages and have undertaken a major reconstruction program. Now there's a lot to see including the splendid temple to Artemis, where work began in 334 B.C. but was never completed. A vast third-century A.D. synagogue rises from the foundations of a Roman basilica destroyed by a devastating earthquake. Nearby are a handsome Roman gymnasium with marble court and a two-story portico, a Byzantine church and acropolis, and a number of shops.

*Ephesus, capital of Roman Asia, is Turkey's best known and most developed ancient site. Americans from Mark Twain to Hillary Clinton have marveled over the remains of this wealthy city, like the handsome Celsus Library.*

Western Anatolia is studded with impressive remains of ancient city-states that flourished under Ionian rule. Freya Stark writes of the "depressing" number of earthquakes that ravaged the area but notes: "Ionia may be said to be strewn with marble, clothed in a vesture of civilization which, however ruined, is radiant and delicate as the world has never seen again."[12]

At first these city-states welcomed the Persians, who liberated them from the Lydians. Then they called on Alexander the Great, who freed them from the Persian yoke and in the process took control of all Anatolia and Persia as well. At Alexander's death in 323 B.C., his empire split up into rival Hellenistic states, only to be reunited under the Roman Empire in 25 B.C. In A.D. 330, Roman Emperor Constantine established his capital at Byzantium, renamed Constantinople, which was to rule over the Byzantine Empire for nearly twelve centuries.

Among these city-states, Ephesus was an important commercial, financial, and religious center as far back as the second millennium B.C.

Ephesus owes much of its fame to the Apostle Paul, who spent a good deal of time here preaching and writing. Before Paul, the Ephesians revered the Great Mother Goddess, known as Artemis or Diana. The magnificent temple to Artemis built at the time of Alexander the Great was considered one of the Seven Wonders of the World. After a succession of wars, earthquakes, and looters, virtually nothing was left of the temple or the rest of the city. By the ninth century, the port of Ephesus was choked by silt and the inhabitants moved inland to what is now the town of Seljuk.

Ephesus was reborn by accident in the mid–nineteenth century when a British railroad engineer, John Wood, discovered the site of the old port and extensive ruins. For the past century, Austrian archaeologists have systematically explored and restored the main monuments. Today Ephesus is the most developed archaeological site in the country, but the Austrians say there is still a good deal more in the ground. Visitors can see the great theater where Paul denounced the pagan gods and was spit upon, the lovely Temple of Hadrian, the beautifully restored library, marble streets, several churches, a vast gymnasium, the agora with its great fountain, and a good deal more.

Usually the place is jammed with tourists, but I was privileged to cover Pope John Paul II's visit in November 1979, when only a select group was admitted to the site. The most moving moment was the pontiff's visit to the House of Mary, where a group of Polish workers employed in Turkey had come to pay respects to "their" pope. According to local tradition, the Apostle John brought Mary to Ephesus around the year A.D. 40, and she is said to have spent the rest of her life here. On a wooded hill, a few miles south of Ephesus, a chapel stands on the site of the House of Meryemana, and has become a popular place of pilgrimage for Muslims as well as Christians. Nobody here seems to heed the alternative tradition that the Virgin Mary's tomb lies in Jerusalem.

The Turks again closed off Ephesus to the public the spring of 1996, this time in honor of Hillary Clinton and daughter Chelsea. My friend Toni, who was recruited as an archaeological guide for the occasion, says that Ephesus was the only place the First Lady insisted on seeing during her fleeting visit to Turkey. Toni didn't get to show President Clinton Ephesus during his visit in November 1999. But she was charged with the B list of VIPs, led by U.S. Secretary of State Madeleine Albright and national security adviser Sandy Berger.

My favorite Greco-Roman center is Aphrodisias, now called Geyre, located inland from the Aegean resort of Kuşadası. Aphrodisias was originally dedicated to local fertility goddesses and later Aphrodite, the Greek goddess of love and beauty. Aphrodisias enjoyed a lengthy Golden Age extending from the first century B.C. to the fifth century A.D. and has many well-preserved archaeological treasures to show for it. Among these are sections of the Byzantine city walls, a huge stadium for 30,000 spectators, a handsome theater of the first century B.C. with 8,000 seats, the Baths of Hadrian with six large halls, the Temple of Aphrodite, transformed into a Christian basilica in the fifth century, two Byzantine churches, and a Bishop's Palace. This land of milk and honey supported a flourishing school of sculpture, which obtained fine white and blue marble from quarries in the nearby mountains.

Although French and Italian archaeologists briefly excavated Aphrodisias at the turn of the century, most of the discoveries have been made since 1961 by the late Kenan T. Erim, a Turkish-American archaeologist, under the auspices of New York University. When I first discovered Aphrodisias in 1982, it wasn't on the tourist map and nobody was around except excavators working on an imposing three-story colonnade with reliefs dedicated to the glories of Imperial Rome. Dr. Erim later told me the discovery of this building complex, known as the Sebasteion and dating from the first half of the first century A.D., "ranks among the major archaeological events of this century."[13]

The reliefs appear familiar to anyone who has seen the film *I Claudius*, says Toni, pointing out that all the members of the Julio-Claudian family are pictured here, from Augustus to Claudius.

George E. Bean systematically and sympathetically traveled around western Turkey in the 1960s, and his chronicles are now classics. In his book, *Turkey's Southern Shore*, Bean, who is not given to hyperbole, writes of the second-century A.D. theater at Aspendos: "It is in fact the best-preserved Roman theater, indeed the best preserved ancient theater of any kind, anywhere in the world."[14] Bean also notes that the rest of the site is worthy of attention and ventures to describe the very fine aqueduct as "probably the best surviving example of a Roman aqueduct." I was enchanted by Aspendos, and it was nice to have confirmation by an expert.

Historians record other overlapping kingdoms in eastern Turkey. The Urartians, said to be native to the region, established their capital at Van, which they called Tushpa, early in the first millennium B.C. Their powerful state flourished until sometime after 639 B.C., but then what happened remains a mystery.

In his scholarly work, *Ancient Turkey*, archaeologist Seton Lloyd writes:

> We are today so copiously well informed about the ancient state of Urartu that it seems hardly credible that our information should have been so recently acquired. From the sixth century BC onwards all knowledge of its history, and even of its location, seems to have been expunged from the records of human memory with only occasional, distorted survivals in Armenian traditions. Only its name, wrongly spelt as Ararat, survived in the Old Testament. A first step leading to its rediscovery was taken in 1827, when a young scholar called Schultz reported finding rock inscriptions and other ancient remains near the city of Van in eastern Turkey. Schultz had the misfortune to be murdered before he could return home, but the careful copies which he had made of forty-two cuneiform inscriptions safely reached Paris and were published in 1840.[15]

Lloyd says it took another sixty years to decipher the Van texts, but meanwhile excavations linked to the British Museum were launched in 1879, followed "by a campaign of illicit digging which brought damaged Urartian antiquities to many European museums." German and Russian archaeologists worked in the area, but little was done until after 1938, when Soviets discovered the ruins of a Urartian city near Yerevan in what is today Armenia, Lloyd writes. Since then, he notes, many sites have been excavated in eastern Turkey and a good deal learned about this wealthy nation, which at its peak ruled a vast area as far west as the Euphrates, including much of Armenia and Iranian Azerbaijan, only to abruptly disappear.

According to Toni Cross's research, the downfall of Urartu could have been caused by Scythians, Medes, or Babylonians. But she hastily adds that the kingdom could have been weakened by Assyrians and Cimmerians or perhaps by civil war. "In short, no proof [exists] at all as to who destroyed the Urartian kingdom or when," she emphasizes.

Armenians, who claim to be descendants of the Urartians, later occupied the area. By the first century B.C., the Armenian Kingdom, which was centered at Van, extended from the Mediterranean to the Caspian

Sea. Unfortunately for the Armenians, this land was coveted by their neighbors, and they became vassals successively to the Romans, Persians, Byzantines, Arabs, and finally Seljuk Turks. The culmination of the Armenian tragedy occurred during World War I, when the Armenians sided with Russia, which had supported Armenian nationalism. In 1915, the sultan ordered most of the Armenian population removed from the strategic border area. Armenians—as many as 1.5 million—died from disease, starvation, and attacks by Turks and Kurds during the long march into exile. Others managed to flee to Russia, and en route killed thousands of Turks.

Van is still an important trading center and military post. Today's rebels are not Armenians (those who remain live concentrated in İstanbul) but Kurds who are fighting for much the same territory the Armenians claim. The principal reminder of the Urartian civilization is the citadel with its crenellated walls and towers and large esplanade, built on a huge rock rising from the plain. Originally, the rock stood on the shore of Lake Van, but the waters have receded. Here too are ancient tombs, some with cuneiform inscriptions dating back to the Urartian period.

The only visible remains of the Armenian past are the distinctive Armenian-style churches around Lake Van. Most of them are pretty much in ruins, but the Akdamar Church on an island in the lake is well preserved and has become a popular picnic site for locals as well as foreign visitors. Built in the tenth century under the Seljuks, Akdamar has the typical high cupola and wonderful carvings of biblical life on the walls of the church.

Another magic mountaintop in south-central Anatolia is Mount Nemrut. Assembled here are a score of giant heads of King Antiochus and his favorite Greek and Persian deities, their severed bodies nearby, flanked by guardian lions and eagles. The group decapitation was owing to several earthquakes but appears as though some mischievous force sought to cut down to size the monumental ego of the monarch. This astonishing pagan memorial was put up in 30 B.C. by Antiochus I, ruler of the short-lived Kingdom of Commagene, which stretched from the Taurus Mountains to the Euphrates River. Commagene, the last independent stronghold of Anatolia, was incorporated into the Roman province of Syria in A.D. 72.

Mount Nemrut towers 6,500 feet over the desolate ridges of the Anti-Taurus Mountains. At its peak stands a 150-foot mound of limestone gravel, and it is believed that hidden somewhere deep inside lies the royal

*It looks like the end of the world on top of desolate Mount
Nemrut, surrounded by gigantic heads and headless bodies
of gods and kings. This is a monument to the huge ego of
King Antiochus I, who reigned over Commagene in
eastern Turkey in the first century* B.C.

burial chamber, yet to be excavated. The statues of Antioch, Zeus, Apollo, and other gods sit as if holding court on terraces cut into the rock at the base of the pyramid, with most of the kingdom stretched below them.

Much of the excavation has been done by the late Theresa Goell, who began working at Mount Nemrut in 1953 for the American School of Oriental Research of New Haven. According to Ms. Goell's reports, the inscriptions explain that Antiochus had his tumulus built on this peak so that his soul would have an easy ascent to join Zeus and the other deities in the heavenly sphere.

In 1987, UNESCO declared Mount Nemrut a World Heritage site, but nothing was done to preserve the remarkable monument, which has suffered from the ravages of time and tourism. A Dutch architect, Maurice

*Cappadocia in central Anatolia is a vast, lunar landscape with thousands of caves cut into rocky towers, cones, and mounds, where early Christians used to hide, live, and worship.*

Crijns, has established a foundation for the restoration and protection of the giant statues. After Crijns signed a protocol with the Ministry of Culture and a Turkish foundation, restoration work on Mt. Nemrut began in early 1999 and is to take five years.

The most extraordinary reminder of Turkey's Christian past is Cappadocia, a place of rock churches, cave-chapels, and underground monasteries where early followers of Christ sought refuge. Cappadocia is a plateau of soft volcanic rock, formed by a massive explosion of the Mount Erciyes volcano and sculpted by millions of years of erosion.

When I first visited Cappadocia in 1980, I had the surreal site almost to myself (it was the year of the military coup, which was bad for tourism). But even now that the place has been discovered by tour groups, it has not lost its strange excitement. Actually, Cappadocia is a triangle, about twelve miles across, extending from Neveşehir on the west to Ürgüp on the east and Avanos on the north, with Göreme in the center.

The best way to explore this lunar landscape of natural towers, cones, pyramids, chimneys, and caves is on foot. But it takes time because hidden in the rocky maze are innumerable chapels and monks' cells and more than 400 churches, some with wonderful frescoes dating back to the second century. In addition, scores of underground cities have been located in the area, going down eight stories or more, with effective ventilation systems, storage depots, churches, and dwellings.

Although Cappadocia is known essentially as a Christian refuge, some of the underground cities were built as early as the fourth century B.C. This means the local inhabitants could have begun building sanctuaries against the Persian and Macedonian armies long before the Christians hid away from persecution by Romans, Arabs, and Turks.

Islam arrived in Anatolia with the Seljuk Turks, who came from Persia and Mesopotamia, defeated the Byzantine army at Manzikert north of Lake Van in 1071, and soon dominated most of Anatolia. They established the first Islamic sultanate at Konya in the central Anatolian steppes. Originally called Iconium and dating back to the Hittites in the third millennium B.C., Konya knew its greatest glory under the Seljuks from the eleventh to thirteenth centuries. Their legacy remains in the magnificent mosques, *medreses* (Koranic schools), and caravanserais, solid brick or stone buildings, adorned with cupolas and pyramids, fluted towers, carved arches, great wooden doors, Islamic green tiles, and swirling calligraphy.

Konya became one of the holy cities of Islam in the mid–thirteenth century when the great mystic poet Mevlâna Celaleddin Rumi founded the order of Whirling Dervishes. A native of Balkh, Afghanistan, Celaleddin and his family fled the Mongol invasion and finally settled in Konya in 1228. His father was a university professor and adviser to the sultan, and the young Celaleddin soon became a prominent poet and scholar. Legend has it that one day he passed by a goldsmith's shop and heard the beating hammers ring out the name of God. Chanting Allah! Allah! Allah! he broke into a whirling dance and soon reached a state of ecstasy there in the middle of the street.

Despite Republican efforts to eliminate religious orders, Celaleddin is still widely venerated. The emotional beauty of his poetry, the music, and dance gave a new dimension to the austere practice of Sunni Islam. It is believed that the religious orders filled a need of Anatolians, who for so many centuries had been imbued with the chants, poetry, and ritual of Christianity.

The power of the poet is felt today as you enter the mausoleum where Celaleddin, his family, and main disciples are buried. Officially a museum, this shrine attracts more than a million visitors a year. Unlike other museums, people must remove their shoes and put on slippers as though they were going into a mosque. Except when interrupted by noisy tour groups, the atmosphere is usually one of pious meditation. Wafted by sounds of a haunting reed flute, some believers mutter prayers in front of a box supposedly containing a hair from the Prophet Mohammed's beard. Others gaze admiringly at the exquisite hand-painted Korans on display. Some Mevlevi, as his followers are known, can be seen kneeling in prayer before the mystic's tomb.

At the entrance to the mausoleum is Celaleddin's message of universal love:

> *Come, come whoever you are,*
> *Infidel, pagan or fire worshiper,*
> *Come to me.*
> *Our convent is not a place of despair.*
> *Even if you have broken*
> *Your vow a hundred times*
> *Come to us again, come.*

Seljuk rule ended in the late thirteenth century, weakened by the European Crusades and the rise of independent Turkic tribes and defeated by Mongols. One outstanding tribal leader, Osman, gradually took over other principalities and fragments of the Byzantine Empire to found the Ottoman Dynasty. The Ottoman Empire lasted six centuries and at its height in the sixteenth century stretched from Mesopotamia to the gates of Vienna. The early Ottomans were militant Muslims dedicated to the propagation of the Islamic faith and culture. Noted authority Bernard Lewis writes that "the Ottoman Turks had identified themselves with Islam—submerged their identity in Islam—to a greater extent than perhaps any other Islamic people."[16]

It is said that on May 29, 1453, the day he conquered Constantinople, Mehmet II visited Haghia Sophia and gave the order to transform the Orthodox Basilica into a mosque. There was no question of destroying this glory of the Byzantine Empire first consecrated by Emperor Constantine in A.D. 325. In fact, the long succession of Ottoman rulers embraced this holy monument as their own, rebaptizing it Aya Sofya and using the court as a royal burial ground. Over the years, the sultans embellished Aya Sofya, adding four majestic minarets, grand candelabra, an Imperial Gallery, decorative tiles, and gilt calligraphy.

Recognizing that Aya Sofya belongs to the national patrimony, Atatürk drafted a special law turning it into a museum in 1935. Thus it remained until the summer of 1980, when then–prime minister Süleyman Demirel opened the somewhat dilapidated imperial waiting room for prayers. Bitter controversy ensued, with secularists denouncing the move as an electoral ploy, even a betrayal of Atatürk, and devout Muslims demanding the whole place back. Finally tempers calmed. Aya Sofya continues open to all as a museum and part of the universal culture. Worshipers can still pray in the waiting room or go across the park to the grandiose Sultanahmet Cami, better known as the Blue Mosque, or one of many other imperial mosques still functioning from Ottoman times.

"Aya Sofya for me represents the great strength of Turkey," Toni Cross asserts. "It was a Byzantine Orthodox Church, then an Ottoman mosque, and now a Republican museum. The land and the people are the same but have evolved and adapted to changing times."

Lloyd puts it this way: "Tribal migrations, the sweep of conquering armies, earthquakes, floods, or famines have been transient misfortunes whose memory has eventually faded, leaving unchanged the traditional pattern of domestic behaviour and the timeless image of Anatolian man."[17]

I would simply add—and the Anatolian woman.

# 7 ⟋

# The Kurdization
## of Turkey

I remember the furtive looks, the stony silences, and whispered confidences when I first traveled to the stark, mountainous area in southeastern Turkey that Kurds call Kurdistan. It was a place of sullen anger and resentment. Many Kurds lived in terror of the secret police and were afraid to speak their language in public.

According to most accounts, the Kurdish uprising got under way in 1984, but the seeds of rebellion were there long before I visited the desolate region in 1980. Painted on the mud-brick houses in the poor neighborhoods were the words (in Turkish): "Freedom for Kurdistan." Whenever I escaped from official view, people would hasten to assure me they were Kurds, not Turks. I was shown anonymous tracts and posters calling for an independent Kurdistan.

Officials at the time conceded there were a dozen "illegal organizations"—bureaucratic euphemism for Kurdish nationalist groups—stirring unrest among the local population. But the spate of violence then was attributed to family feuds or the right-left conflicts troubling the rest of the country, not a nationalist rebellion.

Turkish authorities were adamant. There were no Kurdish incidents. There was no Kurdish problem. There were no Kurds. There were only Mountain Turks living in Turkey.

Not until much later, after thousands of Kurds had been killed by the Turkish security forces and many more arrested and tortured and their villages destroyed, would Turkish officials admit there was a Kurdish problem.

None of the experts can say how many Kurds there are, but according to general consensus, they make up 20 percent of Turkey's population (now 65 million) or about 13 million. Another 12 million or so are spread around Iran, Iraq, Syria, Lebanon, and many have sought refuge in Europe.

Although a geographical entity called Kurdistan was known as early as the thirteenth century, the Kurds never formed an independent state but lived independently as tribal clans in remote mountainous areas under the Ottoman and Persian Empires.

An old friend and colleague, Jonathan Randal, provides a fascinating personal account of the Kurds' long struggle for an independent homeland in his book *After Such Knowledge, What Forgiveness?* A dramatic photographic and archival record of the Kurds' difficult odyssey is *Kurdistan in the Shadow of History* by Susan Meiselas. I will confine my observations to the Kurdish problem in Turkey.

Turkey's visceral opposition to any form of talks on the Kurdish question and any kind of international mediation stems from the 1920 Treaty of Sèvres, never ratified nor implemented, but still very much alive in the minds of Turkish nationalists. This pact, drawn up after the Allied occupation of İstanbul (then Constantinople) and signed by the sultan, set up an independent Armenia and an autonomous Kurdish region in eastern Turkey and allocated much of the rest of Anatolia to the British, French, Italians, and Greeks. Any European suggestion of peace talks or an internationalization of the Kurdish issue immediately revives a national Sèvres complex, particularly among Turkish military leaders.

Atatürk's Kurdish policy could be summed up in one word: assimilation. Those who refused were dealt with forcefully. Sheik Said, a charismatic religious leader, engineered the first major rebellion against the new Republic in 1925; he and his followers were executed. Throughout the 1930s, various Kurdish revolts were brutally repressed, entire villages burned down, and their inhabitants deported to western Turkey. Finally by Atatürk's death in 1938, all was quiet on the eastern front. It was forbidden to use the words Kurd and Kurdistan; Kurdish music and the Kurdish language were banned.

For a time, Turks believed the Kurdish problem was resolved. But with the introduction of multiparty democracy in 1950, many ethnic Kurds were elected to Parliament from the southeastern provinces. In the liberal times of the 1960s, Kurdish publications appeared but were quickly banned. Political parties on the right and the left, which sought votes in the Kurdish region, expressed concern over social conditions and under-development in "the East." The Marxist Workers Party of Turkey went so far as to call for the recognition of the Kurdish language, an act that led to closure of the party and was one of the reasons behind the military coup of 1971.

To a certain degree the policy of assimilation has been successful. Some of Turkey's leading statesmen have been of Kurdish stock, like Atatürk's close friend and successor İsmet İnönü and the late president Turgut Özal. In fact, many people were astonished to learn not long ago that the greatest contemporary writer in the Turkish language, Yaşar Kemal, is of Kurdish origin.

The classic Kurdish success story is that of Hikmet Çetin (CHET-in). He was born in 1947 in the Kurdish town of Lice in the southeastern Di-yarbakır province, and his father was an ağa, a Kurdish feudal lord. Çetin rose through the ranks of the left-wing political parties to become foreign minister and in 1997, president of the Turkish Grand Assembly (Parliament), the second highest office in the Republic. Throughout his long po-litical career, Çetin has always considered himself a Turk, endorsing by his silence the fifteen-year-long military offensive against the Kurdish rebels in the southeast, even the razing of his birthplace Lice.

Already in 1980, it was evident to any observer that the southeast was a different world from the rest of Turkey. In fact Diyarbakır and other Kurdish towns and cities were living under martial law. Here was a con-centration of unassimilated Kurds who did not feel Turkish and were not allowed to be Kurdish. Once an outsider gained people's confidence, they would generally identify themselves as Kurds and refer to Turkish au-thorities like an occupying force. Naturally I could not disclose my Kurd-ish sources for fear they would be arrested and jailed on the catchall charge of "separatism."

Even Diyarbakır's elected mayor, the independent Mehdi Zana, spoke to me guardedly as if he were under constant surveillance. Turkish politi-cians told me Zana was considered to be a Kurdish nationalist and ac-cused of favoring Kurds for municipal jobs. A few months later, after the military coup, the mayor was arrested on charges of speaking Kurdish and advocating separatism and sentenced to thirty-five years in prison (later he was released, although his wife, former parliamentarian Leyla Zana, arrested in 1994, is still in jail).

In those days, the great majority of Kurds lived in miserable conditions, but even those who had attained middle-level civil servants' jobs spoke bitterly of being treated as second-class citizens. Most ordinary Kurds I talked to did not speak of independence. What they asked for was the freedom to live as Kurds with their own language and culture. What they wanted was a better deal from Ankara, more jobs, more investments, schools, hospitals, roads.

It was fertile terrain for a militant nationalist group like the Kurdistan Workers Party, known by its Turkish initials PKK. On my tours of the southeast, I had heard vague references to the PKK, a clandestine Marxist-Leninist group, and one of several illegal Kurdish organizations. Not until after the 1980 military coup and clampdown on all political organizations did Turkish authorities acknowledge that the Kurdistan Workers Party was a force to be reckoned with.

The existence of "a Kurdish threat" was officially recognized in connection with a mass trial of Kurdish militants in the spring of 1981. For the first time, military authorities disclosed there was an extensive clandestine Kurdish organization aimed at establishing an independent Kurdistan. The nation was astonished to learn that some 2,300 suspected PKK militants had been arrested and were to be tried on charges of trying to provoke armed rebellion and establish an independent Kurdish state. Some of the suspects were also accused of murdering more than 240 people, including thirty security officials, over the last three years. These deaths had been reported as part of the general "extreme left-rightwing violence" prior to the military intervention.

For the first time, military sources informed the public that the PKK had gotten its start as early as 1974, as the Ankara Democratic Patriotic Association of Higher Education, and later set up secret organizations throughout the eastern part of the country. Military intelligence reportedly had alerted the government to the Kurdish activity, but the politicians were reluctant to alienate Kurdish voters. Besides, the southeast was far away and had been under martial law for some time.

To show they meant business, the military junta put on trial the former minister of public works, Şerafettin Elçi, on charges of "making Kurdish and secessionist propaganda." Elçi, a Social Democratic deputy, was sentenced to two years and three months in prison, without appeal, merely for saying "I am a Kurd. There are Kurds in Turkey." Elçi told a Turkish friend of mine at the time that he was not a "separatist." What he wanted was an end to the ban on the use of the Kurdish language and alleviation of the poverty and underdevelopment in the eastern regions. But no one would listen to him.

Under the military regime, many other Kurdish politicians and journalists suffered Elçi's fate for similar offenses. In the southeast, all the secret Kurdish organizations were crushed, except the PKK, whose leadership managed to flee to Syria. Things were then quiet on the Kurdish front. In fact the entire country was a political desert until the military junta decided to return to a controlled democracy with restricted elections at the end of 1983.

Meanwhile, the PKK's charismatic, self-styled Marxist leader Abdullah Öcalan (OH-ja-lan) ingratiated himself with Syria's authoritarian President Hafez al-Assad and won a safe haven in Damascus and military training facilities in the Syrian-controlled Bekaa Valley of Lebanon. Thus it was that Öcalan, often called by his nickname Apo, launched a surprise guerrilla offensive against various military and police posts in southeastern Turkey in August 1984.

At that time no one believed the PKK's motley group of young volunteers would be any kind of match for the Turkish army. But the PKK turned out to be a ruthless, determined force and has held its own with just a few thousand guerrillas. It was aided by an increasingly sympathetic or intimidated Kurdish population inside Turkey and the use of bases in northern Syria and Iraq. Although some countries like the United States have classified the PKK as a terrorist organization, it has garnered considerable international support, particularly in Europe.

Only for a brief time in the early 1990s was there a glimmer of hope that the fierce cycle of insurgency and counterinsurgency could be broken. The late president Turgut Özal demonstrated he had the vision and the courage to stand up to the army and civilian hard-liners to seek a nonmilitary solution to the spiral of violence. Under his presidency, there was noticeable liberalization on this taboo issue. People could raise the Kurdish question without automatically being punished as traitors. The use of the Kurdish language was legalized for the first time since Atatürk's days. Kurds began to come out of the closet and acknowledge their Kurdish origins. Kurdish cassettes were sold openly on the streets of İstanbul, and Kurdish publications proliferated.

Many journals were promptly closed for propagating Kurdish propaganda, but the ice was broken. A group of Kurdish deputies split away from the Social Democrats to form their own political party. In October 1991, a group of eighteen Kurds was permitted to take seats in the Turkish Parliament. Their party was rapidly shut down on "separatist" charges, but was succeeded by another Kurdish party and yet another.

It was the Gulf War that focused the world's attention on the Kurds. Özal was the first local leader to respond to the United States' call for a coalition against Saddam Hussein in August 1990 and later led the campaign for a safe haven for Kurds in northern Iraq. His motivation was clear: to stave off the massive influx of Iraqi Kurds into Turkey's troubled southeast and to win American understanding for Turkey's interests in the area. In return, Washington turned a blind eye to repeated Turkish military incursions into northern Iraq to destroy alleged PKK bases.

At the same time, Özal took steps to find a political solution to the cancerous Kurdish problem. In an unprecedented move, Özal met with Iraqi Kurdish leaders to try to work out some kind of modus vivendi. In March 1993, he went so far as to consider the PKK's unilateral cease-fire and offer of a peaceful solution. But on April 17, 1993, Özal unexpectedly died of a heart attack. No other Turkish political figure has had the will or the way or the stature to pick up where he left off.

It has never been easy to assess the Kurdish situation because reports on the conflict reaching Ankara and the outside world are sketchy, controlled, and often contradictory. Even foreign diplomats, who followed the Kurdish issue, complained of lack of access to the area. One Western envoy, with close contacts to the military, noted that the situation was so insecure at the end of 1993, he was not authorized to drive from Erzurum to Elazığ—a 230-mile journey in what was not supposed to be guerrilla territory.

One of the best-informed Turkish journalists on the military situation is Mehmet Ali Kışlalı, brother of Kemalist Ahmet Taner Kışlalı, and an old friend who worked part-time for the *New York Times* many years. He is author of a book, *Southeast—Low Intensity Conflict* (in Turkish), on the Kurdish upheavals, starting with the uprisings in the 1920s and 1930s to the present insurgency.[1]

Kışlalı is critical of the army's approach in dealing with the PKK up to late 1992, when Chief of General Staff General Doğan Güreş increased the number of troops in the area. "The Turkish General Staff had failed to adopt the proper counter-guerrilla methods," he stressed. "Then, with a huge injection of forces and implementation of small units counter-guerrilla warfare tactics, Turkey was able to turn the situation around."

Abandoning conventional warfare, the army cleaned out large areas once dominated by PKK guerrilla groups. By late 1996, the chief of staff, General İsmail Hakkı Karadayı, had doubled the size of Turkish forces in the area to 200,000, issued new rules of engagement, and "achieved an acceptable low level of violence," according to Kışlalı.

Every week, military dispatches still reported twenty, thirty, ninety or so PKK terrorists killed in action. But more terrorist acts around the country were claimed by the PKK. Increasingly Turkish political and business leaders and even some army commanders had begun to concede there was no military solution to the Kurdish question and call for economic and social measures. The Human Rights Association in Ankara released monthly statistics showing continuing high levels of deaths by torture, mystery killings, detentions, and people killed in clashes—mostly in the Kurdish areas.

To see for myself what was happening on the Kurdish front, I returned to Diyarbakır the summer of 1996 with an American photographer friend.

The dusty frontier post, encircled by powerful Roman ramparts, on the banks of the Tigris River has changed unbelievably over the past few years. Ungainly, hastily built cement apartment blocks and administrative buildings have sprawled out of control beyond the city walls. Along every street and vacant lot, children and men were trying to eke out a livelihood selling whatever came their way: pencils, paper tissues, chewing gum.

Government sources claim that since 1990, Diyarbakır's population has swollen from 200,000 to about a million today, but human rights organizations say it's closer to 1.7 million. The population influx comes from villages and hamlets that have been forcibly evacuated "for security reasons."

This formerly bustling market center is now the capital of a wasteland, where some 3,000 villages have been declared off limits or destroyed. In an attempt to eradicate Kurdish insurgents, the Turkish armed forces have emptied large areas inhabited by Kurds, turned them into a no-man's-land or forbidden military zones. Villagers, suspected of supporting guerrillas or refusing to participate in the official militias known as Village Guards, are forced to leave their homes and farms. These are then usually burnt to keep guerrillas out.

Aside from occasional patrols down main streets and soldiers stationed at key points on top of the Roman walls, the military presence in Diyarbakır was not overwhelming. We walked freely about the city, even in the evening. The atmosphere was generally relaxed with crowded mosques, markets, and street cafés where men sat on low stools, sipping tea or coffee late into the night. (Women still tend to stay at home in this conservative Muslim society.)

Yet the Turkish colleagues we contacted appeared extremely nervous and unwilling to discuss anything beyond the weather. We were advised to go to the Foreign Press Office for any information and for the special press pass needed to travel anywhere outside Diyarbakır.

The director of the Foreign Press Office gave us passes but no information. He said only the super governor is authorized to speak about "regional security"—and he was out of town.

Hoping the super governor would return, we decided to get a look at the countryside. Friends had suggested the bus trip to Mardin, seat of an ancient Christian community, near the Iraqi border. During the journey of about sixty miles, we saw no civilian traffic and no one working on the land. We passed five military posts equipped with either armored personnel carriers, troop carriers, or tanks. At two checkpoints, soldiers with assault rifles entered the bus to verify everyone's identity. We were told not to travel at night.

Mardin, topped by sprawling ancient fortifications, hangs precariously on a hill overlooking the Mesopotamian Plain and is said to date back to 3000 B.C. It's like a vast beehive, layers of flat-roofed adjoining brick houses with arched windows and doorways. A whole new city of modern apartment buildings is rising at the base of this natural fortress. We wondered how displaced Kurds could afford these solid middle-class dwellings but were told they were destined mainly for families of the police and military. Clearly the security forces were settling in for the duration.

It came as no surprise that the state tourism office and most of the tourist sites at Mardin were closed. The only other visitors we met were Turkish soldiers strolling in formation along main street, apparently on a shopping expedition. We visited a school in one of the Christian churches and learned there were still sixty Syrian Orthodox families and ten Chaldean families in this tenuous border area. Outside of town, the eighth-century Syrian Orthodox Deyrul Zaferan Monastery is still functioning with a handful of monks. The name comes from the Arabic words meaning Saffron House—a reference to the antique golden color of the stone walls.

From this brief excursion, it seemed that the Turkish armed forces controlled Diyarbakır and other cities and towns and the main highways. But at night, we were told the PKK still moved about the countryside at will.

For me the most astonishing change, after all these years of death and destruction, was the attitude of the Kurds. They no longer appeared to be afraid to say they are Kurds or speak Kurdish or openly demand Kurdish rights. This was clear from chance conversations in restaurants, cafés, and the bazaar as well as meetings at Kurdish organizations.

That was another major change. In the early 1980s, there had been no Kurdish organizations or human rights groups defending Kurds. Now there are several groups openly working with Kurds. Although they risk being shut down, they always reopen, sometimes under another name. The Kurdish political parties have been banned and their leaders jailed, but they always rebound.

There was no sign marking the Human Rights Association when I visited the spartan office in a shabby building in the center of town. Yet a large crowd was gathered there, mostly refugees from evacuated villages. Also frantic relatives of prisoners kept coming in to find out what was happening in Diyarbakır's central prison, where they had seen clouds of smoke. (Later, the association said nineteen prisoners had set themselves on fire in protest against prison treatment, and fourteen had died from their wounds.)

A typical case was that of Kadri Bilen, a thirty-seven-year-old farmer who had been forced to flee his village and had come to the association to report the incident. He readily gave his name and did not object to the presence of two American journalists. Bilen owns 200 acres of wheat and barley but was unable to plant this year because of the insecurity.[2]

He told us that on the previous night a group of soldiers had surrounded his village of Hişkamerg, thirty-six miles east of Diyarbakır. Most of the 450 inhabitants escaped with their families and their tractors. Bilen fled with his wife and five children, leaving them in a nearby village. He had to walk several miles through the fields to get a bus to Diyarbakır. Only old and sick people stayed behind and 1,000 sheep, which the military confiscated.

Security forces had raided Hişkamerg many times before because the villagers refused to join the Village Guards, Bilen said. But this time was different. There had been a clash involving people from Hişkamerg; two members of a neighboring Village Guard had been killed. The soldiers said they would burn Hişkamerg so nobody could go back. Under questioning, Bilen admitted that "70 to 80 percent of the village was pro-PKK."

Sara Ara, wearing traditional flowered bloomers and headscarf, had come to the Human Rights Association for medical help. She was suffer-

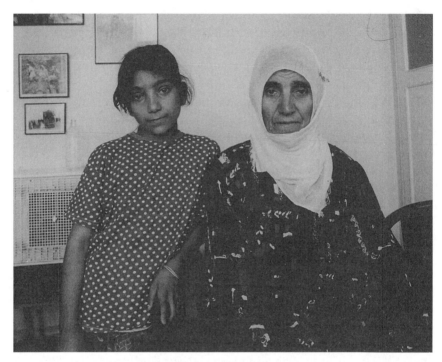

*Sara Ara, whose husband was killed after their village gave food to PKK guerrillas, is one of countless refugees from the Kurdish insurgency in eastern Turkey. Accompanied by her daughter, she tells their story to the Human Rights Association in Diyarbakır.*

ing sharp pains in her chest and stomach. She had been to the state clinic, where she was given a handful of pills, which had done no good.

Mrs. Ara, who doesn't know her own age, was accompanied by an eight-year-old daughter and told her story with little show of emotion through a Kurdish interpreter.[3] She and her husband Hamza had lived with their ten children on a fifty-acre wheat and grape farm at Hüseynik near Lice. The guerrillas had come many times to Hüseynik, and she had cooked bread for them.

One night in February 1995, the guerrillas came to the village to get food and left about midnight. Afterward, her husband went into hiding. At about 7 A.M., soldiers surrounded the village looking for her husband, and she heard gunfire. Later the soldiers took her eleven- and nine-year-old sons and forced them to stay in the icy river until evening. Over the next weeks, she had no news from her husband, and she didn't know what had happened to him.

In May, the military returned and burned all the hundred houses in the village. They warned her if she didn't leave, they would keep her sons. She sent two boys to relatives in Mersin and moved into a cellar in Diyarbakır with the rest of her children. Then eight months after her husband disappeared, a neighbor found his body buried in the cow pasture.

"We have suffered too much," she sighed. "How can we forget?"

On the other side of town, a large sign proudly marked the site of the offices of the People's Democracy Party, known by its initials HADEP. The place was so crowded with volunteers and people seeking help that there were not enough chairs to go around.

"HADEP wants peace and equal rights for Kurds and Turks," said a nineteen-year-old student volunteer, asking me not to use his name. "Even though it's a crime to demand equal rights or read a Kurdish newspaper or look at Kurdish TV, HADEP is the number one party at the university," he asserted proudly.

Abdullah Akın, a thirty-year-old lawyer and chairman of HADEP's Diyarbakır branch, laughed when asked if the army had gotten the situation under control: "That's a comic idea. If things are under control, why have they emptied 3,000 villages? Why have 3,500 civilians been killed in the past three years? Why are more than 10,000 people in jail, including many deputies and writers? Why has the army stepped up operations in the past two years?"[4]

Explaining HADEP's poor showing in the 1995 elections (the party did well regionally but failed to cross the 10 percent threshold nationally required to send representatives to Parliament), Akın said there were difficulties in registering the uprooted population, and military pressures prevented HADEP from opening offices in a number of towns.

"Refah came in first because of the Kurdish vote but Refah's no different from the other Turkish parties on the Kurdish question," Akın said, referring to the pro-Islamist party's victory in 1995. "We'll be better organized next time."

What about the PKK? I asked. The HADEP leader answered without hesitation: "In my opinion and that of the party, the PKK is not a terrorist organization but a resistance movement."

Most people we talked to at the time, from taxi drivers and shopkeepers to teachers, students, and refugees, expressed deep resentment over the prolonged state of emergency and the government's unfulfilled promises. They spoke of the PKK with respect, even admiration. This was the only organization actually doing something to win recognition for the Kurdish people.

"People are very angry," said a Diyarbakır rug dealer, clearly glad to talk to visitors but afraid to give his name. "The politicians promise to change things in the southeast but then leave everything to the military, who can only find military solutions. Refugees from the villages live in the city like animals, more than ten to a room and nobody helps them. America should get the Turkish government to talk to PKK."

Shortly after my eastern tour, the Turkish press reported that the PKK had raided the Altındağ Recreational Facilities a few miles outside Diyarbakır. It was early evening and the group of terrorists with automatic weapons opened fire on the people dining in the garden. Eight persons were killed, including three women and two children, and eleven seriously wounded. Claiming responsibility for the attack, the PKK accused the owner of the establishment of broadcasting anti-PKK propaganda on his private radio station, the Voice of Tigris.

From my cursory visit, I came away with the feeling that the Turkish armed forces have gained the upper hand against the guerrillas. But this does not mean peace. The authorities have a long way to go to win the struggle for the hearts and minds of the local population.

I couldn't help thinking of France's assimilation policy in Algeria, which had produced a brilliant elite of Algerian-born Frenchmen and women, but left the masses outside of French civilization and bereft of their own culture. This loss of identity, Algerian friends say, is the root of the present tragedy.

In today's Turkey, the Kurdish issue is no longer confined to the southeast but has spread throughout the country. Since the early 1990s, large numbers of Kurds have been uprooted by war and what amounts to a scorched-earth policy, and have formed a militant underclass around the main cities. The poor seek shelter and help from extended relatives in southeastern cities: Mardin, Van, and Diyarbakır. Those with some means move westward to seek employment and cram into the shantytowns around large cities like Mersin, Adana, Antalya, İzmir, and İstanbul, which alone counts an estimated 3 million Kurds.

Inevitably there has been a rise in violent incidents attributed to the PKK in cities of western and central Turkey—but not as much as one might expect. İstanbul police have suggested that the PKK was behind a recent series of bombings of tourist sites, ferryboats, shopping centers, and suburban trains in which seven people were injured.

The full impact of this Kurdization of Turkey is only beginning to be understood. Political analysts have suggested that the Kurdish vote may have been decisive in the pro-Islamist party's victory in the 1995 legislative elections.

There is no doubt that the Kurdish problem, which was silenced so long, has taken on national dimensions and is seriously affecting foreign policy. Much to the dismay of Turkey's allies, eight Kurdish members of Parliament were jailed in 1994 on charges of separatism and supporting terrorism.

Among the jailed parliamentarians, the passionately nationalist Leyla Zana, thirty-six, wife of the former mayor of Diyarbakır and mother of two children, has become a cause célèbre. There was a flurry of rumors that Ms. Zana would be released on the eve of an official visit by then Prime Minister Mesut Yılmaz to Washington at the end of 1997. But reportedly, she refused, saying she would remain in prison until a "democratic" solution was found to the Kurdish problem. Turkey's treatment of the Kurdish minority and Ms. Zana in particular is now a primary concern on the international human rights agenda and is seen as the major stumbling block in Turkey's quest to join the European Union.

Since my last visit, the Diyarbakır branch of the Human Rights Association has been closed for making "separatist propaganda" and reopened. The Human Rights Federation opened a new branch in Diyarbakır in mid-1998, but it was promptly closed. Several attempts have been made to close the Kurdish People's Democracy Party (HADEP) for alleged links to the PKK. Its leadership was jailed for eight months, only to be released in July 1999 for lack of evidence. But chairman Murat Bözlak and four party leaders, sentenced to one year of prison on charges of separatism, have been barred from politics for three to five years.

In 1998, two American experts on Turkey, Henri J. Barkey and Graham E. Fuller, brought out what I believe is the first book on the Kurdish issue in this country. *Turkey's Kurdish Question* is a lucid, objective, and knowledgeable policy study of the origins and nature of the problem. Although sympathetic to Turkey's predicament, the authors shatter the official contention that the PKK is simply a terrorist organization, which can be eradicated. On the contrary, they say flatly that it is a nationalist movement that has waged a classical insurgency, using terror and violence, but is primarily a political organization with distinct political objectives.

Above all, Barkey and Fuller suggest various concrete approaches toward a solution, which they sum up as follows:

Major economic improvements and increased democratization in the south-east will help alleviate some symptoms of the crisis, but in the end a solution that addresses the ethnic character of the problem is required. At a minimum that means clear recognition of the existence of the Kurds as a culturally distinct identity, and recognition of the rights of Kurds to express their culture fully under a system of cultural autonomy. This would imply some degree of regional responsibility that permits Kurds to run many of their own local affairs—obviously excluding major national issues such as defense, currency, overall security, national economic policy, and foreign affairs.[5]

The Kurdish question has poisoned Turkish life, resulting in around 40,000 deaths. It has monopolized the attention of the armed forces, drained the economy, changed the demographic map, blackened the country's human rights record, and strained relations with Western allies and neighbors. The capture of the guerrilla leader Öcalan in February 1999 (see Conclusion) has not put an end to the conflict but threatens to provoke more violence among Kurds at home and abroad and seriously impair Turkey's relations with Europeans.

Turkish leaders have finally accepted the fact there is a Kurdish problem and that it cannot be solved by military means alone. Now they must move ahead and come to terms with citizens who have clung to their Kurdish identity through every hardship.

# 8 ⟜

---

## *Silent Minorities*

---

Galata is a crumbling, neglected neighborhood with historical treasures around every corner and underfoot. Over the years, I have paid the ritual visits to the restored twelfth-century Galata Tower (now a tourist nightclub and café), the Neve Shalom synagogue (still used for weddings and Bar Mitzvahs), and the Mevlevi Lodge, where dervishes still whirl. But like most people, I tended to avoid the area with its seedy shops, steep stairs, and dead-end alleys.

Then on a recent visit to İstanbul, my friends the Wildes lent me their Galata flat in a once quite grand nineteenth-century building, complete with close-up view of the Golden Horn. And they introduced me to their friend Mete Göktuğ, an urbane community architect, who helped them with renovations.

A New Yorker at heart, I very quickly felt at home in Galata. It has that wonderful eclectic mix of people that makes some cities so special. In the Wildes' five-story walk-up, there are two Italian nuns who work in the local hospital, a *hacı* (devout Muslim who has made the pilgrimage to Mecca) and two black-shrouded women, an *İmam* (Islamic preacher), a secular Turkish family, two Jewish families, and a large Kurdish family. All seemed to coexist without friction and respect one another's space as well as that of an American visitor.

The most vivid historical portrait of Galata comes from that seventeenth-century Turkish traveler and standard-bearer to the sultan, Evliya Çelebi. The neighborhood takes its name from the Greek word *gala* meaning milk, Çelebi explained, because in the time of the Greek emperors, the area was celebrated for its sheep and dairies. He recounted that the town was "full of infidels"—200,000, according to the conscription lists—and only 64,000 Muslims—"mostly Moors driven out of Spain." There were seventy French, Venetian, and Greek churches, three Armenian churches, two synagogues, 3,008 shops, and 200 taverns and winehouses, "where these Infidels divert themselves with music and drinking." He went on to say: "The Greeks keep the taverns, the Armenians are merchants and bankers; the Jews are the negotiators in love matters and their youths are the worst of all the devotees of debauchery. . . ."[1]

My present-day guide to Galata was Mete Göktuğ, whose architectural studio was built by the British as a jail in the early 1900s and has been tastefully modernized (preserving the prisoners' graffiti). Mete heads the Galata Society, set up in 1994 to awaken people's historic conscience and get them involved in the revitalization of the neighborhood.[2] The main conscience-raising event is the Galata Festival, a huge street party with outdoor theater, dancing, fashion shows, and concerts, held a couple of times a year.

In a thumbnail history of the area, Mete explained that Galata was founded as a Greek city in 600 B.C., and later became an important Genoese trading center. The Galata Tower is part of the ancient Genoese fortifications. Under the Ottomans, Galata was the hub of European life until the nineteenth century. Then it became so crowded that European embassies, merchants, and other foreign residents moved up the hill to Pera district (now called Beyoğlu), and Galata went into decline.

The Galata Society has published a detailed inventory of the main buildings in the district and their state of preservation. Across from Mete's studio stand the Dominican Church and the Monastery of Saints Peter and Paul, built in the twelfth century and recently restored. Around the corner, the Austrian Hospital and the former British Seamen's Hospital, both dating from the nineteenth century, now belong to the Turkish State and are functioning. Down the hill, the Camondo mansion belonged to a Portuguese Jewish family and has recently been renovated as the attractive Galata Apart Hotel. Nearby the German Lycée and the St. George Austrian High School have undergone repairs and are among the city's best schools. At the base of the hill, some grand nineteenth-century neo-Ottoman office buildings have begun to be restored. And recently the state turned over the abandoned Genoese Palace of Commerce to the Galata Society for an Information and Cultural Center. Clearly delighted, Mete said the twelfth-century building is a solid, healthy structure but needs a lot of work.

*Mete Göktuc, community leader, examines the Galata Society's new Cultural Center in the twelfth-century Genoese Palace of Commerce.*

"Finally they're giving importance to history and archaeology," Mete said as he took a municipal inspector and me on a tour of the latest excavations. In a parking lot, workers were digging out the walls of a minaret and mosque, believed to be 600 years old and destroyed in the 1950s. Down the hill, near the old Camondo home, excavators have newly found what could be vestiges of a Byzantine or Roman amphitheater from the fifth century, when the area was known as Sykai—Greek for fig trees.

Now Galata by day has a population of 70,000 but at night the figure drops to only 3,000, Mete told me. Many workshops and small factories thrive here because of its central location and low rents. But it's meant to be a residential area, and there are still remnants of the old society. What Mete wants to revive, along with the buildings, is the cosmopolitan lifestyle of the area—perhaps as some kind of artist's neighborhood—"like Montmartre."

On a recent visit, Mete took me into a dark and dusty workshop inside the Genoese watchtower. There I met Ergin Onar, who like his father is a stonecutter specializing in marble fireplaces. He said a fireplace sells for about $25,000 and takes six months to make, and business was good.

Nearby, we visited the old British Post Office, which was being totally renovated and would become the Galata Film House, a kind of cinema museum.

At the café next to Galata Tower, Mete introduced me to several artists who live in the neighborhood. Among them was Arif Asçi, art historian and photographer, who was making a documentary on his expedition by camel caravan along the Silk Road from İstanbul to Xian.

Another time, Mete took me to lunch at his favorite neighborhood restaurant, run by an Armenian, Vahan Kesker. The restaurateur said that his family originally came from Kayseri, and he is a cousin of the writer William Saroyan. As they talked about the need to restore Galata, more than once Mete called the restaurateur "my brother," and the sentiment seemed reciprocal.

I have visited İstanbul's Armenian, Greek, and Jewish communities off and on since 1980, when the Turkish Armed Forces seized control of the state. At that time, it was the religious minorities who heaved the deepest sighs of relief. Not that these communities had been the target of any kind of pogrom in recent history. In fact, the minorities miraculously escaped most of the ugly political violence engulfing the country in the late 1970s.

But the insecurity was always there. Always the fear that the wave of extremism sweeping other Muslim countries could spill over even to secular Turkey. Concern that the huge Muslim mass would in its pain become vindictive and seek a scapegoat, striking out blindly at the most vulnerable sectors of the population.

Minorities have long memories. The thriving Christian community of 4.5 million under the Ottomans at the turn of the century had declined to about 230,000 out of a total population of 45 million by 1980.[3] The Greek Orthodox community had been sharply reduced by the mass population exchange with Greece under the 1923 Treaty of Lausanne. Most of the remaining Greeks fled in 1955, after anti-Greek riots. The Armenian community had been drastically depleted by forced departures and massacres during World War I, and many more left after the 1995 events, seen as targeting Christians rather than Greeks. There was a temporary swelling of the Jewish community during World War II, when officially neutral Turkey opened its gates to Jews fleeing Nazi decimation. Later many of them left to seek a better life in Israel or the United States.

When minority community leaders spoke publicly of life in Turkey in the early 1980s, it was inevitably in glowing terms. But privately they would voice concerns over the constant hemorrhaging of their members, owing to "external factors." The minorities appeared to be not targets of their Muslim neighbors but hostages to events beyond their control, like Greek planes buzzing a Turkish island, an Armenian attack on a Turkish embassy, a new Israeli settlement in Jerusalem.

Above all there was the common anxiety, in the wake of the Islamic revolution in neighboring Iran, that the upheaval would spread. This was compounded by the nervousness with which they viewed the steady resurgence of Islamic fervor around them in Turkey. Nor did they hide their foreboding over the increasing prominence of Islamist leader Necmettin Erbakan on the political scene—long before secular Muslims became alarmed.

And so it was with a certain apprehension that I renewed contacts with İstanbul's minorities that spring of 1997, when Erbakan was prime minister and Islamists had taken over the municipal governments and were gaining influence in the media and the business world.

I asked myself if the increased presence of the Islamists would be a fatal blow to religious minorities, who had so enriched Turkish life, particularly İstanbul, giving it the cosmopolitan flavor of Lawrence Durrell's Alexandria. In the past, Christians and Jews had told me they would prefer to abandon everything rather than to live in another Iran.

To my surprise, I found the Jewish, Greek, and Armenian communities hanging on and prospering. In fact, the minorities for the most part appeared less worried about a radical Islamic threat than some secular Muslim circles.

Historically Jews have prided themselves on being the most integrated non-Muslim community in Turkey. Unlike Greeks and Armenians, Jews are full Turkish citizens, having waived minority status after Atatürk established the democratic secular republic in 1923.

Even now, many Jews speak with gratitude of how the Ottoman sultan welcomed their ancestors in 1492, when they were forced to flee the Spanish Inquisition. From the sixteenth century, Jews attained important positions in the sultans' courts, in banking and trade, medicine, and the arts and crafts. According to community estimates, there were as many as 200,000 Jews at the end of the nineteenth century, most of them concentrated in İstanbul.

Today's Jewish population numbers between 22,000 and 25,000, or about the same as 1980, despite the rise of Islamists. There are still sixteen functioning synagogues, a Jewish hospital, a home for the elderly, and several youth clubs. Young people still leave to complete their studies abroad, but some return and find good jobs in business, the professions, and the arts. And there is even a Jewish member of Parliament.[4]

In conversations with Jewish academics, I found greater concern over the intransigence of secular extremists than the Islamist threat. Community leaders were more worried about the high rate of intermarriage with Muslims—30 percent—than discrimination. But they are not complacent.

Even during a festive society wedding at Neve Shalom Synagogue nowadays, security is meticulous. No one can forget the bomb explosion at Neve Shalom, which killed twenty-two persons on September 6, 1986, and remains unsolved. These were the first casualties in an attack on a Jewish institution in Turkey. In August 1980, a bomb had gone off in front of the Grand Rabbinate in İstanbul, causing minor damage but no casualties. The deed had been claimed by the clandestine group called Young Muslims, who left leaflets with an ominous threat: "Infidel Israel, get out of Jerusalem. We shall expel infidels from all Islamic lands." Days later, the military carried out their coup, and nothing more was heard from the Young Muslims for quite a while. The last case of anti-Semitism anyone could recall was forty gravestones destroyed in Ulus cemetery in 1995.

Now I sensed a change in the community's mood, more confident and upbeat. The reasons for this altered outlook are complex. For one thing, Jews indicated that the Islamists' participation in power has not proved as negative as anticipated. Then secular Muslims seem to be rallying to the challenge. Above all, the Jewish community has been cheered by the rapprochement between Turkey and Israel. Bilateral exchanges are flourishing at every level, and Israeli tourists are flocking to İstanbul and Aegean coastal resorts.

"It's ironic that the peak in relations between the only two democracies in the region would be under an Islamist-led government," said Susan Tarablus, then editor of the weekly community newspaper *Şalom* (sha-LOM), referring to the recently signed Turkish-Israeli defense treaty.[5] She has since left the paper for a job at the Israeli consulate general, but she said the situation at the paper was basically unchanged.

Celebrating its fiftieth anniversary in the fall of 1997, *Şalom* had undergone major transformations since I first visited its dingy office in the old part of the city in the 1980s. In those days, the newspaper was published in Ladino, a medieval form of Spanish with Hebrew elements, spoken widely in Jewish homes, with only a few columns in Turkish for the younger generation. Today, the newspaper's office is located in a pleasant, airy building in the smart Harbiye district. Only one page is written in Ladino, but this is still a collector's item for language institutes around the world. Mrs. Tarablus admitted she made a mistake in studying Spanish and has forgotten her grandmother's tongue.

She said that her mission, as editor of the weekly paper, with a circulation of only 4,000, was to "keep up Jewish faith and tradition." The paper provides news about the community and the diaspora and avoids politics.

"I'm not a foreigner," Mrs. Tarablus insisted, pointing out that her father's family has lived in Turkey for five centuries. She spoke proudly of her two sons, ages twenty-three and nineteen, a business representative and a student in chemical engineering, "who consider Turkey is their future."

There is an inexorable sadness about the fading Greek Orthodox community, down to fewer than 4,000 from 1.2 million before the population exchange of 1923.[6] An ethnic Greek friend, who has always said Turkey is her home, admits to loneliness now that all her family and Orthodox friends have gone.

But even this tiny minority had cause for optimism. Despite ongoing problems between the Greek and Turkish governments, there were new contacts at the nongovernmental level, mainly among students and businesspeople.

Leyla Üstel is a Turkish businesswoman who has been working with Greek and Turkish friends to improve relations through concrete projects. Cultural exchanges have already happened: concerts, seminars, and fashion shows. And the tourism industry has plans for joint travel packages.

"We like the same food and music and share the same emotions; all we need to do is get together," said Ms. Üstel, whose grandparents came from Kavalla in northern Greece and whose grandfather served in the Greek Parliament for thirteen years.[7]

The heart of Greek Orthodoxy is the Patriarchate, a compound with several buildings, located since 1600 in the now-dilapidated Fener District on İstanbul's Golden Horn. Most of the Ottoman-style wooden buildings have been renovated in recent years, and the patriarchal Church of St. George has been so richly embellished that for this reason alone it is worth a visit.

Invited to an audience with the Ecumenical Patriarch Bartholomew I of Constantinople, I was totally unprepared for the crowd of worshipers attending the morning service. I learned they were mostly Greeks from abroad—Greece, England, Australia, and the United States.

"It is like a family; the children go off and then on special occasions such as Christmas and Easter or when there's a death, they all come back," Patriarch Bartholomew, a Turkish citizen of Greek descent, told me later in a private audience.[8]

I had first met the patriarch in 1979 when he was Metropolitan Meliton, the closest adviser to the late Patriarch Dimitrios I. At that time, he listed the Patriarchate's main concerns as: the continuing drain of Orthodox youth, the deterioration of church property (the authorities generally withheld permission to make repairs), the ban on private colleges, including the Orthodox theological faculty at Halki (an island now called Heybeliada in the Sea of Marmara), and occasional demonstrations by Islamic militants demanding the expulsion of the Patriarchate.

Enthroned as spiritual ruler of Orthodox Christianity in 1991, Patriarch Bartholomew, fifty-seven, spoke to me of the changes. Some of the earlier restrictions were eased under late Prime Minister Özal. For example, authorization was finally given for the construction of a new church and renovation of a dozen other churches. There are 114 functioning churches in five archdioceses in Turkey. Although the Orthodox community continues to decline, those who remain are well respected. There have been few incidents or demonstrations against the Patriarchate, despite the increased influence of the Islamists.

The patriarch emphasized, however, that the problem of Halki is still unresolved. Foremost on his agenda is persuading Turkish authorities to reopen the Orthodox Theological Seminary, closed in 1971 under a law banning private colleges. The law has been relaxed of late, and several private universities have opened.

"It is inconceivable that a school founded under the Ottoman Empire has been closed down during the democratic Republic," the patriarch said, pointing out that all the archbishops serving in the United States, Germany, France, Sweden, and Italy are graduates of Halki. "This is not a school to serve the local population but is needed to prepare the church leaders of tomorrow."

Patriarch Bartholomew actively preaches his message of coexistence and mutual understanding between Christians and Muslims. The patriarch, along with Prince Hassan of Jordan, is one of the leaders of a group called Muslim-Christian Academic Consultation, which meets periodically to discuss problems and cooperation between the two faiths.

Invited by the Turkish/Greek Business Council to give the keynote address at its May 1997 meeting in İstanbul, the patriarch said bluntly:

"Turks and Greeks have sinned against each other," adding, "the time has come when we must confess our sins and put them behind us."

For the first time, the patriarch publicly declared, "In this united Europe there is a place for Turkey. Greece being Turkey's closest neighbor, can work towards this aim." This followed a glowing description of the European Union, "where people, capital, ideas, products, cultures, and religious preferences and ideologies flow freely and unimpeded."

In private conversations, Greek Orthodox sources expressed hope that Turkey would be admitted into the European Union—even though it is public knowledge that Greece has opposed Turkey's membership.[9] "If Turkey gets into Europe, it will have to accept European standards," one church official said. He predicted that when Turkey became part of the union, some Greeks would come back to live in this country and open their own businesses.

It was in a popular Armenian *meyhane*, or tavern, in the spring of 1997 that I learned by chance that the Armenian community has actually been growing in size over the past few years. A Turkish friend, who works in university admissions, noted that the number of Armenian students seeking higher education has been rising.

This is an astonishing development in view of the desperate mood of the community during the troubled times before and even after the 1980 military coup. More than the other minorities, the Armenians feared they could become targets of public outrage. It was the height of the devastating terrorist campaign against official Turkish representatives abroad waged by secret Armenian groups in retaliation for the 1915 massacres. Nobody knows how many Armenians fled the country out of fear of retaliation in the 1980s, but the number is believed to be in the thousands.

The Turkish public was caught off guard by the Armenian violence that erupted in a systematic, highly organized fashion in 1975. The Armenian population, numbering some 60,000 then, was the largest and to all appearances a well-integrated minority. I knew a number of successful Armenians in business, journalism, and the arts, people like the internationally recognized photographer Ara Güler, who is proud of his Armenian ancestry and loves his native city İstanbul and Turkey. Unlike Armenians abroad, most Armenians in Turkey understandably preferred to remain silent about the tragic events during World War I.

For the average Turk in the early 1980s, the Armenian question had ended with the establishment of the Republic. The Ottomans were responsible for the reported slaughter of Armenians, not the Atatürk generation. Also, many Turks were said to have died at the hands of the Armenians. And so there was no question of any kind of apology. Turkish history books largely ignored the subject.

Therefore, Turkish authorities and press tended to discount the claims by Armenians in the diaspora to the wave of terrorist actions and insisted that "other forces" were behind the deeds. Different conspiracy theories pointed to the KGB, the CIA, Greeks, and above all, Greek Cypriots. Many Turks linked the timing of the terrorist attacks to Turkey's military intervention in northern Cyprus in 1974. Cyprus categorically denied the charge.

Armenian religious leaders in Turkey also repeatedly expressed regrets over the attacks on Turkish missions and adamantly denied Turkish-Armenian involvement. Nevertheless, every time overseas Armenians took responsibility for an attack, Armenians in Turkey feared the Turkish public might turn on them.

Various Armenian groups abroad took credit for the anti-Turk campaign, which spanned close to two decades and resulted in the assassination of seventy-two people, including forty-one Turkish diplomats in the United States, Canada, Europe, and Australia.

The attacks actually began in 1973 with the murder of the Turkish consul general and vice consul in Los Angeles. An elderly Armenian émigré was convicted and jailed for the crime, said to be an act of revenge for his personal suffering under the Ottomans. A Beirut-based group called the Armenian Secret Army for the Liberation of Armenia claimed most of the later attacks on Turkish embassies and airline offices. Armenian leaders of this underground organization emerged occasionally to declare they were fighting to liberate the "Armenian homeland," located in what was then part of the Soviet Union, Iran, and southeastern Turkey.

The Armenian campaign petered out in the early 1990s without any formal announcement or settlement. According to unconfirmed reports, Turkish secret agents successfully eradicated the leadership of the Secret Army "Israeli-style." Some Turkish political analysts link the end of the deadly assaults to the breakup of the Soviet Union and the creation of the Republic of Armenia in 1991.

It is certain that tensions in the Turkish-Armenian community diminished significantly after the independence of former Soviet Armenia. Trade and personal contacts have increased with the new Armenia, and many Turkish-Armenians look to Etchmedzian as the seat of the Armenian Orthodox Church.

Ara Koçunyan is editor of the Armenian newspaper *Jamanak*, founded by his great-grandfather in 1908 and said to be the oldest Armenian newspaper in the world. He admitted with sadness that the newspaper's circulation is now down to 1,500 from 15,000 in the beginning.

But the burly, black-bearded newspaperman confirmed that by 1990, Armenians stopped leaving the country, and there are now around 70,000 and the number is growing.[10]

The Armenian community's main aim is to preserve its ethnic identity, Koçunyan says. A specific problem is the lack of enough teachers. The Armenian schools teach the Turkish program in Armenian, and according to the law, it is necessary to be Turkish to teach. Another problem, common to all the minorities, is that an Armenian cannot bequeath his property to an Armenian institution.

On the whole, the editor pointed out, Armenians are "well-integrated" in the life of the country and share the problems of other citizens, like "the democracy problem."

"Like other Turks, we defend the idea Turkey must become more democratic," Koçunyan said. And like Greek Orthodox community leaders, the Armenian editor placed his hopes for the future in the European Union: "This is a great country with a great potential and Europe will be good for the country."

Moving through the broader society, I have met a number of integrated Armenians. One of these is Etyen Mahcupyan, an Armenian Catholic, university professor, and writer, widely respected for his knowledgeable and independent views. He is one of the bridges I talk about later, someone who is quietly working to promote greater understanding between the secularists and Islamists.

Although the other Christians are so few in numbers and not recognized as a minority, I mention them mainly because of the changing attitude toward them.

In the 1980s, other Christians were looked on with suspicion by the authorities and public alike. At best, they were seen as missionaries trying to insert themselves into Turkey's internal affairs, but generally they were viewed as troublemakers and spies for their respective homelands. Their activities were circumscribed and movements controlled in sensitive areas like the far east.

Now in the past few years, Turks seem to have gained a new perception of Christians. The Christians themselves have noticed a change but have been reluctant to publicize it for fear of provoking a counterreaction.

Finally in September 1998, the International Protestant Church of Ankara held the grand opening of its new place of worship in a suburban shopping center with a representative of the Department of Religious Affairs, the American ambassador, and other members of the diplomatic corps as honored guests. The head of Religious Affairs sent a message of good wishes, emphasizing that the three major world religions have a common tolerance and respect for each other.

The Protestant Church, formed in 1990 and attended mainly by foreign businesspeople and families and English teachers, has faced many difficulties. It still does not have legal entity as a church because the Treaty of Lausanne only refers to minority churches, according to Andrew Hoard,[11] an American, who is one of five church elders. At first they held services in a storefront but had to move. Then they met for worship in a garage, but again had to move after hostile neighbors attacked the place with a pipe bomb. They tried to set up a church at Bilkent, a college suburb, but were turned down because the authorities feared the Islamic community would then try to build mosques there.

"Now people are more relaxed toward Christians—probably because they're more afraid of Islamic Fundamentalists," Mr. Hoard suggested. Neighbors at the church's new premises have been "welcoming" and even drop in to listen to the guitar music and singing.

The Erickson family comes from Los Angeles and has lived in Ankara for eleven years. Ken Erickson teaches English, and his wife Norita runs an English-language bookstore, which carries some Christian books. They attend a Turkish protestant church in a storefront that doesn't even bear a sign.

A Turkish protestant church was inconceivable in my day. Although many Turks are secular, they are still Muslim and even more suspicious of Turkish converts than of foreign Christians. Now it seems there are about 1,000 converts, hardly a great danger in this country of nearly 65 million Muslims, and they are allowed to worship freely.

Things have eased considerably since 1988, Ken Erickson told me over cappuccino at his favorite haunt, the Café Latin.[12] At that time, many Christians—mostly members of Jehovah's Witness—were arrested and Bibles seized. Some police in eastern Turkey did not know that the distribution of Bibles is legal. The Witnesses were tried on charges of spreading illegal propaganda, and later everyone was acquitted. After that, there have been occasional arrests, nothing major.

"Since the spread of private television and Internet, everything has opened up," Erickson said. "The authorities have concluded that the churches are not so dangerous and the primary danger is political Islam. They also want to present a good face to Europe."

# 9

## The Headscarf War

It began with isolated protests by a few students and progressively evolved into a full-blown civil rights struggle. What is known as the Headscarf War epitomizes the whole secular-Islamist struggle in this country.

Disputes have erupted over headscarves in other countries—but nothing like the conflict that broke out in Turkey in the early 1980s and still has not been resolved. France banned headscarves in public schools—but then France's population is not over 97 percent Muslim.

An ultimate irony is the fact that many young Western-educated women are in the forefront of the headscarf movement, although Turkish women have acquired more legal rights than any other women in the Muslim world.

Actually the headcovering issue dates back to the early days of the Republic and Atatürk, who considered clothing as part of cultural identity. In his drive to build a modern, Western-type state, Atatürk campaigned tirelessly against Islamic veils and headscarves and went so far as to ban the fez, which he considered to be a symbol of a decadent Ottoman Empire.

The headscarf worn by Islamic activists should not be confused with the traditional headcovering. The former is a voluminous scarf, closely framing the face to leave no trace of hair and knotted or pinned beneath the chin. The latter is a loosely tied bandana, often with locks of hair visible, worn by secular women at funerals and by rural women as a sign of piety or against the sun.

Led by an unlikely alliance between the military and women activists, the secular establishment perceives the "political" headscarf as a symbol of radical Islam, aimed at destroying the Republic and establishing a theocratic state like Iran. The generals call headscarves "the uniform of Islamic extremism" and have demanded their abolishment on university campuses as well as in government offices. Equally committed to the secular ideal are women's groups, acutely aware that women's interests and rights have suffered wherever Islamists have come to power—in Iran, Sudan, Afghanistan, and Pakistan, not to mention the severe orthodox regime in Saudi Arabia.

On the other hand, pious Muslims, led by the now banned Islamic-leaning political party Refah and its successor Fazilet, have adopted the headscarf as a symbol of cultural identity and political protest against what they see as an unjust, un-Islamic system subjected to corrupting Western influences. Some women supporters are devout fundamentalists, who like their Christian and Jewish sisters elsewhere, accept women's submission to men because of "natural" differences. Others have turned to religion as a refuge from the ills of modern life or personal problems. Some have donned the headscarf because of family pressures, others to escape from family pressures.

The Headscarf War first broke out in 1981 and has raged on and off ever since. The armed forces, who seized power in 1980, closed all political parties, trade unions, and other associations and banned headscarves and skullcaps in all public schools. I remember the immediate outcry the headscarf ban provoked: boycotts, protest demonstrations, and denunciations of what was called "an act against Islam."

It wasn't long before the headscarf controversy polarized the country. Leftists united with the religious right against the ban as a violation of religious freedom. Moderate and hard-line Kemalists opposed any kind of religious dress as a betrayal of Atatürk's reforms. Under pressure from all sides, Parliament passed an ambiguous ruling in 1990, stating there would be no prohibition of clothing in universities "unless it violated the law."

One problem was the widespread disagreement on what the law says. Secularists hark back to a 1925 decree issued by Atatürk banning all forms of religious dress in public schools, except in Koranic classes. Islamists insist that although Atatürk abolished fezzes and turbans, there was no specific law prohibiting headscarves. Thus, universities felt free to establish their own policy on the matter, with most preferring to show flexibility. The controversy died down, and headscarves flourished. In stricter schools, some women resorted to wearing wigs—over their headscarves—thereby complying with the Higher Education authorities and a strict interpretation of the Koran.

As was to be expected, the emotional issue of religious clothing was revived during the secular drive against the Islamist-led government at the beginning of 1997. A military-inspired ruling abolishing men's turbans and cloaks was followed by a number of arrests. Turbans and even headscarves declined visibly. Even after Islamist prime minister Erbakan's resignation, the closing of his party, and the establishment of a secular government, the military leaders pursued their campaign against "fundamentalism," their euphemism for any hint of radical Islam. Calling fundamentalism the "foremost threat" facing the nation, the commanders demanded implementation of new "antifundamentalist" legislation, including dismissal of overly religious civil servants, controls on the construction of mosques, restrictions on Islamic foundations, and enforcement of the ban on Islamic dress.

Thus at the beginning of 1998, the Ministry of Education ruled that teachers, officials, and students in all schools and universities must obey a strict dress code—meaning no religious clothing. In a rapid follow-up, İstanbul University's zealous rector specifically barred from campus all female students with headscarves and male students with beards.

Some pious Muslim men wear a trim, short beard, similar to that worn by the Islamic Prophet Mohammed, but it is not considered compulsory. The Koran, however, specifically states that believing women "should not display their beauty," and should "draw their veils over their bosoms."[1] The word *beauty* is widely interpreted to be hair, shoulders, and arms, although some reformists hold that it refers to a woman's private parts, those washed during ablutions.

The dress code ruling unleashed yet another round of angry protests, mass student demonstrations, and criticism even from members of the government. Faced with an incipient rising, the education minister postponed implementation of his controversial directive until fall. İstanbul University's rector followed suit, except for the medical faculty. There as a kind of text case, the ruling was strictly enforced, with results that augured trouble should the authorities try to impose a general ban.

İstanbul University, Turkey's largest university located in the heart of the old city, has become the main battleground for the Headscarf War. In the middle of the main campus, a statue of Atatürk stands vigilant, brandishing a torch of freedom and accompanied by two sparsely clad youths. The university has a total student body of 73,000, including an estimated

5,000 religious activists, who demand freedom to wear beards or head-scarves.

On the front line at the Çapa Medical Faculty, Aysel Ekşi, professor of adolescent psychiatry, keeps the telephone number of the police taped to the computer on her desk—just in case. That spring of 1998, the professor was threatened by a group of some forty bearded men after she barred four headscarved, fifth-year students from final exams.

"I pleaded with my students to take off their scarves, whatever their beliefs, and said we loved them and wanted them no harm, but they simply stared at the floor," Dr. Ekşi (EK-she) recalled.[2] The male intruders, whom she had never seen before, accused her of "poisoning" the young women's minds and warned that she could not force them to uncover. She called the dean, who got help from several doctors to enable the other students to take the exam.

Dr. Ekşi approves of the headscarf ban but argues that it ought to have been imposed a long time ago, lacked the necessary preparation, and should have been done at entry level—not the fifth year.

Acknowledging that some medical students might be sincere in their religious beliefs, the professor emphasized that she knows "many cases" where students have been paid to adopt an Islamic lifestyle. Islamists, she said, have set up virtual enrollment desks at the medical school to attract bright young people with offers of scholarships, accommodations, and even lifetime security. Likewise, employees at the school have admitted receiving gold pieces or a winter's supply of coal just to vote for the pro-Islamic party.

She accused some Islamists of resorting to intimidation not only in her own case but also against her husband Oktay Ekşi, an influential secular journalist, and other Kemalists. She tells the tragic story of Bahriye Uçok, a prominent Islamic scholar who had dared to say on television that covering one's head is not compulsory under the Koran. When they were to-gether at a conference on the Status of Women in Germany in 1993, Uçok confided fears that she would be assassinated by "fundamentalists." Two weeks later, she was killed at home by a package bomb, and the criminal has not been found.

From the outset, Ekşi and a small group of university women were alarmed by events in Iran and the rise of the Islamic movement in Turkey. In 1989, they set up the Association in Support of Contemporary Living (ÇYDD), which aims to defend Turkey's secular and democratic system against militant Islam. They now have more than 10,000 members around the country and are taking their message of secularism to shantytowns, where Islamists have been most active.

A cofounder of ÇYDD, Necla Arat, professor of sociology and philosophy, heads İstanbul University's Women's Studies Center.[3] She is deeply concerned over the large number of headscarved women and girls taking part in recent demonstrations, campaigning for religious schools and even turning out for Women's Day celebrations. She notes that girls in Islamic dress at the university are still a minority, but they can be disruptive. When the university first banned long scarves and sleeves in the Faculty of Medicine, thirty girls were affected but thousands demonstrated and signed petitions.

"We want to protect our Republican rights and improve them," said Dr. Arat, mother of two grown daughters, one a university professor, the other a medical doctor. For three decades, Dr. Arat and her friends tried to raise compulsory schooling from five to eight years, but nobody listened. Only now, after the military became alarmed over the spread of *İmam Hatip* (religious training) schools, was action taken to extend education in public schools.

Dr. Arat called the *İmam Hatip* schools "the great hole in our secular system and against all the liberties we are defending." She cited studies showing that 65 percent of the *İmam Hatip* students want gender segregation in public transports; 80 percent favor a return of Islamic law and many even approve of the heavy black veil for women called *çarşaf*.

Another active Kemalist group is the Turkish Women's Federation, including thirty-five organizations nationwide that deal with issues like women's health, education, and legal rights.

"We've asked the government to please be strict on the headscarf issue," Gültan Das, the Federation president, told me over coffee in her elegant apartment in Ankara.[4] She admitted that the Federation's scholarship program has run into problems in the urban slums, where pro-Islamic party militants have plenty of money to spread around. She gave the example of one of her brightest scholarship recipients caught wearing a headscarf. The young woman tearfully confessed to receiving $200 a week to cover her head and begged the Federation to match it.

Whenever I visit Ankara, I try to see Feride Acar, professor of political sciences at Middle East Technical University and one of the more objective observers of the political scene. When we met at my hotel the summer of 1998, Dr. Acar said there was sufficient support for the headscarf ban in the civil society.[5]

"This is more than a woman's issue. It's not about the right to dress but a political question, a sign of political Islam," Dr. Acar asserted, departing from her usual academic detachment. "We have only to look at the Iranian experience. Women were out in front asking for a more just society. Once the system was installed, women did not receive justice. In fact, gender injustice was legitimized. It could happen here."

But there seem to be just as many Kemalists opposed to the headscarf ban on grounds that it would be counterproductive and not resolve anything. Ayşen Ergin, an aide to the president of Middle East Technical University and an assistant professor of coastal engineering, said there were not many headscarves in the school—only 9 out of 250 students in her department, but she admitted the number was increasing.[6]

"Raising barriers only stirs hostile reaction." Dr. Ergin said over lunch in the faculty dining room. "We have to talk to these young people, win them over, reach out to them through education."

She blames Islamist politicians for using religion as a means to exercise control over their "obedient servants" and religious schools for turning out "fundamentalists with closed minds." But she also faults the secular leadership for "thirty-five years of fluctuation" between Atatürk's way for a truly secular state and the view of religion as a political instrument to reconstruct society.

"We must solve this problem women to women, through persuasion, not prohibition," Sinem Köymen, president of the Association for Research and Study of Women's Social Affairs, told me in her office.[7] This moderate Kemalist group is working with secular municipalities on programs to provide disadvantaged women with education and jobs, competing directly with Islamic social activists. On the other side of the barricades, I found equal passion and resolve that summer of 1998.

Aynur Demirel, the diligent daughter of a Black Sea coal miner, had made it through five years of medical school at İstanbul University. But in the spring of 1998, she was barred from taking the exams, and she might not be able to continue her studies . . . because she wears a headscarf.

"I want very much to be a doctor . . . an opthamologist, but the headscarf is part of my religious belief," Aynur said defiantly.[8] She called the rector's action "arbitrary and unjust," pointing out that headscarved women in other departments were allowed to take exams.

This slight twenty-three-year-old medical student, her round, childlike face enveloped in a large floral-print scarf and a long, shapeless black raincoat, does not appear threatening. But she and many of her class-

*Aynur Demirel (no relation to the president) is a victim of the Headscarf War. A fifth-year medical student at İstanbul University, she was barred from taking her exams because she wears a headscarf.*

mates are determined to keep up their struggle for what they say is a basic human right. Their protests nearly toppled the government and have attracted much public sympathy.

Why would a Western-educated medical student insist on covering her head at the risk of sacrificing her education? To find out, I met Aynur a couple of times on campus, where she had come out to show solidarity with headscarved dental students, also barred from exams. She introduced me to several of her colleagues, who said they had been beaten during the protest demonstrations and showed me official medical certificates to prove it.

Aynur denied any link to the pro-Islamic party and insisted that no one coerced her into wearing a headscarf. She did not see the headscarf as a symbol of male domination. On the contrary, she argued, it is nonpracticing males in traditional Turkish society who dominate women.

"If a man becomes religious, he treats a woman better and for that reason I want to marry a religious man," she asserted. Then responding to my unasked question, she stressed that Turkish women were generally opposed to polygamy, although the Koran allows up to four wives under special circumstances. She also recognized that Atatürk "did positive things for women," and she did not want to give up the rights he had accorded women.

Here was a fundamentalist in the true sense of the word. Aynur said she believes every sentence in the Koran and that covering her body is a religious obligation. "If I uncover, I will be punished in another life; I prefer to have social problems now," she said. She insisted that women were "given justice" under the Koran, and if men have more rights (in marriage, law courts, inheritance, and so on) it is because they are stronger and must shoulder more responsibilities in protecting and supporting women.

Aynur and her covered friends had journeyed three times to the capital—the last time by bus, acclaimed by thousands of supporters. They met with representatives of all the main political parties, even from the government coalition, who expressed sympathy for their cause privately while urging them to uncover.

That fall of 1998, the High Board of Education advised all universities they must apply the Dress Code, that is, no headscarves or beards in classes, and warned that university presidents who did not comply would be dismissed.

At İstanbul University, covered students applying for registration faced lengthy interrogations: When did they begin to wear headscarves, whether their mothers wore them, where they planned to live? Students said they were forced to sign a contract promising not to come to school with headscarves, and those who refused were not permitted to register.

In protest against what they saw as an injustice, thousands of students and their supporters gathered in İstanbul, Ankara, Elazığ, and a score of other cities across the country on October 11 in a Hand-in-Hand demonstration "for respect for beliefs and freedom of thought." It was an orderly movement, but 500 young women were reportedly arrested and held for a day. Six headscarved students from İstanbul were brought before the State Security Court on charges of rebellion.

Aynur and her friends have contacted various international human rights organizations like Cities for Human Rights and Human Rights Watch because they had come to the conclusion they would need outside support in their struggle.

"We're caught between hope and despair," Aynur told me just before the October 11 protest. "All we can do is to wait for the political air to change," she said optimistically, looking forward to springtime elections. "The politicians will have to solve this problem because they've seen the people support us."

She was referring to the general predictions that the new pro-Islamic party, Fazilet, would come in first in the 1999 elections. Fazilet chairman Recai Kutan had publicly denounced the universities' policy as unjust and called the headscarf ban "a human rights issue."

(Fazilet did not win the elections. The new secular government clamped down on headscarves more firmly than ever. A discouraged Aynur began looking into the possibility of studying abroad but feared she would lose credits for four years of medical school in Turkey.)

In Ankara, I came to know several veterans of the headscarf movement, including Hayrünnisa Gül, wife of the pro-Islamic party deputy Abdullah Gül.[9] With her large dark eyes and fair skin framed by a navy blue headscarf, Mrs. Gül possesses the serene beauty of Ingrid Bergman in the film *The Bells of Saint Mary*. Softly, without recrimination, she told me her story over dinner one evening with a group of women friends, who work for Ankara's Islamist mayor.

Mrs. Gül, now thirty-two, began wearing a headscarf at age thirteen. She was married at fifteen and barred from receiving her high school certificate because of her headscarf. Seventeen years later, after raising three children, she obtained her high school certificate. But her plans to go to university have been dashed by the new headscarf ruling. She displayed bitterness only when she spoke of problems facing her son and daughter over the closure of religious schools.

Her husband, member of Parliament from the central Anatolian city of Kayseri, however, protested publicly when she was barred from registering at Ankara University's Department of Arabic Language and Literature, which gave secularists grist for saying it was a political gesture.

Ankara's Islamist mayor Melih Gökçek has recruited a number of bright headscarved young women and given them senior positions in different departments at City Hall.

Each one has a different story. Ayşe Yılmaz, who has a serious intellectual air, is a new mother and works for a conservative think tank, devising solutions to Turkey's problems with a focus on foreign affairs. An honor student at prestigious Bilkent University—President Demirel shook her hand on graduation day—Ayşe praised Bilkent's policy of flexibility on headscarves that she hoped would continue, despite the ban.[10]

"Turkey is going through a period of transformation, the elite thinks it knows what's best for the people and for that reason we see a clash over moral values," Ayşe said in a discussion over the headscarf struggle. "If the secular society is tolerant, we will be tolerant and there will be no clash."

Sema Özdemir, a pale, mild-mannered young woman, shows deep anger when she recalls her expulsion from Middle East Technical University in 1994.[11] One of her professors told her, "You don't belong here; why don't you go to Konya [a religious center]?" In response she sued the school's administration. She succeeded in collecting many signatures of support, including unexpected backing from a blind atheist student who said, "What is the problem? You have every right to an education."

Then there's İnci Mercan, thirty-seven, who looks like a student, is married, has two children, and works on new projects for the mayor in the department of International Relations and Finance. İnci comes from Eskişehir, an industrial city 140 miles west of Ankara, where her father was a police officer and her mother a civil servant, both nonpracticing Muslims. After obtaining her master's degree in industrial engineering from Eskişehir University, İnci married a colleague.

The young couple took off for the University of Florida, where he worked on his MBA and she discovered religion. For the first time, she recalls, she had access to many books on Islam and guidance from an American Muslim professor of anthropology. Her husband, who comes from a traditional family, also exerted discreet pressure, indicating he would like her to cover herself in public.

"At the same time, I felt freer in the States, away from peer pressure and people staring at what you wear and asking why do you pray," İnci told me.[12] By 1990, before giving birth to their second child, she felt she was ready to cover herself. She was already wearing a scarf when she prayed and thought it was "just hypocritical" to take it off afterward.

Some of her husband's academic and military friends had urged her not to cover, warning that it could hurt her career. The problems started as soon as they returned to Ankara, where her husband accepted a job as associate professor at Bilkent University. Half a dozen international companies interviewed İnci, and all of them turned her down because she wears a headscarf. It was only after the pro-Islamic party won municipal elections in 1994 that İnci got the job at City Hall, even though she is not a party member.

Now İnci is worried about the increased pressures against Islamic activists: the closing of religious schools, the ban on covered medical students, beating students wearing headscarves, putting the mayor of İstanbul on trial for reading a poem. "They'll turn moderates into radicals and radicals into fanatics," she predicted glumly.

As I found positions hardening on both sides of the headscarf dispute and the larger secular-religious conflict, I looked up women who in the past had talked about compromise and reaching out to the other side.

Secular friends had introduced me to Selime Sancar as one of the new generation of Islamic women activists. Selime, who was working on her doctoral thesis on Ottoman Women for McGill University in Montreal, had returned to İstanbul and appeared regularly on a moderate Islamic television channel. She had attracted public attention as an articulate representative of Rainbow, a platform for Turkish Islamic women's groups, at the Montreal conference for the International Year of the Family in 1994, and later at the Women's NGO Forum in Beijing in 1995, and Habitat at İstanbul in 1996.

When we first met the spring of 1997 at a tea garden near her home on the Asian side of the Bosphorus, Selime stressed that she did not speak for Rainbow "but for myself," which was fine by me. Wearing a white silk headscarf, smart jean jacket, and pants, she looked as though she had just stepped off a luxury yacht.[13]

In her late twenties, with unwavering, clear blue eyes, Selime is an unlikely heroine of the Headscarf War. She was born in Knoxville, Tennessee; her mother was a graduate student from Ohio and a Methodist; her father, a Turkish industrial engineer and a nonpracticing Muslim. But the Sancars (SAN-jars) wanted to raise their three children in Turkish culture and so returned to Turkey.

Selime first put on a headscarf at age fifteen. In answer to my question why, she said: "The covered head is more spiritual; I consider it a kind of aura, an identity which is peaceful and shows I am a woman who is trying to have a direct relationship with God."

In 1986–1987, she lost a semester at Marmara University because of an earlier headscarf ban. When she refused to take off her headscarf, she was given a warning and decided not to return until the situation improved. The following semester, some of her covered friends took off their headscarves, some wore wigs, some were expelled, and a few left school. Selime came back wearing a turban, a kind of fashionable bonnet, and was accepted as "a foreigner" (an exception no longer allowed in 1998).

"Why are we fighting so hard to stay in the university?" Selime asked. She emphasized that all of her women friends wanted to get jobs and be financially independent; many were becoming doctors, dentists, lawyers. Things were being blown out of all proportion, she said, referring to both secularists who warned that Turkey risked becoming *another Algeria* and Islamic fanatics who feared Turkey was becoming *too European.*

"We're a synthesis; secularists have to know their grandmothers wore the *hijab* and Islamists must remember part of Turkey is in Europe and the country has been Westernized ever since the sultans brought Europeans here," Selime had insisted. If the two sides couldn't agree on other issues, they should focus on women's problems, like the double standards for women and men in education and the abuse of women.

But by the summer of 1998, Selime seemed depressed. Women who wanted to wear headscarves were caught up in a power struggle. She knew many cases of women who have been forced to cover and others forced to uncover. "In essence it's the same; it's the male authority deciding what women should wear. Both sides are not ready to hear what women are saying."[14]

I heard similar concerns in progressive secular circles. Pınar İlkkaracan and her sister İpek are co-coordinators of Women for Women's Human Rights, which seeks to raise women's consciousness of their legal rights through workshops and literacy courses, particularly in İstanbul's shantytowns.[15]

Pınar was deeply worried by what she sees as a dangerous power struggle between the Turkish Armed Forces and Islamic fundamentalism, with women as the immediate target. Her main fear was that Islamists and their allies would win a majority at the polls, which would provoke another military coup. Defending the right to wear a headscarf, Pınar is opposed to the ban as "bad politics," serving only to reinforce fundamentalists. "The State should pull its hands out of women's dress and Fazilet should keep hands off too," she stressed.

We talked of the organization's recent research into the life of women in eastern Turkey.[16] According to these findings: Half the women are illiterate; early marriage and polygamy are still prevalent; forced marriages still take place and arranged marriages are the majority; domestic violence is common and honor-killings the customary penalty for women or girls suspected of sexual relations outside of marriage.

What a pity, I thought, so much time and energy spent on headscarves when there is so much to be done to bring many women into the twentieth, let alone the twenty-first, century.

# 10 ～

---

## *Marriage of Inconvenience*

---

Without doubt history was made that summer of 1993, when Tansu Çiller was catapulted to the post of prime minister of Turkey. Turks across the political spectrum and particularly women were excited over the event. Here was an attractive young woman with a smashing smile, an American-educated economist (who speaks better English than Turkish), and an avowed secularist who could give this Muslim country a fresh new image in its struggle to break down European barriers.

"We were very happy when Çiller came to power. It was a blow to all those male politicians on TV and to patriarchal domination. She represented democracy," Şirin Tekeli, a leading feminist, recalls the initial reaction to Çiller's nomination.[1] But it wasn't long, Tekeli emphasized, before Çiller showed that what she had learned in the United States was "mainly greed and how to handle the mass media."

Even Birgen Keleş, a former deputy from the ideologically opposed Social Democratic Party, said she was hopeful at first. "I wanted Çiller to succeed, but she proved she wasn't ready for the post. She was completely ignorant about politics and had no idea how the system and the state work."[2]

Because Çiller had so much going for her at the outset, the pain was so much greater when she failed to achieve her lofty goals of economic and political reform. To make matters worse, her immense personal wealth was questioned openly in the press and in Parliament.

Her shortcomings as prime minister might have been forgiven had she remained true to her proclaimed secular principles. But many of Çiller's

*Tansu Çiller, Turkey's first woman prime minister, was the hope of secularists—until she formed a coalition with the Islamist leader, Necmettin Erbakan.*

erstwhile admirers and supporters could not excuse what was widely seen as a betrayal of Atatürk and the secular cause. After all, she had specifically presented herself at home and abroad as the only barrier to the Islamic fundamentalist flood.

In one of politics' most astonishing turnabouts, at the end of June 1996, Çiller, the symbol of secularism, formed a coalition government with her former archenemy, Islamic leader Erbakan. Under a power-sharing agreement, Erbakan was to serve as prime minister two years, then turn the post over to Çiller, who meanwhile would act as foreign minister and deputy prime minister.

Defending the unlikely alliance, Çiller pleaded the need for national stability and suggested that hers would be a restraining role to assure that the government remain within the path traced by Atatürk. Later, when she saw she had lost much of her secular support, she draped herself in the freedom-of-religion banner and even occasionally donned a headscarf when expedient.

What might have been interpreted as a positive move toward national reconciliation very soon looked like an astute political deal. With support from her Islamist partners, Çiller was formally cleared of all corruption charges and the parliamentary inquiry closed.

Çiller's swift rise to power and riches is still something of a mystery. Initially she appeared as Demirel's disciple, the new face of his aging True Path Party. But he grew suspicious of her personal ambitions and made it clear he did not favor her succession as party leader. Later persistent rumors suggested she was the United States' *card*, had acquired American nationality, and even served as a Central Intelligence Agency recruit—allegations promptly denied by all concerned.

Turkish newspapers have published detailed reports alleging Çiller's involvement in illegal land deals, the diversion of government funds, and other improprieties, all of which she has adamantly denied. She has yet to come up with a convincing account as to the source of her multimillion-dollar fortune, including a million dollars' worth of real estate in the United States.

By way of explanation, she claimed having received more than a million dollars' inheritance from her mother (described by others as a woman of modest means), several hundred thousand dollars from her father, interest on smart investments, and substantial refunds from the U.S. Internal Revenue Service. But there are many unanswered questions that won't go away.

Çiller's biography up until 1990 is quite unexceptional. Born in İstanbul in 1946, the only child of a senior civil servant, she received a good education and was clearly destined for an academic career. After attending the American High School for Girls, she went to prestigious Robert College, graduating in economics in 1967.

"Tansu had been interested in economics since she was a young girl because she remembered her father saying that it was the economy that was going to save Turkey from all its troubles," says an old friend, who asked not to be named. This friend said that Çiller used to read books on economics like novels.

While still in school, she married a classmate, Özer Uçuran, a grocer's son, who agreed to her father's request that he take the name of Çiller. The young couple went to the United States to do postgraduate studies. Ms. Çiller often recalled that when they got to the States, she "didn't have the money to buy a Coca-Cola."

She obtained a Ph.D. from the University of Connecticut and did post-doctoral studies at Yale in 1971. After teaching three years at Franklin and Marshall College, Çiller went home to the post of assistant professor at Bosphorus University, as Robert College had been renamed. Rapidly promoted to professor, she headed the school's Department of Economics from 1976 to 1979. Then she served as consultant to the İstanbul Municipality, the State Planning Organization, and other institutions, while continuing her university lectures. Çiller first attracted public notice with articles and reports attacking Özal's populist economic policies. She is not known to have accumulated any great wealth until after she held public office.

My friend Gülter Kolankaya remembers meeting Çiller at a friend's place in Washington, D.C., the spring of 1990, when she was still an anonymous economics professor.

"She was so cute and very polite and talked mostly about her diet, but I could see she had a quick mind because she asked clever questions," Gülter recalls. "I had a sixth sense about her; she was almost too sweet, her smile was too warm, and her eyes were cold and lifeless."[3]

In the fall of 1990, veteran politician Demirel invited Çiller to attend his True Path Party's congress, and her political career was launched. Demirel apparently felt his party needed a new look to face its liberal rival Motherland Party in general elections the following year. Elected to the party's executive board, Çiller was appointed deputy chairman for economic affairs and her name put high on the list of parliamentary candidates.

"True Path was losing votes. Demirel wanted to renew ties with the cities, women, and youth," Tekeli explains.[4] "Çiller was able to unite these forces behind her I Want My Radio campaign, against the state broadcasting monopoly.

Reenergized, True Path came in first in the 1991 election, although it did not win a parliamentary majority. Demirel took over as head of a coalition government with the Social Democrats and named Çiller minister of state in charge of the economy. She held this post until Özal's death in 1993, when Demirel became president of the Republic, leaving the positions of party leader and prime minister vacant. Contrary to general expectations, Çiller was elected chairman of the True Path at an extraordinary party congress and as such, was asked to head the new government.

Meanwhile, her husband had gone into business, first as the administrator of a large holding company, then director general of an İstanbul bank that went bankrupt, but he was quick to rebound. The word in inner circles was that Özer is a keen businessman and has had a hand in many deals over the years. More important, it is said that his wife always listens to him.

Çiller's performance as prime minister was not distinguished. She was unable to get a grip on inflation, which soared to 150 percent in 1994. She also failed to implement the urgently needed austerity program and achieved poor results with her privatization package. Under European pressure, she engineered minor reforms in human rights legislation but gave the military free rein to pursue their war against Kurdish insurgents.

The prime minister's top priority, to the exclusion of almost all else, was the battle to win a Customs Union agreement with Europe, the first major step toward membership in the European Union. Çiller personally traveled through the corridors of Europe, effectively using her photogenic charm and powers of persuasion. Her message was simple: If Europe rejected the Customs Union, Turkey would succumb to the wave of Islamic fundamentalism sweeping the region. In response, the European Parliament put aside demands for substantial democratic reform and voted overwhelmingly for the Customs Union with Turkey on December 13, 1995.

A fortnight later, the Turkish public gave a clear signal that it was unimpressed with Çiller's European success and in fact was turned off by traditional politics. In national elections, none of the parties won a clear governing majority. The Islamists' Refah Party came in first with 21.3 percent of the vote, while Çiller's party came in third with 19.2 percent, after the liberal Motherland with 19.7 percent.

Islamists were ecstatic. After three-quarters of a century spent in the political desert or along the fringes, an Islamist leader had at last been given a popular mandate to govern.

Almost everybody else, including most foreign diplomats and observers, read the election results as a sound 79.7 percent victory for the parties devoted to secularism. Experts even begrudged the Islamists their one-fifth of the vote, insisting that about half of Refah's poll could be considered a political protest and not an endorsement of the Islamist platform.

Nevertheless, President Demirel, a stickler for the law, called on Erbakan as leader of the winning party to form a government. After lengthy negotiations, none of the secular parties was prepared to join Refah in a coalition.

Under strong pressure from business circles, the press, and the military, Çiller and her archrival Mesut Yılmaz, leader of the liberal Motherland

Party, finally agreed to put aside personal hostilities and form a coalition aimed mainly at keeping the Islamists out of power. Yılmaz would serve as prime minister the first year, and then the post would rotate to Çiller.

Angered at being sidelined after victory at the polls, Refah went on the offensive. In a carefully mounted campaign, the Islamist party, which controlled the largest number of deputies, introduced a series of motions accusing Çiller and her administration of massive corruption and demanding parliamentary investigations. Specifically, Refah asked for an inquiry into charges that during her short time in government, Çiller and her husband irregularly amassed wealth estimated at $50 million, including property in the United States worth over a million dollars. Other charges involved financial misdealing associated with state-owned utilities as well as the disappearance of some $6 million from the prime minister's discretionary funds.

Çiller's party retaliated with a call for parliamentary investigations into Refah's supposed abuses, including misuse of contributions, secret training camps, Erbakan's substantial assets, and alleged involvement in heroin smuggling. This motion was rejected with Motherland and the Democratic Left parties supporting Refah.

Yılmaz's uneasy coalition with True Path fell apart when Motherland deputies sided with Refah in voting to open investigations against Çiller, paving the way for her to be sent before the Supreme Court. Çiller threatened to join the opposition in a confidence vote against the government, forcing Yılmaz to resign. Demirel again turned to Erbakan to form a new government.

Meanwhile, contrary to all appearances and logic, there were rumors of rapprochement between Çiller and Erbakan. The first concrete sign of this strange political twist was Refah's vote to turn down its own motion for a parliamentary investigation into Çiller's misuse of discretionary funds.

By the end of June 1996, the unthinkable was a fait accompli. Refah and True Path had agreed to establish a new coalition with Erbakan serving as prime minister for two years to be succeeded by Çiller the next two years. Çiller would act as deputy prime minister and minister of foreign affairs.

Nearly a score of Çiller's parliamentary group refused to vote for the new alliance, and some of them left the party. One of these deputies, Ayseli Göksoy, former head of the National Women's Association and a former True Path deputy, told me later, "Tansu lost the trust of the nation when she entered a coalition with Refah because she was afraid of impeachment."

Some Refah deputies also threatened to leave their party but then thought better of it. There was some criticism of Erbakan for allying himself with someone his party had denounced for corruption, but these voices were muted. İlnur Çevik, editor-in-chief of the *Turkish Daily News*, who favored giving Refah its chance at governing, warned that the Islamists would lose their credibility as "a clean party" if they went along with a corruption coverup just to hang onto power.[5]

Çiller's old friend says, "She was a dream, the perfect role model, the new political figure we were all looking for, but then she became an ordinary power-hungry politician." She went on to describe the two Tansus. "On the one hand, there's the childish, caring young woman, who likes sports—soccer, swimming, jogging, skiing, tennis—who loves beautiful things and wants to enjoy everything. Then there's the ambitious, demanding woman who has her own plans and doesn't accept contradiction."

The friend, who has taken her distance since the pact with Erbakan, insists that Çiller is not particularly religious. She had only one reason for joining the coalition: the parliamentary inquiry into her wealth. "She wanted to control the investigations, so she opened the gate to power to the Islamists," the friend remarked.

This was an extremely pragmatic ménage à deux. Although there were divergences, particularly in foreign policy, Çiller and Erbakan carefully avoided rupture, keeping their eyes on the prize, political power. Disregarding sniping from all sides, the unlikely couple went about their respective agendas as if there were two separate governments. And at times there were three centers of power, as the military played an increasingly active political role.

In those early days of the coalition, Çiller assumed the role of watchdog bent on keeping her partner from straying from Turkey's traditional pro-Western path. But she soon demonstrated that no matter what her unpredictable partner might do, she was not about to abandon the coalition.

A seasoned politician, Erbakan made no move to carry out his preelection threats, like leaving NATO, closing down U.S. military facilities, or breaking off relations with Israel. Clearly aware of his limits, the Islamist leader refrained from making any basic policy changes. But he did try to implement an array of measures designed to consolidate his party's position.

Erbakan immediately embarked on a populist economic program, raising civil servants' wages by 50 percent and then increasing the pretax minimum wage by over 100 percent. Generous subsidies were distributed to hazelnut, grape, cotton, and other agricultural producers. Financial markets reacted uneasily, and the powerful Turkish Business and Industrialists Association and the Employers Confederation warned against such official munificence.

Çiller hastily reassured all who would listen that Turkey would remain true to a free market economy. Disregarding her partner's money-printing spree, she insisted that Turkey was ready to accept any "bitter medicine" prescribed by the International Monetary Fund and the World Bank.

Moving on another delicate front, Erbakan's Refah Party sent out feelers for a Kurdish peace campaign. The plan included amnesty for PKK insurgents, dialogue with Kurdish intellectuals, and lifting the ban on the Kurdish language on radio and television.

Turkey's military leaders reacted coldly to what they saw as a project to open peace talks with terrorists. They let their displeasure be known through not-so-veiled press reports. Çiller rapidly disassociated herself and her party from her coalition partner's Kurdish initiative. Erbakan beat a hasty retreat, denying any intention of negotiating with the PKK.

Surprisingly, Erbakan, who had been harshly critical of Israel to the point of being considered anti-Semitic, made no attempt to reverse the blossoming relations between Turkey and the Jewish state. He duly signed a defense industry cooperation agreement with Israel, then turned over this new alliance to the military who had promoted the rapprochement in the first place.

On most foreign policy matters, Erbakan gave his foreign minister free rein. Çiller tried to resume her personal crusade to get Turkey into the European Union. But Europeans, who remembered her impassioned warnings of an Islamic threat, listened to this junior partner in an Islamist-led government with some skepticism.

The European Parliament assailed Turkey for failing to fulfill Çiller's earlier pledges to deal with human rights, democratization, Cyprus and the Kurdish problems. The Europeans threatened to halt all aid to Turkey, and the European Socialist Group suggested reconsidering Turkey's membership in the Customs Union.

In swift response, Çiller actually succeeded in producing a new democratization and human rights package. But it was largely window dressing and not enough for the European Parliament, which decided to freeze aid to Turkey. Worse, the European Union Commission made public its list of potential new member states, and Turkey was not included.

Foreign Minister Çiller also faced difficulties on another Western front with Turkey's principal ally, the United States. Erbakan soon made it clear that his main foreign policy objective was to reinforce ties with the Islamic world. Plans for his first official visits included Iran, Libya, and Sudan with goodwill missions going to Iraq and Syria, all on Washington's blacklist.

The State Department bluntly advised Erbakan not to go to Iran, warning of sanctions should he go through with the projected $23 billion natural gas and pipeline deal with Tehran. Refusing to bow to such overt U.S. bullying, Erbakan went to Iran, signed the pact (which had been worked out by the previous Çiller government), and reaped credit with a wide spectrum of Turkish nationalists.

But the Libyan visit turned into a fiasco and caused a serious rift in the coalition. Qadhafi received his Islamic brother Erbakan with honors, but publicly castigated Turkey's Middle East policy and demanded independence for the Kurds. Erbakan hastily returned home to a political whirlwind. His government barely survived a censure motion; one True Path deputy resigned in protest and others openly questioned the validity of the coalition.

Even with growing opposition all around, this unnatural alliance might have muddled along, were it not for a fatal car crash one night in November 1996, near a village called Susurluk south of İstanbul. Initially it appeared to be a banal traffic accident until the identity of the victims was made public: a senior police official, a heroin smuggler wanted by Interpol, a former beauty queen, and an MP from Çiller's True Path Party (the only survivor) together in the same car.

Recognizing the enormity of the scandal, the chief prosecutor launched an investigation to determine why a police chief and an MP would be traveling together with a known Mafia boss. A few days later, Interior Minister Mehmet Ağar, a close associate of Çiller, resigned, citing his son's ill health. Political commentators generally linked the minister's resignation with what became known as the Susurluk Affair.

Opposition leader Mesut Yılmaz denounced True Path's links to the Susurluk scandal and called for Çiller's resignation. Again Çiller denied any wrongdoing.

Finally Erbakan ordered an investigation into the Susurluk Affair. Subsequently, six police officers were removed from their positions. It became clear, however, that the official investigation would not go very far. Refah introduced a new bill to tighten restrictions on the press in a blatant attempt to discourage scrutiny of official scandals. Shortly afterward, the ministry of justice, headed by a Refah stalwart, rejected an application to remove parliamentary immunity from former minister Ağar, implicated in the Susurluk Affair.

At the same time, the Refah-led parliamentary commission investigating corruption charges against Çiller concluded with a recommendation that there was no reason for her to appear before the Supreme Council.

Many Turkish and foreign observers were appalled by what appeared to be a monumental coverup of the Susurluk Affair and its implications of government links to death squads and drug trafficking as well as financial misdeeds.

"After Susurluk, we saw the danger, the hidden evil," says political scientist Feride Acar. "Corruption was worse than it had ever been. We heard corruption stories involving politicians almost daily and yet Parliament turned a blind eye. Somebody had to stop the slide. At first the media had supported the True Path–Welfare government but after Susurluk they turned against the coalition in a kind of chain reaction. Then the Army decided to act step by step."[6]

# 11 ～

---

## Secularists Stand Up

---

The Fatih district is known as the heart of fundamentalism in İstanbul. Even before talk of Islamic revival, I recall meeting devout Muslims in religious garb at the great Fatih Mosque complex, built by Mehmet the Conqueror. In recent years the streets have been overrun with headscarves, çarşafs—long, black hooded robes—and skullcaps. Although the Islamic theological schools and library have long been closed, neighborhood mosques, religious bookstores, and even prayer halls are thriving.

This is an inconceivable site for a new coeducational community center sponsored by a group of dedicated secularists. Yet in the heart of Fatih, the Turkish Education Volunteers Foundation (TEGV) has converted an enormous Byzantine cistern into a center specifically designed to counter the spread of Islamic fundamentalism.

The place is generally crowded with young people working on computers, taking part in modern dance, theater, and music groups, studying English or German, and playing chess, Ping-Pong, or basketball. Their elders can be seen in the center's literacy courses and library. The center has 13,000 members and is open to all residents of the neighborhood for a small family fee. But few headscarves are visible.

"Normally these kids would be on the street or in Koranic schools," Halide Pek, a professor at Marmara University and director of the center, told me on my first visit. "We're offering them an alternative."[1]

Ms. Pek, who describes herself as "an ideologue of Kemalism," said the idea for the center first came from the Turkish businessmen's federation TÜSİAD in 1995. The project became a reality with the help of Fatih's then-secular mayor (he gave them the site), a group of university teachers, and 200 volunteers—mostly housewives. Now other mayors from as far as Samsun and Van have come to look at the TEGV experiment and plan to set up similar centers.

As mayor of Fatih, Saadettin Tantan became a kind of role model for secularists in their fight against Islamists. His election was cited as an example of how secularists, when they unite, can defeat Islamists even in an Islamic stronghold. A former police chief with a reputation for clean and efficient administration, Tantan ran as candidate for the liberal Motherland Party with backing from other secular parties and won. That was in the 1994 local elections, when Refah made such a strong showing elsewhere.

A grizzled man who seems to be in perpetual motion, Mayor Tantan talked to me about his ambitious plan to refurbish the entire historical district of Fatih, where some half-million people live.[2] The mayor conceded there was no money in the district coffers for this kind of rehabilitation project. Nor did he receive any cooperation from the Islamist mayor of Greater İstanbul, but had to go around him to get anything done. In fact the Islamist party actually fought against the opening of the TEGV center.

Undeterred, Mayor Tantan turned half his office into a workshop for architects from the city's main universities. Winning support from UNESCO and the European Council for some of his projects, the mayor then appealed to Turkish industrialists for financial help.

The determined mayor built a modern cultural center in the ancient Zeyrek mosque compound and began restoring 165 traditional wood houses in the degraded Byzantine quarter. He also opened a new clinic, cultural center, and café in the religious neighborhood of Yavuzselim, repaved the main street in the old Jewish quarter of Balat, and set up a sports arena and botanical garden near the city walls at Silivrikapı. His plans included converting unused Islamic schools and lodges into "useful" places, like a drug rehabilitation center, diabetes clinic, crafts school, and home for the elderly. A long-term project is to transform the ruins of the Byzantine Tekfur Palace into an outdoor theater.

Mayor Tantan told me his primary aim was to put some 10,000 unemployed people in his district to work. By restoring historical sites, he hoped to attract more tourists, which meant more jobs. If he succeeded, Fatih would be a powerful showcase for secularism.

The Fatih challenge is part of what can be called the Secular Revival, which got started in the mid-1990s. There was growing recognition that Islamists had become an important force that could threaten the foundations of the modern Turkish state, if something weren't done to stop them. Most people were at a loss for what to do and as in past crises, suggested that the military would take care of things.

But for the first time, a number of secular individuals and civic groups began to confront the Islamic movement where it has made the greatest gains: as patrons of social services and defenders of democracy. Refah's accession to power the summer of 1996 was the spark needed to ignite the disparate secular movement. It hasn't been a coordinated assault, but rather guerrilla warfare with sniping from all sides.

Turkey's powerful industrial groups were openly alarmed by Erbakan's populist policies and Islamic thrust. Rahmi Koç, head of the largest industrial holding, engaged in a public war of words with the Erbakan government, warning that the private sector had no choice but to take matters into its own hands. This rebellious mood echoed through - İstanbul's secular business establishment. The government was not governing, and so private enterprise was ready to support any viable opposition to the coalition in power.

Early in 1997, the influential Turkish Industrialists' and Businessmen's Association (TÜSİAD) issued a soul-searching analysis on what had gone wrong in the Turkish Republic. Viewing the Islamists' electoral victories as a protest against the system, TÜSİAD urged the elimination of certain "deficiencies" in Turkish democracy. The 200-page report calls for freedom of religion, thought, and expression, and recommends giving Kurds the right to instruction in Kurdish.

Even more daring, the report suggests eliminating the National Security Council, the organ through which the armed forces can intervene in any aspect of government policy. It also advocates that civilians no longer be tried in military courts and military commanders be subordinate to the civilian Defense Ministry. Reaffirming TÜSİAD's commitment to Atatürk's principles and reforms, the report says without ambiguity: "We need to take the developed Western democracies as our model. We should see that, by adopting a more broadly based democracy in Turkey, political and economic stability would be strengthened."[3]

These apparently reasonable recommendations caused a political uproar. The democracy issue was now on the table. Halis Komili, president of TÜSİAD and a leading industrialist, was called to task by the military leadership and subsequently resigned. Rhami Koç and other prominent businessmen took their distances from the revolutionary report. Komili's successor, Muharrem Kayhan, steered the association back to its immediate goal, getting rid of the Islamist-led coalition. "We would prefer a government that is as broad-based as possible which would produce solutions to the country's problems," he told the press.

The Turkish media took up the ball. Initially the mainstream press and television stations had been willing to give a chance to the Erbakan-Çiller tandem. But as the government stalled over the Susurluk scandal and other high-profile crimes, the media was increasingly thrust into the position of the political opposition. Revelation followed revelation about slick racketeers, shady businessmen, criminal gangs, druglords, and gunmen with links to the state security services.

"It's like Italy all over again; the Mafiosi eroding the establishment and the state powerless to react," a Turkish newspaper friend remarked. As parliamentary investigations led nowhere because of the Refah–True Path majority, prominent journalists embarked on relentless Watergate-type investigations into the murky world of official scandals and coverups.

The media was now engaged in a collision course with the Islamist-led coalition. The broad spectrum of the press, radio, and television, with the exception of the handful of openly Islamic papers and stations, attacked the government for almost every action and inaction.

In response, the authorities lashed out with virulence that threatened the fragile freedoms of the Turkish press. Scores of journalists were detained or arrested, and legislation was introduced that would severely restrict the press's freedom to investigate official sources. Then in what was considered a blatant attempt to intimidate media critics, the owner of a radio station was killed and a band of armed assailants attacked a TV station.

The dangers of the situation were highlighted in an international conference on "Media and Democracy," sponsored by a private think tank, the Turkish Economic and Social Studies Foundation, and the leading *Milliyet* and *Sabah* newspaper groups.[4] A distinguished panel met for three days at İstanbul's Hotel Marmara to discuss political and economic pressures on the world media and the new threats to freedom of the press in Turkey.

"The democratic system is not working" said Okay Gönensin, editor-in-chief of the İstanbul daily *Yeni Yuzyıl*, noting that the judicial system was not functioning properly, the administration was not doing its job, the unions have been weakened, and the left-wing opposition was not taken seriously.

Nail Güreli, president of the Turkish Journalists' Association, said the media was trying to fill the vacuum. He accused the authorities of attempting to scare the press into submission, citing the attack on Flash TV, the recent arrest of eight journalists, and other harassment. "What is needed is a new democratic constitution," Güreli concluded.

Dr. Haluk Şahin, news coordinator at Channel D that had led the investigations into the Susurluk Affair, recounted how government ministers had accused the station of being "an enemy of the Republic." He went on to say that the Turkish media in general was "the target of a concerted government campaign."

Recalling the dark period after the 1980 military coup when freedom of expression, politics, and press had been banned, Peter Galliner, former director of the International Press Institute, spoke soberly of the efforts by the present government "to bring the press under control." He concluded: "I'm still hopeful democracy will prevail. If it does, it will be thanks to the courage and professionalism of Turkish journalists who are helping keep democracy alive."

Women's groups had been fighting against Refah's influence for some time, but the formation of the Islamist-led government gave them a new sense of urgency. For the first time, secular women took to the streets in Ankara, chanting slogans like "No to *Sharia*" and "Join Hands for Democracy." Ayseli Göksoy, former president of the 200,000-member Turkish Women's Association, was a key participant in the secular movement. Deputy Göksoy broke with Çiller when she formed the coalition with the Islamists and became an active MP for the Democratic Turkey Party grouping True Path dissidents.

"We're not going to be another Iran," Göksoy vowed over coffee and sweets at her comfortable Ankara flat, overflowing with plants and chinoiseries.[5] Acknowledging that Refah has made inroads among the poorest sectors, she insisted that the threat was not Refah but "the money it gets from Iran, Saudi Arabia, Turkish workers in Germany." With these funds, she explained, Refah has won over a core of youth and provided incentives and price supports to peasants.

A direct consequence of the political crisis was an extraordinary flowering of civil associations and foundations in the past few years, many of them founded by women seeking ways to respond to the Islamist challenge. It was an uncoordinated piecemeal movement with a powerful potential.

Feride Acar, professor of political sociology at Middle East Technical University, told me the faculty association gave out some 6,000 scholarships a year to needy students, who would otherwise turn to Islamists for help. Women faculty members and wives were also collecting second-hand clothing and holding yard sales to raise money.[6]

The Anatolian Modern Education Foundation was founded in 1995 "to help modernize the secular education system in Turkey," according to its president, Ayla Hatırlı.[7] The foundation led a fax campaign to extend compulsory schooling to eight years and restrict the number of religious schools. It also runs adult literacy and vocational training courses and preschool classes in two of Anakara's slum neighborhoods.

Another volunteer group, the Contemporary Women and Youth Foundation, opened a Public Center in Ankara's vast shantytown Mamak district in 1995. This center provides free health care, literacy courses, kindergarten and day care services, a library that offers coaching for exams, and professional training for women.

The Mother Child Education Foundation (MOCEF), founded in 1993, runs Turkey's first home-based preschool education program for mothers and children in disadvantaged environments. More than 24,500 mother-child pairs have taken part in this program, which is available in thirty-four provinces. MOCEF also operates a Functional Adult Literacy Program, which reaches 1,500 people.

At a symposium organized by MOCEF in May 1997, Nermin Abadan-Unat, a prominent professor of political science at İstanbul's Bosphorus University, warned that the country was faced with "a serious conflict of values" between those who want education based on religious values and those who believe in reasoning. Dr. Abadan-Unat appealed to all political parties and social institutions to act together to stand up to those associations and foundations seeking to restore a Muslim culture where women are not equal to men. "We're moving on to the information age," she concluded firmly. "We must abide by secular principles."

Another important sector of civil society to unite against Erbakan's administration was labor. In an unprecedented move, TURK-İŞ, the main conservative trade union confederation, and DISK, the leftist confederation, coalesced in support of secularism and called for the resignation of the Islamist-led government. The influential management organization, the Union of Chambers, and the Employers Union joined them.

"Turkey is headed for either a direct military coup or radical Islamic takeover," DISK's secretary-general Rıdvan Budak told me at the union's headquarters in Ankara.[8] Expressing distaste for either solution, Budak said workers and employers had joined forces "to open the way for a modern democratic government."

Artists also joined the fray. At the drop of a hat, any concert, ballet, or art exhibit would turn into a rallying stage for the struggle against Islamic fundamentalism.

From the outset, some Islamist mayors openly disapproved of Turkey's lively art scene, which is heavily influenced by Western productions and ideas. Subsidies for art festivals disappeared, a couple of statues were pulled down, a museum threatened, the head of İstanbul's municipal theaters removed, and many secularists in the Ministry of Culture lost their jobs. It was not exactly a declaration of war on the art world, but many Turkish artists and their followers felt threatened.

Painter Bedri Baykam was one of the first artists to denounce the Islamists and their agenda and continues to do so at every possible occasion. That spring of 1997, he was again openly defying the Islamist authorities with an exhibit glorifying the left. Occupying a whole floor of the vast Atatürk Cultural Center, Baykam's show, "The 68 Years," featured popular leftist icons like Deniz Gezmiş, a Turkish student activist executed in 1972. There were also international heroes like Che Guevara, Fidel Castro, Martin Luther King, Mohammed Ali, Marilyn Monroe, John and Robert Kennedy, the Beatles, and the Rolling Stones. The large photo-paintings and canvases were accompanied by songs of the sixties and interviews with student leaders, journalists, soldiers, and politicians of the times. It was an extraordinary show of freedom of expression and clearly demonstrated that the military power was no longer concerned with the left.

After ten years as director of İstanbul's six municipal theaters, Gencay Gürün had been dismissed by Islamist mayor Erdoğan for allegedly ignoring Turkish playwrights in favor of foreign authors.

"The mayor was misinformed," she said angrily, when we first met in the spring of 1995 at her elegant apartment overlooking the Bosphorus. She stressed that out of the 109 plays she had put on, 60 were Turkish. Ms. Gürün had not taken dismissal easily. She opened her own theater and was a big success with plays like *Auschwitz* by Scottish writer C. P. Taylor.

"We feel embattled. We are pro-Western, secular and of course we don't want soldiers in control but better the military than Refah," Ms. Gürün told me. "That is why Europe is so important to us; the main thing for Turkey is to become part of the modern democratic world."

When I saw her again in the spring of 1997, Ms. Gürün had gone into politics to promote legislation to defend the arts.[9] Critical of Çiller's alliance with Refah from the outset, Ms. Gürün left her True Path Party in protest and was serving as an independent deputy. Refah, she said, had gotten control of Çiller's party and together they had hushed up the Susurluk scandal. Refah's friends were getting lucrative business contracts and building permits. Other people in the arts had been sacked, among them the director of the Council of Historic Sites. Secular events like İstanbul's annual Music Festival were no longer getting official help.

"This has been the most difficult year in the history of the Republic; all our principles are in danger," Gürün said glumly. She was particularly resentful of Erbakan's courtship of Islamist nations like Libya and Iran, which she said "was alienating" Turkey's friends in the region as well as the United States and Europe. Parliament, dominated by Refah–True Path, was inoperative, she continued. Islamists were working hard; opening Koranic courses everywhere, sending their children to *İmam Hatip* schools. Fundamentalists were gaining new courage and appearing in their robes despite the ban. "We've been sleeping—like England slept," she declared. "This has to be stopped."

It became clear to me that the Islamist-led coalition's days were numbered when the different protest groups turned into a generalized crusade.

First there was the Lights Out Movement. It began in February in Ankara as an unorganized, grassroots demonstration against corruption and went on for about two months. Every night, ordinary citizens turned off their lights for one minute in a symbolic protest against all the scandals shaking the country. The movement spread around the country like brushfires and soon turned into a campaign to preserve "democratic and secular Turkey." Islamic authorities were critical of the movement, and religious neighborhoods visibly failed to take part in the mobilization.

Other protests occurred when large crowds of secularists got together. Performances of the Turkish oratorio "Yunus Emre," which preaches religious tolerance, turned into a political event. A Beethoven concert in the Ankara sports stadium became a plebiscite for Western culture, with people chanting, "No to *Sharia.*"

Official celebrations of Youth Day were transformed into rallies for secularism. People thronged to Atatürk's mausoleum bearing flowers for the leader's tomb. The crowd whistled down the Islamist prime minister and cheered President Demirel, who had pointedly refused to shake hands with Erbakan and his coalition partner Çiller. Later half a million people gathered at the Ankara sports stadium for a pop concert and wildly acclaimed the leftist musician Zülfü Livaneli, who sang in honor of Atatürk. The crowd chanted: "Turkey is a secular country and will stay that way."

If there is a spokesman for the arch-Kemalists, someone who articulates the profound apprehensions of the secular elite, it is probably Yekta Güngör Özden, former chief judge of the Constitutional Court and now head of the Atatürk Thought Association. His views weighed heavily in the legal action to close down Refah Party and sanction Islamic extremists.

Suffering from a severe case of flu, Dr. Özden nevertheless showed up stoically for our appointment at his office on Atatürk Boulevard in Ankara.[10] But he's that kind of a man.

When had he personally become conscious of an Islamist threat in Turkey? I asked, expecting the usual response: at the time of the 1994 local elections or the national elections the following year.

Not at all. The bushy-browed judge said he had become aware of an Islamist movement as early as 1947, when he was in high school. And by 1952, as an activist in the Republican People's Party (founded by Atatürk) youth organization, he had understood the Islamist threat. It was Menderes's Democrat Party that had given concessions to the Nurci and other religious orders.

"Already Islamic militants were committing aggressions against Atatürk's statues. Some deputies in Parliament were asking for the restoration of prayers in Arabic and the return of *Sharia*," he recalled.

In modern times, Refah became the focus of antisecular activities and its aim was to change the legal state, according to Dr. Özden. "If *Sharia* were restored, the Republic would die," he underlined, citing his forty-three years of experience as a lawyer. "It would mean the end of equality of men and women. Education would be largely religious. The legal system would be based on a double standard. Democracy would go."

The judge claimed there was evidence that Islamists have been using mosques and *İmam Hatip* schools to mobilize students. *Sharia* people were trying to get control of the universities through the headscarf movement. Some of the militants have been paid to create turmoil. Some have been brainwashed in the United States. Some deputies have even threatened that people who do not think the way they do would be killed. Armed camps have been found in the regions of İstanbul and Bolu. But most important, Islamists have widely penetrated the state and local bureaucracies.

Dr. Özden said he told Prime Minister Çiller at the end of February 1994 that nearly half the governors and administrators, three-quarters of the security force, nearly half the teachers, and one-third of the judges and prosecutors were involved in the pro-*Sharia* movement.

"She said okay, she would take action, and now four years later nothing has changed," he recalled bitterly. "The danger is still there and increasing in the security forces, provincial governments, universities, and bureaucracy. Some municipalities are out of control. But recently the army has kicked out a number of officers accused of Islamic sympathies and some mayors are in prison and under investigation. The State must control financial institutions. Islamists must be removed from security positions and the bureaucracy."

Was there no room for compromise? I asked hesitantly in the face of this anti-Islamic deluge. Or is political Islam completely incompatible with a democratic secular system?

"We have moved to enlightenment and civilization with Atatürk. We are secular but there is 100 percent freedom of religious belief in this country," the magistrate asserted. "Islam and democracy are not compatible. If Islam becomes political, this democracy becomes Islam."

# 12 ~

## The Military Moves

Historians will probably conclude that on February 28, 1997, Turkey's military leadership carried out yet another coup or at least the first phase of a coup, which terminated with the resignation of Islamist prime minister Necmettin Erbakan nearly four months later.

Three other times in modern history, the generals found it expedient to intervene in the political process: 1960, 1971, and 1980. Each time, they justified their undemocratic action citing the constitutional obligation to defend Atatürk's secular republic. And on the earlier occasions, they could invoke the pretext of widespread political violence and the need to restore order.

This time was different. Although the Islamists sometimes committed rhetorical excesses, their demonstrations were pointedly peaceful and seemingly patriotic.

Responding in kind, the Turkish General Staff did not draw their arms but waged their assault on the Islamist enemy through recommendations, briefings, and warnings.

It was a highly sophisticated type of cold warfare, difficult to imagine in any other setting or with other armed forces. This was not your classic coup, no bloody open-ended takeover. Once they achieved their aim, the ousting of the Islamist leader, Turkey's army commanders backed off and let the democratic process take over.

Not to say that Turkish military cannot be as bloody-minded as the next. I had lived through the 1980 coup. In the name of democracy, a six-man military junta suspended Parliament, arrested the main political leaders, closed all parties, trade unions, and other associations, established strict press censorship, made mass arrests among dissidents, and produced a new restrictive constitution.

Through it all, the general public had given the junta the benefit of the doubt. For most Turks, what counted was that the extreme left-right terror had been crushed, violence in schools ended, and gangs of extortionists disappeared. Most politicians and journalists, who had directly suffered in the crackdown, accepted the coup as a necessary ill and agreed that changes in the political system were needed.

Although the military leaders did everything they could to sanitize the state and produce a new system, by 1987 all the old politicians were back leading parties with new names, and it was almost business as usual. The main difference from earlier coups was the severe 1982 constitution, giving the authorities far-reaching powers to defend the integrity of the secular Republic. The preamble, as amended in 1995, states:

> No protection shall be given to thoughts or opinions that run counter to Turkish national interests, the fundamental principle of the existence of the indivisibility of the Turkish state and territory, the historical and moral values of Turkishness, or the nationalism, principles, reforms, and modernism of Atatürk, and that as required by the principle of secularlism there shall be absolutely no interference of sacred religious feeling in the affairs of state and politics . . . [1]

Actually, some seasoned observers had expected the fourth military coup a year earlier, when Islamist leader Erbakan came to power after his party had won national elections with 21 percent of the vote. It was no secret that Erbakan, with his openly anti-American, anti-NATO, anti-Europe, anti-Israel, and pan-Islamic positions, was anathema to the armed forces.

But the military leaders were reluctant to intervene. Turkey's main partners, the United States and countries of the European Union, had made it amply clear they would not condone another military intervention in the name of democracy. Times had changed, and the Western democracies could no longer turn a blind eye to behavior tolerated during the Cold War. Although NATO governments were unhappy about the prospect of dealing with an Erbakan government, they were wary of the alternative. The bloody conflict in Algeria was on everybody's mind as a catastrophic example of what might happen when an Islamist party was deprived of its victory at the polls.

Furthermore, the military had considered the mathematics of the situation. Maybe Erbakan's party had come in first, but nearly 80 percent of the country had voted for secular parties and were represented in Parliament. Besides, Erbakan's secular coalition partner, Tansu Çiller, had advised her supporters that she would be a watchdog and hold the Islamists in check. In the military mind, it was up to the secular majority in Parliament and outside to put the Islamists in their place, that is, out of government.

This turned out to be a faulty strategy for the basic reason that Çiller, fighting against parliamentary investigation into corruption charges, became Erbakan's virtual hostage. And because of the personal power wielded by a party leader, True Path's parliamentary group did her bidding.

For the first six months, Erbakan "behaved," military sources told me privately. Contrary to expectation, the Islamist leader did not charge into his new office like a bull in a china shop. Treading gently around Turkey's pro-Western foreign policy, he made no basic changes and toned down his Third World rhetoric. Reneging on campaign promises, Erbakan went so far as to approve the new defense agreement with Israel and endorse U.S.-British use of a Turkish base for overflights of Iraq.

In fact, Erbakan and Foreign Minister Çiller, themselves at odds over foreign policy, appeared to step aside and let the military handle key issues. Army chief of staff General İsmail Hakkı Karadayı personally took over the warming relations with Israel and was received there like a head of state by the president and prime minister as well as top military personnel. General Karadayı also took up the long-simmering Greek problem, announcing publicly that the Turkish armed forces were determined to end the deep mistrust between the two countries.

His deputy, the personable English-speaking General Çevik Bir, went to Washington and in meetings with U.S. officials, discussed the dangers of increasingly militant Islam. The candid general went so far as to condemn Iran publicly as "a terrorist state," countering his prime minister's efforts to improve relations with that unpredictable Islamic neighbor.

On domestic policy, Erbakan gave reassurances that his government had no plans to alter the constitution. The way he put it, he simply wished to "correct certain deficiencies" in the implementation of the law.

Nevertheless, the armed forces displayed increasing impatience with Erbakan's governance. Although it was difficult to pin him down on specific changes of policy, it soon become apparent that he was unabashedly using his office to expand his party's power base in the bureaucracy, state

*General Çevik Bir was the chief spokesman for the movement to oust Prime Minister Erbakan and clamp down on radical Islamic activities.*

institutions, and the voting public at large. (Actually this is a Turkish tradition, but appeared more alarming to the ever-watchful army chiefs when it involved Islamists.)

The military leaders were in a real bind, sources close to those habitually aloof quarters told me privately. The commanders' main fear was not that Erbakan would fail but that he just might succeed. After all, the Islamist mayors had generally proved to be less corrupt and more efficient at the local level than some of their secular predecessors. Islamist success at the national level, in the military view, would have devastating consequences for the future of a Western democratic Turkey.

The chief dilemma facing the army commanders, according to these sources, was whether to give Erbakan and his friends the possibility of trying to resolve the Kurdish problem their way. Erbakan's initial approaches to the "Islamic brothers" in Iran, Iraq, and Syria had been slapped down as consorting with the enemy. And those Islamists who had made exploratory contacts with Kurdish militants outside the country were denounced for what amounted to treason.

The Kurdish conflict has always been a military prerogative, and, in line with the prevailing dogma, only the army could resolve it. Now here was a serious civilian effort to put an end to the war. What if Erbakan's diplomatic moves successfully isolated the Kurdish fighters? What if his government actually engaged in a social-economic program to improve living standards in the Kurdish-inhabited area? And what if they made good on electoral promises to respect Kurdish cultural rights?[2]

These concerns would explain why the military lashed out with such persistent intransigence at any Islamic gesture by the prime minister. For example, Erbakan's controversial visits to Iran and Libya were widely condemned. Yet other Turkish leaders like Özal had been praised as pragmatists for enhancing ties with these oil-rich states.

No less offensive was Erbakan's dinner for some forty leaders of *tarikatlar* (religious brotherhoods) during the Muslim holy month of Ramadan. Military sources privately viewed this incident as a deliberate challenge. They could not countenance the opening of the prime minister's residence to Islamic *sheiks*, who had been banished by Atatürk and were still only tolerated. It was tantamount to desecration of Atatürk's memory, a criminal offense.

Other seemingly minor moves by Erbakan, clearly aimed to placate his Islamist constituency in lieu of policy changes, also stirred the wrath of the military. These included an unsuccessful attempt to end the ban on headscarves, plans to build a mosque in İstanbul's central Taksim Square, and the proposed opening of a land route to Mecca (which would multiply the number of pilgrims traveling to Islam's main holy places).

Then there was the highly publicized Sincan incident, which looked for a time like it might have triggered a real coup. The Islamist mayor of Sincan, a working-class town near Ankara, hosted a rally to mark Jerusalem Night at the end of January 1997. The Association for Solidarity with Jerusalem, a radical pro-Iranian group, had organized similar events in the past with little impact. This time was different, essentially because the mayor of Sincan was a member of the ruling party and because of the country's close new alliance with Israel. In the heat of the moment, Mayor Bakir Yıldız actually suggested the restoration of *Sharia* in Turkey—a criminal offense. The main speaker was the Iranian ambassador, who predictably attacked Israel, its leaders, and its policies, as he had done on other occasions. The small but militant crowd chanted radical slogans, denounced the Israeli government and PLO leader Arafat, and later assaulted a Turkish woman journalist.

Outraged over this seemingly flagrant act of Islamic provocation, the army delivered a clear warning several days later. A unit of tanks and armored cars rolled through Sincan presumably "en route to exercises" in the area. Sincan's mayor was promptly jailed, and a fortnight later the Iranian ambassador and two other diplomats were summarily deported. Erbakan's minister of justice promised to investigate the incident, but nothing came of it.

Sincan was apparently the last straw in what the military saw as an alarming drift toward Islamic fundamentalism, with the acquiescence if not the connivance of the government.

The generals fired the first round of their coup-in-progress at the National Security Council meeting at the end of February 1997. The council, a military-dominated watchdog agency, presented Erbakan with an ultimatum in the form of eighteen "recommendations." In so many words, the military ordered the Islamist prime minister and his coalition government to crack down on Islamic groups and activities or face the consequences (widely understood to mean direct military intervention).

It was an impossible situation for Erbakan, who risked losing his credibility and the support of his main constituency. The military gave top priority to the closure of illegal Koranic schools and the establishment of eight-year compulsory public schooling (ending intermediary religious education). Most devout Muslims adamantly opposed the closure of religious schools. Other sensitive measures included tightening controls on religious brotherhoods and Islamic businesses and cracking down on Islamic dress.

Even more difficult was the demand for government action to prevent "the entrenchment" of so-called fundamentalists in state and municipal offices. The government was also told to end all exploitation of religious issues for political reasons, monitor antisecular broadcasts by radio and television, terminate attempts to provoke the armed forces, and prevent Iran from interfering in Turkey's domestic affairs.

For several days, Erbakan resisted the council's orders. In an unusual show of defiance, the prime minister stated, "Governments are formed in Parliament not in the National Security Council; laws are made in Parliament." He had obviously hoped to shift the purview of the recommendations to Parliament, but parliamentarians refused.

In the end, Erbakan signed the orders without fanfare.

Later, in a meeting with Turkish writers, the prime minister blithely accused the media of "blowing up" the current political crisis. Acting as though he and his party were not targets of the recommendations, Erbakan acknowledged there were some minor militant Islamic groups, "who must be dealt with through education." He said the government would discuss the recommendations and prepare legislation if necessary.

But Çiller, speaking for the coalition, said, "We will implement all Council decisions in a serious manner." This was followed by some token arrests of men in religious garb and the closing of unregistered Koranic courses. Then nothing, and it appeared that the government thought the military and their recommendations would go away.

For their part, the generals insisted both publicly and privately that they did not want to use force, but expected the politicians to ensure their orders were carried out. Their main hope was in a "parliamentary solution." This meant that either Çiller could be persuaded to pull her party out of the coalition or enough dissidents within her party would see the writing on the wall and join the opposition to topple the government.

There were indeed prominent defections from Çiller's party that spring, including the ministers of trade and health, who resigned over the government's failure to implement the National Security Council's decisions. But it was a slow process.

Meanwhile tensions between the government and the armed forces increased to the point of personal insults. One senior officer went so far as to call the prime minister "a pimp" for going with his family on the pilgrimage to Mecca as guests of Saudi Arabia. When Erbakan urged the military to sanction the officer, they refused.

Erbakan also used colorful language in an attempt to show he was not intimidated by the military mystique. In one speech to party stalwarts, the prime minister reportedly invoked the pharaoh-and-elephant metaphor in a not-so-veiled allusion to the army. Noting that pharaohs believe they have "a right to act cruelly," Erbakan added, "If being strong meant being in the right, elephants would be right all the time."

But the strains between the military and civilian authorities were no laughing matter. Dramatically illustrating their loss of confidence in the government, the armed forces launched a major offensive in mid-May against Kurdish rebels in northern Iraq without advising the government. Erbakan commented ruefully that he had learned about the operation, involving 50,000 troops, in the newspapers. A senior military commander acknowledged they had notified the government twelve hours after the campaign was under way out of fear the information would be leaked and the separatists forewarned.

The crisis reached its peak on May 11, 1997, when Erbakan's supporters went on the offensive, organizing the largest rally anyone could remember at İstanbul's historic Sultanahmet Square. It was an orderly, well-run show of Islamic strength. A crowd estimated at over 100,000 men, women, and children from all over the country waved Turkish flags and gave a resounding "no" to the army's top demand: eight years' compulsory state education and closure of intermediate religious schools.

Unused to such open defiance, the generals proved all the more determined to fight against religious "extremism." According to sources close to the military, they viewed the Sultanahmet demonstration not as an expression of popular will but as a potential problem of street violence. The threat could be contained at present, but the urgency to curb the Islamists' mobilizing capacity was evident.

Cautiously and deliberately, the military proceeded to put into motion phase two of their intervention. At an extraordinary meeting of the Supreme Military Council in late May, Erbakan was obliged to endorse the cashiering of 161 officers and noncoms for alleged links with fundamentalists. Later Erbakan explained to his parliamentary group that he was faced with two options: challenging the army's position and stepping down from government or trying to persuade and reach a compromise. He said he had chosen the second way for the good of the party and the country.

At the end of May, the National Security Council held its regular meeting to review the implementation of the February 28 decisions and made its dissatisfaction clear. The military commanders served the government notice: It must do their bidding at once.

But Erbakan again upstaged his adversaries, seizing the headlines. The following day, the prime minister and his coalition partner announced an accord to exchange places and prepare the way for early elections. They assumed that if the Islamist leader stepped down and gave the reins of government to his secular partner, the military would relax its pressures.

Dismissing the Çiller-Erbakan pact as a ploy to avoid carrying out the antifundamentalist measures, the generals moved on to phase three of the coup. In early June, General Karadayı personally gave the green light for the operation, ordering all military commanders to remain in the country through August, in case it was needed to call an emergency meeting of the National Security Council.

Then the military staged an extraordinary show of their own, a whole week of "briefings" for selected audiences with one overriding objective: convince influential sectors of civil society that the threat of political Islam had reached a dangerous level and must be halted.

Prosecutors and judges turned out in great numbers for the first briefing, defying a ban by the Islamist minister of justice. The media and university circles, labor unions, and other civil organizations and teachers followed them. The briefings were held at the Turkish General Staff headquarters in Ankara and usually presented by the chief of General Staff Intelligence and the head of counterintelligence.

Judging from the press briefing, the military had amassed an overwhelming catalog of circumstantial evidence, which did indeed demonstrate the significant growth of the Islamic movement and the sympathy it enjoyed from the ruling pro-Islamic Welfare Party. But, in the opinion of neutral legal observers, they failed to produce any real proof of a plot to overthrow the regime or even of wrongdoing, aside from the much-touted cases of Jerusalem Night and the prime minister's dinner for the *sheiks*. Even the evidence of foreign involvement—Iran, Libya, Saudi Arabia, and Sudan—was hardly convincing, based mainly on prisoners' confessions and press statements. What was to be taken seriously was the charge that the government had done nothing to implement the February 28 antifundamentalist measures, and consequently, the military was prepared to take up arms to fight fundamentalism if necessary.

A new element in this mass of allegations was the army's decision to challenge Islamic capital. The military denounced 100 "Islamist bosses" who were said to be exploiting religious beliefs on behalf of some thirty radical organizations. The government was accused of favoring so-called fundamentalist companies in the privatization of state companies. Separate press reports disclosed plans of the armed forces to blacklist 100 companies, allegedly financing the spread of radical Islam. Targets of the boycott included İhlas Holding, the largest Islamic group with interests in fifty-five companies from banking to soft drinks, and Kombassan, a Konya-based conglomerate with interests in thirty-five companies, including machine tools and Liquefied Petroleum Gas.

Even Western diplomats, who sympathized with the Turkish army's concern over the spread of Islamic fundamentalism, reacted negatively to the briefings. The military have not come forth with any evidence that fundamentalists were preparing an armed rebellion, a senior diplomatic envoy told me privately. Another diplomat categorized the moves against the Islamic businesses as "an outrageous interference in the private sector." But other foreign observers tended to minimize the crisis, saying the Turkish army was fully aware that armed intervention would be a devastating blow to any hopes for full membership in the European Union.

Washington took the crisis seriously. "We have made very clear that it is essential that Turkey continue in a secular democratic way," Secretary of State Madeleine Albright told the press in mid-June. She added that the Clinton administration had also made it very clear that any changes "have to be within a democratic context and with no extraconstitutional approach."

Earlier Deputy Secretary of State Strobe Talbott had flown to Ankara and conveyed Washington's position personally to Deputy Chief of Staff General Çevik Bir. Sources close to the Turkish military said General Bir had responded candidly: "We're doing what we have to do."

The American press was blunter. "Military Meddles in Turkey" was the headline of an editorial in the *New York Times*, which called the military action "a backdoor coup against parliamentary democracy." The *Los Angeles Times* quoted a White House official as saying, "First we don't like coups. And second, it is unlikely to undercut the appeal of Erbakan."

Although some Turkish newspapers had interpreted Talbott's visit as a sign of support for the military against the Islamist-led government, İlnur Çevik, editor-in-chief of the *Turkish Daily News*, wrote: "The American message is loud and very clear. The era when the West accepted military regimes in Turkey is over. Whoever wants to stage a coup has to do it without the backing of the United States and the European states."

Faced with relentless military and civilian pressure, Erbakan resigned on June 18, 1997, citing the need for early elections. He could also see that his coalition's parliamentary majority was in doubt, as Çiller's True Path Party continued to lose deputies concerned over the government's feud with the military.

In a last-ditch attempt to retain power, Erbakan urged President Demirel to transfer the office of prime minister to Tansu Çiller. Clearly aware the military would not accept such a maneuver, the president called on the main opposition party leader, Mesut Yılmaz, to form the new government. Yılmaz, a moderate secularist, formed a right-left coalition, which he described as government of "reconciliation"—with no Islamists.

The coup by recommendation was complete. The military leadership had achieved its goals without risking the widespread condemnation of an armed intervention. The democratically elected Islamist prime minister had voluntarily relinquished power. A new secular administration was in place with the implicit mission to carry out the National Security Council's bidding. Civilian prosecutors had embraced the task of investigating and prosecuting all organizations or individuals accused of anti-secular activities. These included Erbakan and his Welfare Party, their youth group known as the National View Foundation, Islamic mayors and governors, and Islamic businesses and financial institutions.

There was a palpable change in atmosphere with the secularists back in power, a relaxation of the tension that had been building up over the past few months. Whereas the generals withdrew from center stage, they made it very clear they were not ready to repair to their barracks. Even though the Islamist prime minister was out, that was no reason to ease their vigilance regarding antisecular activities. And given the past performances of the politicians, a military presence was needed to prod the process along.

The National Security Council continued to meet periodically, but now they discussed the agenda beforehand with the prime minister. The West Working Group, a body composed of intelligence chiefs set up to report on the Islamic threat, let it be known there would be no slack in its investigations into Islamic efforts to infiltrate the army, the media, business, and schools.

The military commanders, who had apparently enjoyed the recent experience of virtually running the country's foreign policy, indicated they would keep a hand in foreign affairs, for security purposes of course. Now, however, they tended to work with the Ministry of Foreign Affairs rather than strike off on their own, as they had under the Erbakan administration. For example, when some Nordic countries openly supported Kurdish dissidents, the military urged the Foreign Ministry to reconsider relations with countries that demonstrated a "negative attitude" to Turkey. They specifically let it be known that defense purchases would be used as a foreign policy tool, with friendly countries getting the big contracts.

There was little opposition to these military moves.

To be sure, every Friday after prayers, Islamists organized protests against the closure of religious schools, but nothing like the demonstrations when a sympathetic Erbakan was still in office. Some Islamist figures railed at President Demirel for not acting "constitutionally" in ignoring the Erbakan-Çiller deal and against politicians and prosecutors for their "undemocratic" acts.

Never timid, former deputy prime minister Çiller went so far as to declare at a rally that the public "wants the military to get out of politics and stick to soldiering." She also urged her party to call for a parliamentary commission to investigate the military's secretive West Working Group. Her party refused the suggestion, which bordered on treason.

Probably the main reason for the mild reaction to the soft coup was that a large segment of civil society agreed with the military commanders on the need to get rid of Erbakan and was generally relieved that force was not necessary.

My friend Gülter Kolankaya, who like many secularists looks to the military as the last resort to protect the gains of Atatürk's revolution, put it this way: "It's happened before. We go to the edge of the precipice and then wake up. There was so much turmoil; it looked like the state was losing control. Then the military appear and without bloodshed order is restored."[3]

For all their tendency to hover about the political scene, the armed forces have remained the most highly respected institution in Turkey, according to opinion polls. In the wake of all the political changes, a poll by a national cultural and scientific foundation revealed that 78.37 percent of Turks considers the army "the most reliable institution" in the country.

Despite the obvious temptation to extend their own mandate, four out of five of the military commanders retired in August when their time was up. This respect for hierarchy and promotions sets Turkey's military apart from other armed forces that have found it necessary to intervene in politics.

I had been curious for some time about the unique role of the military in Turkish society. Several friends suggested retired General Kemal Yavuz, an executive with TEMA, the country's leading private environmental agency, could provide some answers.

In an interview in his İstanbul office, General Yavuz pointed out that the Ottoman Empire was founded by warriors and had accorded the military a special place in the state structure. Ottoman Turks seeking to rise to positions of influence chose the military profession, leaving industry, trading, and the arts to the minorities.

"Despite limited resources, important investments have always gone to military education," said General Yavuz, a distinguished white-haired man wearing a sporty checkered shirt.[4] He explained that during the reorganization of the Ottoman army in the nineteenth century, young officers were sent abroad, mostly to England, to learn Western information and technology. "Thus," he said, "the military were involved in all innovation and modernization efforts that went on under the empire.

I understood then that it was no coincidence that Atatürk, the war hero, had assumed his mission to modernize the state and its society. It was military tradition, although no other leader had undertaken such wide-ranging reforms, from language and law to dress and attitudes.

The tradition of excellence and discipline continues at the Turkish War College today, General Yavuz stressed, noting that the curriculum was updated each year with material particularly from the United States, Germany, and England.

Another way the armed forces has earned the respect of the people, the general continued, is through strong internal checks from bottom to top, "so that everything is socially, financially, and legally correct."

Asked about the current threats to Turkey, General Yavuz gave a succinct rundown of external dangers, sounding very much like an American military strategist. To the west, he noted, are the "volatile" Balkans and "difficult" Greece. To the north, there are the Caucasus, "where problems may always erupt," and Russia, "a country with which we have had and will have conflicts." To the east and south are "societies not socially developed into modern states."

General Yavuz described the primary internal threat as *irtica*—extreme political conservatism—another expression used to refer to political Islam. The armed forces are particularly sensitive on this subject, he said, because certain religious groups have fought against the state since the beginning of the Republic.

This former commander of the Second Army, based in the Islamic center of Konya, did not underestimate the significance of Islam in people's lives but blamed the politicians for the growth of political Islam.

"As an eastern nation marching to the West, religion is still very important in our society," General Yavuz said. He stressed that the military leaders who took charge in 1980 were aware of this fact and wanted to improve the quality of religious instruction. For this reason, they opened more religious schools—and not, as often rumored, as a deliberate move against the left. Claiming that the military's good intentions were "abused by politicians," the general said that the parties appealed to religious sentiments, promised more religious freedoms, and used any means to get votes.

General Yavuz believes the people increasingly turned to religion because the politicians didn't live up to their words. Since the 1970s, he noted, parties with different ideologies had come to power: Social Democrats, the center and the right, and none could meet the public's expectancies.

"Then the Islamists came up with their Just Order and for many Turks this was a great new hope," the officer said. Again, the politicians—this time the Islamists—were unable to provide solutions to the country's problems. The public was disappointed once more, and a lot of people realized they had made a mistake.

Declaring that the Islamist danger is more obvious now, General Yavuz said that the state apparatus "has been widely infiltrated." Under suspicion, he said, were half the provincial governors, many subgovernors, some police chiefs, and officials in the State Planning Office responsible for distributing credit.

The general was not very optimistic about the prospect of enforcing strong secular laws in the near future. With elections on the horizon, he said, the politicians would be more involved in party politics than dealing with the problems of the country.

"Nobody in his right mind can think elections will produce a useful result unless the political parties change," General Yavuz said, not bothering to hide his exasperation. "What Turkey needs are new political leaders, new parties, and new ideas."

# 13 ～

---

# *Another View of the World*

---

Turkey is obsessed with Europe. It's nothing new. A century ago, the Ottoman Sultans who sought to reform the decaying empire looked to Europe as the source of enlightenment and progress. Later Atatürk was driven to emulate all things European, from law and politics to music and dress, as he laid the foundations of the new Turkish Republic.

Modern Turkey has joined every European and Western organization possible, starting off as a founding member of the Council of Europe in 1949, becoming the only Muslim country in the North Atlantic Treaty Organization and the Organization of Security and Cooperation in Europe, and entering the European Economic Community in 1963 as an associate member.

The aim of full integration into the new Europe has been the cornerstone of Turkish foreign policy ever since then. In 1987, Turkey formally applied for membership in the European Community. Successive governments never had any doubt but that one day the country would gain admittance to this exclusive club. After a tough fight, the European Union approved of a Customs Union with Turkey, which went into effect the beginning of 1996 and was widely seen as the antechamber to the EU.

Nobody thought accession to the European Union would be easy, with archrival Greece a member and in position to veto. In fact Greece has successfully blocked more than $450 million of EU financial aid intended to ease Turkey's debut in the Customs Union (Spain and Portugal did receive this kind of assistance). But somehow, the Turks were convinced their cause would prevail and the other Europeans would force the Greeks into line.

Turkey's European fixation reminds me of Portugal's decade-long struggle to gain admittance to the European Community. Having divested itself of fascist rule and a colonial empire in the April Revolution of 1974 and concerned over the rise of an aggressive Communist party, Portugal looked desperately to Europe for political identity and as guarantor of Western democracy. Economic considerations were secondary.

For Turkey's secular establishment, haunted by the specter of Islamic fundamentalism and Arabization, Europe appeared as a political safety net. Even Islamists, who initially looked at Europe as a hostile Christian camp, came to see European democracy as a shelter from Turkey's harsh secular rule.

Only in this light is it possible to understand what Europe's rejection has meant to many Turks. This was the *no* of a fiancée, the only love that modern Turkey has ever known, and the impact has been devastating.

The first public slap came from European Christian Democrats who declared in the spring of 1997 that Turkey was not a candidate for membership in the European Union, *not short-term or long*. The main reason given was the *difference in civilizations*. This official statement coming from a meeting that included such prominent Europeans as German chancellor Helmut Kohl, Spanish prime minister José Maria Aznar, and Belgian prime minister Wilfred Martens sent shock waves around Turkey and the region. Here were responsible Christian Democrats taking up Huntington's controversial "clash of civilizations" theory.[1]

Tansu Çiller, then foreign minister, who had embraced EU membership as her personal cause, was furious. "Turkey is the member of NATO with the second largest army after the United States of America. It has the fastest growing economy in Europe. It is the only country with a customs union with the EU. None of the other countries [Eastern European countries including Hungary and Poland] fit these criteria. Yet Turkey is not mentioned for membership. This is something we can't understand. This is something the Turkish people can't accept."

Later Çiller suggested that if Turkey were not accepted as a candidate for the EU, Ankara could veto NATO's expansion plans to include Eastern European countries. Cooler heads prevailed, and this tactic was dropped when Europeans and the United States made it clear that such blackmail was unacceptable.

Many prominent Turks blamed the European fiasco on the Islamist-led government. Emre Gönensay, a former foreign minister who broke with Çiller over her coalition with Erbakan, told the *Turkish Daily News,* "It seems to me because of this government—to use a Churchillian phrase, 'an iron curtain is descending' between Europe and Turkey. This government is responsible for it. And this is the biggest betrayal to the Turkish Republic since its foundation. You have a party, which is not only unconcerned about relations with Europe and the West, but its ideology is to break those relations, break away from the West. A Prime Minister who thinks Europe is the 'infidel' and who has close and warm relations with terrorist countries, which are bent on destroying the West by terrorism. And if you have a Deputy Prime Minister and Foreign Minister who has lost all credibility in Europe . . . "[2]

Reactions differed, but no one was indifferent to Europe's closing door. Cem Duna, a former ambassador who heads an investment consultants firm in İstanbul, told me: "The mood has changed from an American can-do outlook to what's going to become of us?" Duna said Turkey should deal with its very real stumbling blocks to European membership like Cyprus, the southeast (Kurdish question), democratization, income disparities.

A more radical response came from Akın Önger, CEO of the Garanti Bankası, who predicted that Europe would never accept Turkey as a full member because of cultural differences. "Turkey shares European land and history but it is not part of European culture," the banker told me. He went on to say that Turkey didn't need to belong to Europe but can become a partner. What is important is to belong to the European market through institutions like the Customs Union.

At about the same time, the International Olympic Committee excluded İstanbul from its shortlist of candidates for the 2004 Summer Games. For ordinary Turks, it was comparable to the EU's rebuff. *Turkish Daily News* editorialist İlnur Çevik said the problem was Turkey's "rather poor image abroad," the poor image on human rights, which he said had been worsened by military coup rumors and attempts by "a handful of fundamentalists to turn Turkey into a religious state."[3]

In early December 1997, Europe did in fact exclude Turkey as a candidate for the foreseeable future. This was not the Europeans shutting out an Islamist-led government—Erbakan had been long since gone. It was a repudiation of the Republic of Turkey. The meeting in Luxembourg announced membership talks would open the following March with six candidates: Poland, the Czech Republic, Hungary, Estonia, Slovenia, and Cyprus. Negotiations would begin later with other countries: Romania, Bulgaria, Slovakia, Lithuania, and Latvia.

Europeans suggested various reasons for leaving Turkey out of their expansion plans, namely, human rights abuses and the repression of Kurds. Germany, already wrestling with the problem of 2.5 million Turkish immigrants, raised the usual objections to the prospect of a mass influx of Turks on the labor market. And Greece brought up the Turkish occupation of northern Cyprus, among other problems.

Being barred from Europe was bad enough for Turks. That the Greek-dominated island of Cyprus, which has never come to terms with the Turkish minority in the north, should be accepted as candidate was adding insult to injury. In fact, the EU had agreed to a Cypriot candidacy back in 1996 as a sweetener to get Greece to accept Turkey's admission to the Customs Union and in hopes it might help unite the divided island.

An angry Prime Minister Yılmaz announced that Turkey would break off all political contacts with the European Union and intensify the integration process with the Turkish Cypriots in the northern zone. Meeting with a group of American journalists before leaving on an official visit to Washington, Yılmaz said bluntly that the main reason for Turkey's exclusion from Europe was "religious discrimination."

A few days later Deputy Prime Minister Bülent Ecevit declared, "We must leave it to time. I believe if Turkey uses its potentials in an effective way there will come a time when the EU will feel bound to invite Turkey to become a full member."[4]

In a lengthy interview, Ecevit defined Turkey's foreign policy for the postrejection period. "We are a very important country in a very important part of the world. We should never give up our objective of full membership in the EU. We should not withdraw our application but it may remain suspended for an indefinite period and in the meantime we should solidify, extend, and deepen our other international relations not only in other parts of Europe and Asia but also with the United States."

Some Europeans, namely France and Great Britain, expressed sympathy for the Turkish position and called on Ankara not to sever ties with the EU. British prime minister Tony Blair went so far as to declare that his government saw Turkey as a natural part of Europe and would apply all diplomatic means to improve relations between Ankara and the EU. Even a leader of the German Social Democrat Party, which has been critical of Turkey's human rights record, urged Turks not to abandon their "European perspective." Rudolf Scharping, on a visit to Ankara, stressed that Turkey's Muslim religion should not be an obstacle to EU membership. He said Turkey had made considerable steps toward democracy and human rights, and more steps in this direction would ease the way into Europe.

Strongest support came from the United States, which has for some time urged the European Union to take a more positive stand on Turkey. A State Department spokesman, Jim Foley, declared categorically that as far as the United States was concerned, Turkey was a part of Europe.

An editorialist in the *New York Times* slapped Europe, saying, "The European Union erred this week by rebuffing Turkey's longstanding membership application for poorly disguised reasons of ethnic and religious prejudice." But the *Times* urged Turkish leaders "to look more critically" at their human rights problems. If Ankara wanted to be part of the West, the editorial continued, it must respect Western values, namely, curb the military's role in politics, respect the rights of the Kurdish minority, and stop imprisoning parliamentarians, journalists, artists, and ordinary citizens for using free speech.[5]

Some six months after the Great Snub, Turkey seemed to have put Europe on hold. Turkish diplomats insisted that the country considered itself European and was not looking for alternatives. They argued that Turkey is more eligible and better off socially and economically than some Eastern European candidates.

"Once we have put our own house in order we should be ready to continue our relationship with the EU," Farouk Lolloğlu, deputy under secretary in the Foreign Ministry told me.[6] In an interview at the home of a mutual friend, the official underlined that certain internal problems must be overcome first, including human rights, the Kurdish issue, and weaknesses in the democratic institutions.

The Turkish diplomat said some progress has been made in these areas: human rights courses in the police academy, improvement in detention conditions, attempts to reform the penal law, and relaxation of restrictions on expression, except in cases of incitement to violence. Noting there were no insurmountable obstacles in the economic sphere, he suggested a realistic timetable for full EU membership would be "between the years 2010 and 2020."

Lolloğlu acknowledged that Greece has given no signal that it is prepared to accept Turkey in the European Union, although it has made a

Turkish Reflections
956.1
Set

few conciliatory statements. "The Greeks' problem is they still view İstanbul, the Aegean, the Black Sea, and Cyprus as part of the Hellenic Universe; what motivates them is their desire to regain their lost lands," Lolloğlu said.

In my own contacts with Greeks, I have observed a general obsession with Turkey and Turks. Not so much nostalgia for Alexander the Great's empire but a very real fear of their big, nationalistic neighbor.

Greece's relations with Turkey always seem on the brink of catastrophe. Any kind of incident—the skirmish over a rocky islet in the Aegean, unannounced military maneuvers, and recently, the Greek Cypriots' decision to purchase S300 missiles from Russia—could provoke a major confrontation.

The Cyprus crisis—which is part of the overall Turkish-Greek dispute—dates back to 1974, although the frictions go back much earlier. An attempt by Greece's military junta to annex Cyprus in 1974 was followed by the Turkish invasion and occupation of the northern third of the island to protect the Turkish minority. A United Nations peacekeeping force has kept violence to a minimum between the Greek and Turkish Cypriot communities ever since. But U.N.-mediated negotiations have failed to find an acceptable formula for the reunification of this divided island, about half the size of Hawaii with a population of 700,000.

On several visits to both sides of the island, I found most people eager to break down the artificial barriers. Although the Greek southern part of Cyprus is internationally recognized and prospering, many Greek Cypriots lost homes and land in the north and want to return. The Turkish army, which still occupies the north, gives the Turkish Cypriot minority a sense of security. But only Ankara recognizes the so-called Turkish-Cypriot Federal State of Cyprus, and so trade and other communications with the outside world are very difficult.

The European Union's recent acceptance of Cyprus as a candidate for membership has only hardened the division. Turkey contends that, as a guarantor for the island (along with Greece and Great Britain), its approval is required for EU candidacy. This is hardly likely with the EU refusing to consider Turkey as a candidate.

Most probably, the broader Greek-Turkish feud must be resolved first before Greek and Turkish Cypriots can get together. The main question is the Aegean. Greece claims its territorial waters extend twelve nautical miles around its 3,000 islands. Turkey argues this would make the Aegean a Greek lake and refuses to respect this claim. Heightening the tension, Greece has militarized its islands near the Turkish coast, and Turkey maintains an Aegean Army outside its NATO-integrated forces. The underlying problem in the Aegean is the question of seabed mineral rights, namely, oil, an untapped resource.

Thus far the two countries even differ on the forum for resolving their disputes, with Turkey urging bilateral negotiations and Greece insisting on submitting all the claims to the International Court of Justice at The Hague. A minibreakthrough did occur in June 1998, when Greece and Turkey agreed to take certain confidence-building measures. The main part of the agreement consisted of a halt to all military maneuvers in the Aegean during summer months, because of tourism. But these good-will gestures have been dwarfed by Greece's open support to the Kurdish nationalist movement in Turkey.

Turkey's vision of the world had already begun to change in the early 1990s, with the internationalization of the Kurdish problem, the Islamic revival, and the fall of the Soviet Union. Since then Turkey has been engaged in a reappraisal of its international relations with the aim of formulating a more independent foreign policy. Now the European rebuff imposed new horizons.

Europe's slammed door is not the end of the world for Turkish policymakers. It has reawakened Turkey's need to diversify its foreign policy. Turkish officials do not consider the United States as an alternative to Europe but would like to see a strengthening of already close relations. For half a century, ever since the Truman Doctrine of 1947, the two countries have developed close bilateral economic relations as well as common strategic interests in the North Atlantic Treaty Organization.

Faced with Soviet claims on its eastern border, Turkey became a key player in the Cold War. In response to a common threat from the Soviet Union, Ankara allowed the United States to maintain electronic and radar intelligence posts and use several air bases for the deployment of tactical aircraft. In return, Turkey became the third recipient of American military assistance, after Israel and Egypt. This close cooperation was upgraded to the status of Improved Partnership in 1991, after Turkey gave decisive backing to the United States during the Persian Gulf crisis.

For a time, Turks feared their country's geostrategic importance might decline with the end of the Cold War. But it soon became clear that Turkey was still on the front line in an even more dangerous era with increased instability in the region, the rise of radical Islam, and a revival of Russian irredentism.

If reassurances were needed, they came at the annual conference of the American-Turkish Council in Washington, D.C., in February 1998. Denouncing the European Union for its "ostracism" of Turkey, guest speaker Senator Jesse Helms of North Carolina called for closer ties with Ankara and said: "Turkey is more important to the United States than it was during the Cold War."

Addressing the same conference, Assistant Secretary of State for European and Canadian Affairs Marc Grossman said Turkey was at the "center of U.S. interests" from the Balkans to the Caucasus and the Middle East and played a "key" role in combating such global threats as terrorism, crime, and drug trafficking.

A thorn in the relations between the two allies is the severe indictment of Turkey's record in the State Department's annual report on human rights around the world. It is to Washington's credit that it does not gloss over the failings of its close friend and to Ankara's credit that it listens to these denunciations and is ready to discuss them with American officials.

The 1998 report states that "torture remained widespread" despite government denials that it is systematic. It denounces "serious human rights abuses" by security forces and curbs on freedom of speech and press. Criticizing limits on religious freedoms, the report says the closure of Refah is a "troubling" development for the future of Turkish democracy.

In response, the Foreign Ministry issued a mild comment on the American report, declaring that the Turkish government considers human rights "a priority." The official statement said that "despite efforts toward a balanced approach, space was given to some unfounded claims"—but did not specify which.

Other snags in generally positive U.S.-Turkish relations, like restrictive trade quotas or a temporary embargo on special military sales, are seen by Turks as the work of influential Greek and Armenian lobbies in Washington.

Turkey's new partner in the region is Israel. Bilateral relations are growing at such a fast pace that this could change the geopolitical balance in the Middle East. Turkey was in fact the first Islamic country to recognize Israel in 1948 and had always maintained ties with the Jewish state, despite pressures from other Muslim countries.

In a way it is surprising that Israel and Turkey had not established a special relationship much sooner. These two countries have so much in common; they are the only democracies (albeit imperfect) in a largely hostile neighborhood. Both states have fought to defend their territorial integrity and still suffer terrorist attacks. Their societies are generally religious, but their states are secular and Western-oriented. They share the same best friend (the United States) and common enemy (the former Soviet Union) and face the same troublesome neighbors: Syria, Iraq, and Iran.

But Turkey's foreign policy experts are for the most part of the Atatürk school and have tried to remain aloof from Middle Eastern conflicts, at least publicly, keeping an even-handed posture between Israel and the Arabs. When Israel invaded Beirut in 1982, Turkey did downgrade, but not sever, diplomatic relations with Israel.

Then in the early 1980s, the late president Turgut Özal developed his own brand of an Opening to the East, with the blessings of the generals. Although preserving Turkey's goal of membership in the European Union, Özal forged advantageous economic ties with Middle Eastern countries, the Soviet Union, and later the new states of Central Asia. As deputy prime minister, Özal launched a major export drive to the Middle East, opening the Turkish economy to Arab investors. In the name of shared Islamic values, Özal brought a new dimension to Turkey's foreign relations. Turkish goods, Turkish entrepreneurs, and Turkish workers could be found throughout the oil-producing Muslim countries. Turkish military leaders, who looked favorably on a revival of moderate Islam as a counterweight to leftist forces at home, approved of Turkey's enhanced role in the Middle East as economic realism.

Breaking with the tradition of nonimmixation in Middle Eastern conflicts, President Özal supported the U.S.-led coalition against Iraq after its invasion of Kuwait. Although the Turkish military commanders refused Özal's request to send forces into Iraq, they allowed Americans to use the İncirlik Base for air raids over Iraq. And at great cost, Turkey complied with UN sanctions by closing down two pipelines carrying Iraqi oil to the Mediterranean. In the wake of this war, a protected zone was set up for Kurdish refugees in northern Iraq, monitored by British and American aircraft.

After Özal's unexpected death in May 1993, Turkey's leadership concentrated on the struggle for Europe, putting the Islamic connections on the back burner. In reality, Özal's successors were at a loss as to what to do about their "rough neighborhood"—a reference usually to Syria, Iraq, and Iran but not excluding Greece.

The power vacuum in northern Iraq has turned into Turkey's worst nightmare: an autonomous Kurdistan divided into hostile fiefdoms of

Iraqi Kurds, pro-Iranian Kurds, and Turkish PKK guerrillas, with their changing alliances. Turkish armed forces make periodic forays into the area, wreaking havoc but failing to eliminate rebel sanctuaries. A U.S.-brokered accord between the two main Kurdish factions in 1998 and talk of federation has given the Turkish Foreign Office the jitters.

At the same time, Turkish military intelligence has repeatedly denounced Iranian assistance not only to the PKK but also to the Islamic fundamentalist movement inside Turkey. Tehran has denied the charges, but Iranian aid still flows.

Another problem is Syria, which for a long time allowed PKK leaders to keep their headquarters in Damascus and use a training base in Lebanon's Bekkaa Valley. Turkish envoys have appealed directly to Syrian president Hafez al Assad to end his support to PKK terrorists. The Syrians, on the other hand, have longstanding territorial and water claims.

By the fall of 1998, Ankara's patience had run out. First Turkish army commanders, then President Demirel and senior government officials warned Syrian authorities to halt all aid to the PKK or face the consequences. The war of words between the two Muslim neighbors became so heated that Egyptian and Iranian leaders rushed to the scene in mediation efforts. It was clear the Turks meant business, and so Syrian officials agreed to meet with their Turkish counterparts in the southern city of Adana, where they signed an agreement to cooperate in the struggle against terrorism. The first concrete result of this accord was Syrian pressure on PKK leader Öcalan and his entourage to leave Damascus at least temporarily, which cooled things down.

It was in fact the continued hostility shown by Syria that led to Ankara's decision to reinforce ties with Israel in the first place, according to senior Turkish diplomats. The timing of the rapprochement, however, was precipitated by Refah's victory in the 1995 national elections. Concerned that an Islamist-led coalition might balk at signing a defense agreement with Israel, top Turkish military commanders flew to Israel to conclude the pact, without informing Parliament of its contents. Later Foreign Ministry officials tried to minimize the event, saying that Turkey has twenty-seven such military cooperation accords, including eight with Arab countries.

As prime minister Erbakan soon demonstrated his Islamic tilt, making his first official tours to Iran, Pakistan, Malaysia, and Indonesia, followed by Libya. His government fully espoused the cause of the Muslim victims in Bosnia, Kosovo, and Chechnya. Turkey volunteered to coordinate assistance to Bosnia from members of the Organization of the Islamic Conference.

These Islamic initiatives no doubt encouraged the military to intensify relations with Israel. Even before the fall of the Islamist-led coalition, it was clear that Ankara's new multidimensional foreign policy would be based on a strategic partnership with Israel. There is no doubt that Turkey and Israel have mutually benefited from the enhanced relationship in everything from military training, defense procurement, and shared intelligence to technical cooperation, cultural exchanges, bilateral trade, and a major influx of Israeli tourists in Turkey.

To balance these moves, Mesut Yılmaz's secular coalition made efforts to strengthen ties with "like-minded" Arab countries, namely, Jordan and Egypt, because of their shared hostility to Islamic fundamentalism and friendly relations with Israel. Despite sporadic border problems, the government sought to restore relations with Iran on a new and friendly footing. The two countries actually signed a security cooperation agreement focused on their common struggle against drug smuggling and terrorism. As a sign of good faith, Iran agreed to extradite to Turkey a number of Turkish Kurds who were described as PKK terrorists.

No longer threatened by a superpower on its eastern border, Turkey moved to establish friendly relations with Russia, signing various economic and technical agreements, even sharing intelligence. Balancing the close partnership with Washington, Prime Minister Mesut Yılmaz warmly received Russia's then–prime minister Viktor Chernomyrdin for wide-ranging talks on cooperation and the conclusion of a $13.5 million natural gas agreement.

Parallel efforts have been made to promote the Black Sea Economic Cooperation Organization. But this has been slow to get off the ground because of longstanding disputes among the members, namely, Greece and Turkey, Armenia and Azerbaijan, and Moldova and Ukraine, as well as regional conflicts within Russia and Georgia.

Turkey's new frontier is Central Asia, those young republics with their staggering oil reserves and other mineral resources that burst on the world scene after the collapse of the Soviet Union. Suddenly not just Turkish politicians but entrepreneurs, educators, merchants, bankers, and ordinary workers were rushing off to the Turkic republics of Kazakhstan, Kyrgzstan, Turkmenistan, and Uzbekistan and Farsi-speaking Tajikistan.

It is like the 1980s, when Özal opened up the Middle East. Now nearly everybody I know has a relative somewhere in the Caucasus or Central

Asia, opening a gas station, running a supermarket, working on an oil project. A typical sign of the late 1990s is the advertisement in the local press from Ankara's Gazi University offering courses in dialects unheard of a decade ago: Uygurian Turkish, Turkomanian Turkish, Kirghizian Turkish, Uzbekian Turkish, Tatarian Turkish, and others.

Actually President Özal had envisioned Turkey's future links with Central Asia even before the breakup of the Soviet Union. Cem Kozlu, CEO of Turkish Airlines, accompanied Özal on several trips to Baku and Almaty to start up a regional service. He recalls Özal's words at the time: "We want to make İstanbul the gate to Central Asia and Central Asia's window on the West."[7]

Turkey became the first foreign nation to open embassies in the new states. Then Prime Minister Süleyman Demirel visited the region in 1992 to promote economic, cultural, and technical relations and was to return many times. His primary aim, however, was to present the Turkish model as a modern Muslim country and democratic alternative to the radical Islamist regime in Iran.

At first the Turks let their common sense be overwhelmed by the euphoria of having rediscovered a vast Turkic world stretching from the Caucasus to China. But it soon became evident that the Central Asian states were still very dependent on Russia and not about to provoke Moscow's wrath by joining some kind of Turkic Common Market. Neither Turkey nor Iran had the kind of development capital that the new states needed, and so it was clear that a multinational effort was required, including Russia, the United States, and China. Turkey did succeed in bringing the Central Asian republics Azerbaijan and Afghanistan into the Economic Cooperation Organization, a regional Islamic trade pact with Pakistan and Iran.

Without pushing too hard, the Turkish model has worked rather well. By and large, the new countries have kept secular systems, adopted the Latin alphabet, hope to achieve democracy, and are deeply hostile to Islamic fundamentalism. In fact, in some cases like Uzbekistan, the authorities are emulating Turkey's strict secularist policies, including the ban on headscarves in the university.

Turkish firms are involved in all kinds of construction activity in the new developing eastern countries, from highways and housing to factories. The Koç Holding, for example, sees important prospects for its household appliances and other consumer goods in the emerging markets of the Caucasus and Central Asia as well as Russia. In this connection, they have opened Ram Stores—the equivalent of their popular Migros supermarket chain at home—in Baku and Moscow, with considerable success.

"Central Asia was virgin ground; it lacked everything from components to financial institutions," Hasan Subaşı, who heads Koç's Consumer Durables Group, told me, referring to plans for new investments and joint ventures in the area.[8]

The summer of 1999, Koç Holding opened a $32 million hypermarket cum indoor ice-skating rink at Almaty, the new capital of Kazakhstan. It was Koç's eighth retail operation in the one-time communist world, which is avid for Western capitalism.

Increasingly İstanbul is becoming a regional center for international firms seeking to expand into the Caucasus and Central Asia. Although Russia still dominates the area and many foreign companies prefer to work out of Moscow, more and more are setting up regional operations in İstanbul, where there are frequent flights to the new markets, good telecommunications, and it costs less to do business.

"Moscow is far ahead politically . . . but İstanbul's success in business suggests that Turkey is pulling ahead in the race for markets and profits," Hugh Pope wrote in the *Wall Street Journal.* He noted that about half of the 253 American companies with investments in Turkey have set up regional headquarters in İstanbul.[9]

The Coca-Cola Company, which opened its first bottling plant in İstanbul in 1964, now has ten plants in Turkey. In 1993, Coca-Cola chose İstanbul as its administrative center for operations in the Caucasus and the Central Asian Republics.

Cem Kozlu is Coca-Cola's managing director for the entire region and recently resumed his post as head of Turkish Airlines as well. He said Coca-Cola has set up joint ventures mostly with state companies and now operates seven plants in the Caucasus and Central Asian Republics. At first Turkey supplied bottles, cases, caps, labels, and trucks, but now many support industries have also moved into the region.

Turkey's big advantage in Central Asia and the Caucasus is resilient workers who can get along in difficult conditions, Kozlu told me in an interview over lunch in the company canteen at Coca-Cola's headquarters on the Asian side of the Bosphorus.[10] He recalled that in the early 1980s, Özal had pushed Turkish businessmen to increase exports and construction contracts in the Middle East. "These were difficult markets but we learned to operate in tough schools," Kozlu said. The main lesson was patience, he said, remembering his own experiences selling olive oil in

Libya, when he used to be kept standing four to six hours waiting for an appointment.

The main project, which has fired imaginations inside and outside Turkey for several years, is the route to Central Asia's rich natural gas and petroleum reserves. The Caspian Sea region contains 2.2 billion tons of proven oil reserves and 8.7 trillion cubic meters of natural gas. Feasibility studies are currently under way on a natural gas pipeline from Turkmenistan either through the Caspian Sea or crossing Iran.

Energy poor and eager to reduce its dependence on the Middle East and Russia, Turkey has developed a proposal labeled the Caspian-Mediterranean Oil Route. This plan, which has the support of the United States and Azerbaijan, involves the construction of the Baku-Ceyhan pipeline, with an annual capacity of 70 million tons of Azeri and Kazakh crude oil. The 1,080-mile pipeline would run from Baku on the Caspian Sea to Midyat, near Mardin in southeastern Turkey, where it would connect with the pipeline from Kirkuk in Iraq that goes to the Mediterranean port of Ceyhan (also called Yumurtalık).

The most attractive (economically) alternative route is the Black Sea project, backed by Russia, Germany, and the American producer Chevron, which has a joint venture with Kazakhstan. Some Kazakh oil is already transported by pipeline to the Russian port of Novorossiisk and by tankers through the Bosphorus Strait, but increased production would mean the construction of another pipeline, and of course more tankers. Turkey wants to avoid at all costs any increase in the already dangerously busy Bosphorus traffic. And both Ankara and Washington would like to break the Russian monopoly on the distribution of Central Asian oil and gas.

During celebrations for his seventy-fifth birthday in May 1998, Azerbaijan's president Haydar Aliyev told President Demirel, who had gone to Baku for the event, that he endorsed the construction of a pipeline through Georgia and Turkey and not the Russian project to the Black Sea.

The strongest endorsement yet for the Turkish project came from the leaders of four Caspian countries: Azerbaijan, Georgia, Kazakhstan, and Uzbekistan, gathered in İstanbul for celebrations of the seventy-fifth anniversary of the Turkish Republic at the end of October that same year.

But the dozen oil companies operating in Azerbaijan have balked all along at the $2.4 billion Baku-Ceyhan pipeline on the grounds that not enough oil is being produced in the region to warrant the cost of the new pipeline through Turkey. Alternative routes through Russia, Georgia, or Iran are estimated at about half the cost of the Turkish pipeline.

*President Süleyman Demirel talks of Turkey's place in the world in*
*an interview at the Presidential Palace.*

A compromise being discussed leaves Turkey in the waiting room. It is
the Black Sea route but with a variant, a pipeline that goes from Kazakhstan through Georgia and not Russia or Turkey.[11] It is a solution the United
States can live with since it involves neither Iran nor Russia. Keeping their
feet in the door, the companies would postpone any commitment to the
Turkish pipeline until such a time that production justified the cost.

Following in Özal's footsteps, President Demirel has taken the lead in
expanding Turkey's frontiers eastward and regularly attends Turkic summit meetings. The Turkish president has described this "Turkic World" as
a vast area englobing 200 million Turkic-speaking peoples stretching from
the Adriatic to the Great Wall of China.

"Turkey has historical, fraternal, cultural, and linguistic ties with Azerbaijan and the Central Asian States," President Demirel told me in an interview in the ornate Presidential Palace in Ankara.[12] "It is committed to
sharing its experience of democracy and free market economy with these
countries and is extending every possible assistance to them for their integration with the outside world."

Reviewing Turkish foreign policy at the dawn of the twenty-first century, President Demirel said: "Momentous changes that have occurred in

recent years in and around Europe have placed Turkey on a new political and strategic platform. Because of its enhanced strategic importance and active diplomacy, Turkey is increasingly being perceived as a regional power now."

Declaring that a primary goal of Turkish policy remains full membership in the European Union, Demirel stressed that high on the foreign policy agenda is the development of friendly relations with neighboring countries on the Black Sea, in the Balkans, the Caucasus, Central Asia, and the Middle East.

Defining his vision for the country in a nutshell, the president said: "Turkey as a democratic secular Muslim country and due to its geostrategic location, pursues a multi-faceted foreign policy and constitutes a bridge between East and West, North and South."

# 14 ～

## Anatolian Lions

Of course they don't roar like Asian tigers. Maybe it's still more of a meow . . . but Anatolia's "lions" are making themselves heard these days.

Traditionally any kind of development has been concentrated around İstanbul and İzmir and other centers of western Turkey. The appearance of thriving poles of development in the Anatolian hinterland caught most people by surprise. Even more astonishing is the fact that some of these new industrial centers are located in the southeast, which in recent years has been associated more with devastation, poverty, and insecurity.

Now Konya, famous for its Whirling Dervishes and Seljuk architecture, has become a hub of paper and packaging, machine and construction industries, food marketing, cattle and poultry farms. Denizli, once considered little more than a point of access to the wondrous springs of Pamukkale, has become a major textile exporter and a synonym for Turkish towels. Yozgat, not known for much of anything, boasts one of the largest integrated meat, dairy, and stockbreeding centers in the world. Adana, which gained attention with the American presence at nearby İncirlik air base, is becoming a base for food, textile, and plastics industries. Kayseri and Kahraman Maraş, important trading centers from Hittite times (second millennium B.C.), are now expanding as hubs for textile, electrical, and other industries.

But the most visible boom city is Gaziantep, formerly known as a medieval focal point on trade routes from Europe to the East and before that as an important Paleolithic site. Within the past decade Gaziantep has become the economic capital of southeast Anatolia. There are now three industrial zones, and a fourth is under construction with a broad range of factories: plastics and synthetic fibers, flour, pastas and processed nuts, soaps and perfumes, furniture and paper products, shoes and other leather goods, cotton yarn, and machine-made carpets.

The heart of this economic miracle is the GAP, Turkish acronym for the Southeastern Anatolia Project, which has been described by foreign observers as one of the Wonders of the Modern World.[1, 2] Stephen Kinzer of the *New York Times* calls it "one of the most ambitious development projects ever attempted."[3]

In poetic terms, the goal is to transform the parched, impoverished Mesopotamian Plain into the Fertile Crescent that flourished in ancient times between the Tigris and Euphrates Rivers.

Actually it was that visionary Atatürk who first articulated the need to regulate the country's water resources and established the Electricity Survey Administration in 1936. Extensive surveys were made along the Euphrates and the Tigris, and works were carried out on several hydroelectric plants and irrigation networks. The large Keban Dam was completed in the early 1970s. The various schemes relating to the Euphrates and Tigris basins were merged into the Southeastern Anatolia Project in 1977 and consolidated as the GAP Regional Development Organization in 1989.

Estimated at a total cost of $32 billion, the GAP project consists of twenty-two dams, nineteen hydroelectric power plants, and a number of irrigation and drainage projects along the Euphrates and Tigris Rivers. The GAP region covers nine provinces or an area of 75,358 square kilometers bordering on Syria and Iraq, and a population of about 5.5 million.

When I first visited the area in the early 1980s, it was still largely a dream—and for some a nightmare. The project had been slow to get off the ground, mainly because of difficulties in obtaining funding. Financial institutions like the World Bank refused to take part in the project, not because they doubted its feasibility, but because Turkey had failed to reach an agreement on the allocation of water with two neighbors to be affected, Syria and Iraq.

In those days, foreign investors and even Turkish private enterprise were skittish about any investments in the southeast. Much of the GAP region lay under emergency rule because of the Kurdish problem.

But Turkish authorities doggedly persisted with the ambitious project, using much of the state's development funds, and in the process fueling the high inflation rate. Works were begun on the key structure, the huge multipurpose Atatürk Dam, in late 1983 and were completed ten years later. Located on the Euphrates forty miles north of Şanlıurfa, the Atatürk

Dam's vast reservoir doomed Samsat, the largest archaeological mound in the area.

Samsat (also known as Samosata) goes back to the third millennium B.C. and was successively capital to Assyrians, Urartians, Medes, Persians, and Hellenes. Before the great tumulus was submerged, archaeological excavations revealed thirty layers dating back to prehistoric times. But most of Samsat's treasures were lost to the reservoir, as were the secrets of other tumuli in the area.

Excavations at Nevali Çori, before the construction of Atatürk Dam, suggest that this may have been one of the world's oldest settlements, dating back to 8000 B.C. Now GAP says the ancient city of Zeugma (Belkıs), downstream from Atatürk Dam, is to share Samsat's fate, as work progresses on the Bireçik Dam. Vestiges of a continuous settlement have been found at Belkıs on the west bank of the Euphrates, dating back to the Hellenistic period. It was known as one of the most important cities of the Commagene Kingdom in the first century B.C., and there are also Roman ruins in the area scheduled to be flooded.

Suddenly by the mid-1990s GAP became a reality. The violence in the southeast had been largely contained. The government and even the Turkish armed forces insisted on the need for economic and social investments to complement the security effort. This time it was not just talk. The first major change was the electrification of all the villages in the area. Then water from the Atatürk reservoir began to flow through the new irrigation network. Now cotton, corn, barley, soybeans, and vegetables have begun to grow on the once-barren Şanlıurfa-Harran Plain. And scores of factories linked to cotton and food processing are going up in the region.

State Minister Salih Yıldırım, who is responsible for GAP, declared in mid-1998 that although terrorism in the southeast has not been overcome, it's time to talk about reconstruction in the region. In a lengthy interview with the *Turkish Daily News*, the minister said the government has plans for tax incentives and credit for small and medium industries in the area. Foreign financial institutions have at last shown interest in investing in GAP, he stressed. But he did not hide the immense health and education problems because of the protracted state of insecurity. He noted that 32 percent of the schools are closed and 45 percent of the teachers appointed to the area refuse to go. There are few doctors in the region, and most of the health centers do not function.

In GAP's shiny new headquarters in Ankara, Servet Mutlu, a senior official, gave me a brief progress report. The project was 40 percent completed in financial terms ($14 billion) and 55 percent completed in terms of power generation capacity.[4]

"We're behind the original schedule, particularly in irrigation," Dr. Mutlu admitted. He noted that the target date had been altered from 2005 to 2010, and financing was the main reason for the delay. But recently, the expert emphasized, international funding has begun to appear: $120 million from the World Bank for a waste treatment sewage plant and additional credits from the Eximbank for power station equipment.

The GAP official said that in the past decade, all 3,800 villages and 8,500 rural settlements in the area have been connected to the national power grid. With completion of two 26.4-kilometer Şanlıurfa irrigation tunnels—the longest in the world—about 80,000 hectares of the Harran Plain have been put under irrigation. In all, 180,000 hectares have been irrigated so far—only 9 percent of the target.

Dr. Mutlu acknowledged that twenty-eight villages had to be submerged and another six were affected by works on the Atatürk Dam and reservoir, which means 50,000 people had to be resettled. He stressed that the villagers were "fully compensated" and given the choice of urban or rural resettlement.

"But the agricultural transformation has started," he said. Three or four years ago, there was no industry at Şanlıurfa, and now there are several agro-based factories. Gaziantep, which already had an industrial base, is becoming a major textile center, with a population close to a million inhabitants. He urged me to go to the area and see for myself.

My archaeologist friend Toni Cross insisted I take a straw hat. The Euphrates Plain could be excruciatingly hot in summer with precious little shade. And so I spent the better part of a day probing Ankara's wide variety of clothing stores before I came upon a straw hat that looked like a remnant of Atatürk's times.

The trouble with the hat was it wouldn't pack and so I had to wear it all during my travels, which instantly branded me as a Foreign Visitor. Maybe straw hats were *de rigueur* at archaeological digs, but I was always the only straw-hatted person around. I admit it was more than welcome on the scorching streets of Gaziantep, at the shadeless castle walls of Şanlıurfa, on the bleak hills around the Atatürk Dam, and the blistering plain around Harran.

My quaint headcovering, in this land of headscarves, also served as a convenient conversation opener. Turks seemed to enjoy explaining The Situation to such an obvious outsider. During the long wait at Ankara's still spartan airport, I encountered a young man reading the *Life of Confucius*. He was a musician with Bilkent Symphony Orchestra, en route to a summer gig at a bar in Bodrum. He had learned English from the BBC and his Russian colleagues, who make up the majority of Bilkent's orchestra. In the fall, the orchestra was going on a tour of the southeast for the first time—a sign that the security situation had improved. They would play Beethoven, Tschaikovsky, and a program of modern classic Turkish music, "which is authentic but not well known." The conversation, as usual, soon turned political. "People have lost hope in the old leaders and are waiting for somebody new," he said, adding that he himself hoped one day to immigrate to Australia.

On the hour-long flight to Gaziantep, a prosperous-looking businessman introduced himself as a Kurd working for an international firm. There were many Kurds in the Gaziantep area, and they were generally treated as second-class citizens, he confided. But now most of them had jobs, and there were almost no violent incidents in the area.

My first view of Gaziantep was an astonishing anomaly. A timeless Middle Eastern landscape of adjoining stone houses with flat rooftops and narrow alleys clustered around a huge mound capped by ancient castle walls. Stretching beyond were modern suburbs, with newly laid parks, high-rise residences and offices, and building cranes everywhere. And lost in the middle, an occasional herd of goats.

Planning to return to Gaziantep, I took the three-hour bus ride to Şanlıurfa, where the regional headquarters of GAP are located. The road runs through straw-colored hills, wheat fields, and green patches of pistachios and vineyards.

Admiring my hat, the young woman beside me said she was a high school biology teacher in the Mediterranean city of Antalya, going to visit friends in Şanlıurfa. If girls wanted to wear headscarves in her school, it was all right, but there were only a few, she volunteered, when I brought up the subject.

"The main question is the teachers; if a teacher wears a headscarf all the girls follow suit," said my companion, who wore the latest skin-tight jeans and nothing on her head. "That's why the school takes strict disciplinary measures against teachers who cover, like docking their salaries or even dismissal."

She went on to point out that if headscarves were a religious matter, why hadn't girls worn them ten years ago? In her opinion, it was the men who didn't want to lose their influence. She stressed that Şanlıurfa was much more conservative than Antalya.

"Men here still have arranged marriages and several wives and want to keep things that way, but nowadays a girl doesn't want to marry before she's twenty-four, and she wants to choose her husband."

Şanlıurfa (SHAN-li-UR-fa) probably looks very much the way it did in Ottoman times, with its many minarets and domes, caravanserais, and vaulted covered bazaar.

But change has come even to Şanlıurfa, according to Mustafa Aydoğdu, who was born and grew up here.[5] One of the bright young engineers working at GAP's regional office, Aydoğdu dates the changes to GAP's takeoff in 1995. That was when water began to reach Harran, and farmers planted the first irrigated cotton. Already peoples' lives have been transformed, the GAP official underlined. Now farmers take cell phones with them when they go to the fields. And there's a long waiting line for Nissan and Opel air-conditioned cars (priced at $20,000).

Even though problems with Syria and Iraq have not been resolved, foreign banks have finally become involved in the project, Aydoğdu said. He noted that Germany's Philipp Holzmann AG heads an international consortium that is building the Bireçik hydroelectric dam, fifty-five miles downstream from the Atatürk Dam. Chase Manhattan Bank in İstanbul has arranged financing for the DM 2 billion project with commercial loans and export credits from various European countries.

The Turkish engineer claimed Syria has already begun to benefit from the regulation of the Euphrates. He pointed out that Syria used to get only 300 cubic meters per second in the summer and as much as 8,000 in winter. Now the average yearly flow is 1,100 cubic meters per second.

"We can grow everything on the Harran Plain except strawberries," boasted Ahmet Lami Çavusoğlu, who heads the GAP research station, north of Şanlıurfa.[6] Cotton is the most profitable crop and is easy, he said. Already Şanlıurfa needs to import labor from Adana at picking time. Most of the production goes to factories in Gaziantep and İzmir.

Engineer Çavusoğlu (CHA-voos-oh-loo) said local farmers want to try new cultures, but for now there are not enough vegetable processing factories in the region. He showed me the extensive experimental plantation, which he runs with the help of students from Harran University's Faculty of Agriculture. There are all kinds of rich crops like pecans, almonds, plums, pomegranates, broccoli, and Chinese cabbage.

Predicting that the fertility of Mesopotamia could be restored "even better than before," the GAP agricultural engineer stressed that it would take time. "We have enough water but we have to give it little by little so the land can get used to it."

Providential irony, I thought. Precautions must be taken not to push irrigation works too fast in the GAP area for fear of salinity. It seems the long delays and lack of international funding have been beneficial after all.

The road to Harran, barely twenty-five miles southeast of Şanlıurfa, is an exciting demonstration of Before and After GAP. It passes through broad stretches of new, bright green cotton plantations—the miracle of irrigation. Then brusquely the landscape changes, becoming a vast treeless desert around the bleak ruins of Harran, once the center of rich farmland, until the rivers dried up.

The real miracle is Gaziantep, one of the fastest-growing cities in Anatolia today, and also one of the oldest settlements. Archaeologists have found many Paleolithic tools dating back as far as 700,000 B.C. in the Duluk caves a few miles north of the city. Gaziantep itself was known as Antep or Aintab (healing spring) and variations thereof. The city won its title of *gazi* (brave warriors) after its citizens put up a heroic defense against the English and French forces in World War I.

I knew of Gaziantep via the American connection. The American Hospital in Gaziantep is said to be the oldest American hospital still in operation in the Near and Middle East. John Chalfant, an educator formerly with the American Board mission schools in Turkey, is now an adviser to the Turkish Health and Education Foundation (SEV), which runs the hospital and three former American schools.[7] I had met Chalfant the previous year in SEV's İstanbul office, behind the Egyptian market, and he had given me a brief history of the American role in Gaziantep.

It all began in the 1820s, when an agreement was reached with the Ottoman sultanate to permit three foreign mission stations in the empire, Chalfant recounted. The British were charged with the Russian Orthodox inhabitants, the French were given the Roman Catholics, and the Americans "got the Armenians," which meant mainly setting up schools for their constituents.

Thus it was that Dr. Azariah Smith, an American medical missionary, went in 1847 to Aintab, which had a large Armenian population. The American Board had asked him to look into the possibility of establishing a modern medical school there. Dr. Smith died of typhus before he was able to achieve his goal, but the Boston-based American Board went ahead to found the Central Turkey College at Aintab in 1876. It was the first institution of higher education in the entire region. The college aimed to inculcate "the highest Christian faith and morality" among its students. By 1900, the student body had reached 135—mostly Armenians. The sixty-acre site on a hill on the west side of Aintab was the gift of a prominent local Muslim, and patrons of the school included Muslims and Jews as well as Protestants, Gregorians, and Catholics.[8]

In 1879, a group of Dr. Smith's former Yale classmates contributed the funds to build an American teaching hospital in his memory linked to the Central Turkey College. Although the college closed down after World War I, with the depletion of the Armenian population, the hospital continued to function through all the upheavals and recently reopened a nursing school.

On my first day in Gaziantep, I walked around the city center to get my bearings. It was July and sweltering, at least 100 degrees in the shade, if you could find any. Seeing a sign pointing up the hill that said American Hospital, I remembered my talk with Dr. Chalfant. This might give me another perspective on the city. I made my way up the steaming narrow cobblestone streets, following the well-placed signs, and was fortunate to find the American medical director, Dr. Barclay M. Shepard, who gave me a personal account of his family history in Gaziantep.[9]

His grandparents, Dr. Frederick Shepard and wife Fanny, were both medical missionaries and had organized the Gaziantep Hospital in 1884. Dr. Frederick Shepard used to ride on horseback to the surrounding villages, which had no medical facilities, and worked out of his tent clinic. Specialized in eye surgery, the doctor performed some 10,000 eye operations using chloroform because it was too hot for ether. Dr. Shepard treated Kurdish bandits and tribal chieftains, Turkish soldiers and devout Muslims, Armenian neighbors, teachers, and church people and later Armenian refugees by the thousands.

Seeing my interest, Dr. Barclay Shepard lent me a book written by his aunt, who vividly describes her parents' day-to-day life in this difficult frontier country. In *Shepard of Aintab*, Alice Shepard Riggs gives a moving account of Dr. Frederick Shepard's efforts to cope with the tragic events following the outbreak of World War I.[10] Most of the native physicians had been drafted, which meant more patients for the already stretched hospital staff. Hospital supplies and medicines were fast used up, and new shipments could not get through because of lack of transportation.

Faced with famine conditions, the hospital opened a soup kitchen for hundreds of poor sick people in the area.

Added to the sufferings of war came the persecution of the Armenians. Riggs writes that when a representative council of Armenians in the northern city of Erzerum refused to join the Turks against the Allies, Turks and Germans united in a horror campaign directed generally against innocent Armenians. "It included imprisonment, torture, and cold-blooded murder of the men, deportation of the women and children sent out at an hour's notice from their homes, to wander over desert paths, robbed of food and clothing, until those who were not actually butchered died of thirst, starvation, and disease."

Ms. Riggs recounts that when the wave of deportations swept over neighboring towns and was threatening Aintab, her father personally appealed several times to the governor general and even to the Imperial government in Constantinople to halt the banishments. But to no avail. On learning of the order to deport the Armenians of Urfa, Dr. Shepard rode on horseback to the city where he had attended many patients and found that only 40 out of 5,000 houses in the Armenian quarter had not been destroyed.

His daughter quotes him as saying: "My heart is broken, I can bear the burdens of Turkey no longer." Not long after this, he died in the typhus epidemic in Gaziantep in 1915.

Continuing the story, Dr. Barclay Shepard said his father, Lorrin Shepard, was born and grew up in Gaziantep. After graduating from Columbia Medical School, Dr. Lorrin Shepard returned to the American Hospital in 1919 to follow in his father's footsteps. But the political situation at the end of the Ottoman Empire was extremely complex, even in the outlying province of Gaziantep.

"When my father arrived, the British had occupied the area under the Treaty of Sèvres," Dr. Barclay Shepard told me. "Then the French moved in bringing with them Senegalese troops. The French persuaded the remaining Armenians if they could strengthen their position, they would be left in charge of Aintab. But the Turks succeeded in driving the French, and with them the Armenians, south to Aleppo in 1920. Father took care of wounded on both sides."

The 1923 Treaty of Lausanne, under which the Allies recognized the borders of modern Turkey, includes an extraordinary provision. Four American doctors were authorized to practice in Turkey, including the medical director of the American Hospital in Gaziantep. Atatürk later issued an edict that only Turkish citizens could practice medicine, but the exception remains even to this day.

Three of Lorrin Shepard's children were born in Gaziantep, and Barclay was conceived there but grew up in İstanbul. From 1927 until retirement in 1957, Dr. Lorrin Shepard held the post of medical director of the Admiral Bristol Hospital, named after the American high commissioner who had strongly supported Atatürk's reforms.

Initially escaping from the family pattern, Barclay Shepard went to the Maritime Academy in Maine and did stints with the merchant marine and American Export Lines, before taking up medical studies and graduating from Tufts Medical School in 1958. Joining the navy, he specialized in chest surgery and spent much of his career with the Navy Surgeon General's Office in Bethesda, Maryland, retiring with the rank of captain.

Dr. Barclay Shepard came back to Turkey in 1995, after his marriage of forty-three years ended in divorce. "I fell in love with the country and wanted to start a new life here," he explained. The American Hospital in Gaziantep was looking for an American doctor at the time. And so in 1996, he assumed the post his father and grandfather had held . . . and inherited their right to practice medicine in Turkey.

As I toured the immaculate, spacious premises, the only other American I met was the nursing education director. Clearly the American Hospital is a Turkish institution, although there is some American support. The Armenians are gone, and the patients are mostly if not all Muslims. The private, nonprofit hospital provides all kinds of care except major cardiovascular surgery and long-term therapy. The sixty-six-bed hospital has been undergoing renovations, with the large wards converted into private and semiprivate rooms, many with bathrooms, TV sets, and air-conditioning, in part funded by local Turkish donors.

An agreement was reached recently with the National Health Care for Retired People to receive fifty to sixty outpatients a day. There are now plans for a new outpatient building. USAID has provided a grant of $100,000, and the hospital is trying to raise the rest locally. The president of a Turkish pharmaceutical company donated a new Mercedes ambulance to the hospital. And the U.S. Military Humanitarian Assistance Program provided $46,000 worth of equipment for the intensive care unit.

The nursing school, which reopened in a lovely old stone building in 1995, had been closed for seventeen years because of changes in the Turkish law on nursing education. Formerly the school had provided junior high school level nurses training, but now it offers a two-year post–high school course, graduating its first class of twenty-five nurses in 1997. In a corner of the nursing school grounds lies a small cemetery, which includes the grave of Fred and Fanny Shepard. Inscribed on the stone are the words: "They live in the hearts of many races."

Sevim Türkân Öztahtacı is a member of the board of the Health and Education Foundation that took over from the American Board in Turkey. Dressed in the latest European fashion, Mrs. Öztahtacı received me for coffee in her comfortable, tastefully decorated home not far from the hospital. She told me proudly of her American ties.[11] Her father was a surgeon in the American Hospital and graduate of prestigious Robert College in İstanbul. Her mother and she were both graduates of the American Board's women's high school at Üsküdar.

Mrs. Öztahtacı's husband, who died in 1993, started the macaroni business in 1960 from his father's flour mill, then bought another mill and later a furniture factory. She leaves business matters up to her son, a food engineer, and son-in-law, who worked with her husband for twenty years as finance manager. OBA is now the leading macaroni and pasta business in Gaziantep and one of the 500 largest companies in Turkey.

"I'm Muslim; I fast but I cannot cover my head," she said when I asked about the headscarf problem in Gaziantep. She acknowledged that more and more young women were wearing headscarves. Her own sister, who is married to a devout doctor, wears a headscarf and went on the pilgrimage to Mecca. "She feels closer to religion, but I think it's better for me to do social works and help out the American Hospital," Mrs. Öztahtacı said.

She herself is an admirer of the İstanbul professor of Islam, Yaşar Nuri Öztürk, who appears frequently on national television. "He reads the Koran in Turkish, and shows that it is a tolerant religion—very different from what the Islamists claim," she stressed.

Several other educated women in Gaziantep talked to me about the work of Professor Öztürk, as a means of reaching out to religious Muslims. Among these, Feliz Bekem, who heads the Gaziantep University Women's Center, said Islam has been "badly interpreted" by Islamists to keep women in a subordinate position.

Şanlıurfa and Gaziantep are still deeply traditional as far as women are concerned, according to Nihal Tütüncüler and Emine Durak.[12] These two young professional women are members of the Gaziantep Women's Platform, set up in 1994 to teach women their rights. The Platform is made up of eighty-four Gaziantep housewives, who give leadership training and reading and writing classes and seminars on health and legal problems. "The problems are the same in Urfa and Gaziantep," Ms. Tütüncüler said. "Many parents in the area still think there is no need to educate girls. As a rule, girls cannot go out at night. And honor killings still occur," she said. She referred to a much-publicized case a couple of years ago when a girl from a nearby village was thrown from a tractor and killed, after her parents learned she had run away with a boy.

It was astonishing for me to think that social mores could be so far behind economic progress. But then one has only to think about the lag between human rights and economic development in China.

Most people I met in the area seemed to see GAP as the panacea to all the local problems. Over and over again, Gaziantep was described as GAP's Western Gate. By this they meant not only the international airport and good connections with Mediterranean ports but above all the city's vigorous entrepreneurial spirit. The Chamber of Commerce, for example, celebrated its centennial anniversary in 1998—twenty-five years older than the Turkish Republic itself.

Although the Turks did not mention Gaziantep's Armenian past, it seemed clear to me that some of the Armenians' business skills had rubbed off on their neighbors. Later, James Wilde of *Time* magazine told me that businessmen in Kayseri, another Anatolian lion, insist with pride they learned their craft from Jews and Armenians.

"This is a city of production. People value hard work and good organization," Gaziantep's mayor Celal Doğan said, receiving me in his office in the severe modern City Hall.[13] A Social Democratic lawyer from İstanbul, Doğan (DOUGH-un) has served two terms, improving roads and waste treatment, increasing green spaces, and extending planned areas for industry and housing. Unlike other Turkish cities, Gaziantep has allocated lands for a rural migration of about 300,000 people. "*Gecekondu* are illegal here; our rural migrants have deeds," he emphasized.

The mayor said the Islamist opposition was unable to put forth a program and so they used religion. Although the campaign for the 1999 elections had not begun, the Islamists were engaged in ongoing political activity through meetings with women's groups, at the university, and in Koranic courses (ten illegal courses have been closed down in Gaziantep). There had been some minor demonstrations over headscarves on campus. "But there've been no problems; we don't force the issue," Mr. Doğan stressed.

Kürşat Göncü, secretary-general of the Ganziantep Chamber of Industry, told me that exports from this area soared to $5 billion in 1998 from $500 million a decade earlier.[14] Gaziantep now accounts for 10 percent of Turkey's exports, mostly to the European Union and the Middle East but increasingly to Central Asia and the Caucasus. He said at present there are 620 factories in the three industrial zones and another 1,000 factories are planned by the year 2000, with 100,000 new jobs.

"We have no unemployment here," Göncü said proudly, emphasizing there is a lack of skilled labor and administrative personnel. "I can provide jobs immediately for electric engineers, mechanical engineers, economists."

The Young Businessmen's Association (it accepts women) broke away from the Chamber of Commerce in 1993 because the group of young businessmen thought the chamber wasn't doing enough to push the city. The association, which has 108 members, organizes an annual fair, receives potential foreign investors, and publishes reports on the local production. German, French, and Israeli firms have already established joint ventures in building, chemical, and textile industries. Several foreign tractor companies and seed producers have also expressed interest in the GAP area.

Emel Tavşancıl handles the business side of Modesan furniture company, and her husband runs the factory.[15] As a businesswoman, she has never had problems in Turkey but admits it's a handicap in dealing with Islamic countries. She used to export to Saudi Arabia and Syria but stopped because it was so difficult. Although she buys much of her wood from Kazakhstan and Turkmenistan, she cannot go herself "because they don't want to do business with a woman." Fortunately they have distributors in İstanbul.

In addition to traditional markets in İstanbul and Ankara, much of Modesan's Scandinavian-type furniture goes to hotels, hospitals, offices, and residences in fast-developing Gaziantep. Annual sales have increased 70 percent to $300,000 in the past five years, Ms. Tavşancıl said. "Now we have only this one-floor showroom but next year, we'll move into our new building with seven floors."

I met Ali Öztahtacı not through his mother but on recommendation of the Gaziantep Chamber of Industry. The thirty-four-year-old chairman of the OBA Group comes across as a man of energy and vision. Like other local businesspeople, Öztahtacı complained about the bureaucratic centralization in Ankara, high dumping duties in the United States and overproduction in his field. But mostly he was excited about "the GAP explosion."[16]

Öztahtacı's immediate plan is to turn his macaroni/semolina factory into a food complex. Profiting from expected high yields of hard durum wheat in the GAP area, he has projects for the production of pizza and cake mixes, flour-based puddings, vacuum-packed pastas, and frozen vegetables. He is currently working with soy flour pasta and encouraging farmers to produce soybeans in the area.

"Our main aim, however, is bio products," he disclosed. He has raised the issue with the Ministry of Agriculture, pointing out that Europeans are increasingly turning to natural foods and urging a ban on the use of insecticides and chemical fertilizers in GAP's new irrigated areas. "We'll do everything necessary to be a European company," he vowed.

Aykut Tuzcu, publisher of Gaziantep's daily newspaper *Sabah* (circulation 5,000), is a jolly, expansive man, who visited the United States on a Young Leader's grant in 1995.[17] He claims that Gaziantep has played an important role in stopping the advance of terrorism. "People who fled here from the southeast found jobs and don't have time for terrorism," he said half jokingly. "And the terrorist organization gets its supplies here and doesn't want to rock the boat."

For all his light hearted facade, Tuzcu gave me some sober insights into the local business scene. "Our entrepreneurs like their independence," he said, noting that 99 percent of the businesses are owned by a family or an individual, no partners or shares. Another problem cited by the newspaperman is "a sheep mentality." If pasta or cotton yarn succeeds, other businesses copy, flooding the market, he said. Some businesses are importing cheap, used machinery, but they need up-to-date technology to compete overseas. They have had the advantage of cheap manpower, but next year there will be problems because they'll have to pay more to labor.

In a move to help modernize local business practices, the publisher persuaded the European Union to open the first EU Information Bureau in Gaziantep in May 1996. "I convinced the EU representative in Ankara that Turkey is not Ankara, and they have now opened ten information bureaus around the country."

"For me, the EU is a lifestyle and my ambition is to bring that lifestyle here," Tuzcu said. He stressed that Turkey's most important problem is the shocking disparity in income distribution. "We now have some 200 billionaires in Turkey while many people are so poor they have no place to go but God."

Noting that religion is still very important in this country, he expressed concern about those people "using religion for political ends." In the 1994 municipal elections, the vote was very close in Gaziantep, and the Social Democratic mayor Celal Doğan, who is very popular, almost lost to the Islamists. He was concerned that Doğan could lose in 1999 because he said Fazilet cadres were generally competent and have been working hard, particularly in the rural areas. (In the 1999 elections, Mayor Doğan defeated his Islamist challenger, although his Social Democratic Party lost heavily nationwide.)

Calling headscarves "an artificial problem," the publisher said Islamists were forcing women to wear them as a political symbol. For example, he said, if 20 out of 200 employees went into the post office with headscarves, all 200 would come out covered because the Islamists would be waiting to intimidate them at the door.

"We're afraid of force," Tuzcu said. "That's how Iran changed and we are trying to stop it from happening here."

There it was, the same apprehension I had heard in Ankara and - İstanbul—and now even in the den of the Anatolian lions.

# 15 ⬤

## The Islamic Agenda

When Islamist leader Necmettin Erbakan surged to power in June 1996, it was on a platform of Islamic-based, anti-Western populism for a new Just Order and rapprochement with the rest of the Muslim world. As prime minister for less than a year, Erbakan, seventy-one, made no basic changes in Turkey's secular, pro-Western policies but succeeded in alarming—and uniting—the country's disparate secular forces.

With their leader driven out of office and banned from politics, Refah (Welfare) Party closed down, and with no letup in the movement against suspected Islamist extremists, Islamic politicians reorganized themselves in the Fazilet (Virtue) Party, under the banner of Western-style democracy.

The beleaguered Islamic activists embraced a new strategy portraying themselves, with some justification, as archdemocrats and victims of a rigid anti-Islamic system. In spite or perhaps because of the continuing crackdown on suspected Islamic radicals, Fazilet—like its predecessor Refah—came out in most polls as the country's number one political party, even in a military-commissioned survey.

With much talk of early elections, it seemed time to take a new look at the Islamic agenda. What were the aims behind the democracy slogans? How did Fazilet's program differ from Erbakan's policies, which had stirred such broad hostility? What were the chances of accommodation between the leaders of the chastised Islamic movement and the increasingly belligerent secular establishment?

During a six-week visit to Turkey the summer of 1998, I talked to a wide range of Islamic activists and found little echo of the old anti-American, anti-NATO, anti-Israel, anti-Europe rhetoric. Instead, even militant Islamists were now asking for basic American rights: freedom of religion, assembly, enterprise, speech, and dress.

Of course many Islamic activists still harbored their Third World view of the United States as an invasive, arrogant, materialistic superpower. This came through in the radical Islamic press like the daily *Yeni Şafak*. And whenever the United States engaged in any anti-Islamic operation, Islamic militants were quick to demonstrate at İstanbul's main mosques and universities, where leftist students usually joined them.

Of late, however, Islamic groups have focused on Western democracy as the panacea to Turkey's problems and their own. They have apparently concluded that this would be in the realm of the possible as Turkey's secular leaders continue to press for membership in the European Union.

Both the United States and European Union countries were strongly critical of the closure of the Islamist party in January 1998, calling it a setback for Turkish democracy and Turkey's bid for EU membership. Probably the single gesture that upset the military the most (and encouraged the Islamists) was the visit by a group of NATO officials to former prime minister Erbakan, at the end of February, after he had been barred from politics and his party shut down.

"The thoroughly antidemocratic closure of the RP is not only Turkey's problem," Erbakan told the press with some satisfaction. "It is the problem of all the world—it is a problem of NATO as well."[1]

Foreign diplomats I talked to subsequently said political as well as religious Islam have been making gains, in part because of an overreaction by Turkey's secular authorities. These observers predicted that if Islamists become the targets of an indiscriminate witch hunt, their popularity would only be enhanced.

Turkey's secular rulers tended to dismiss the democratic pretensions of the Islamists as a ploy to tranquilize the lay establishment while they regrouped in an attempt to regain political power. But the civil and military authorities differed on how to handle the Islamic challenge.

That summer of 1998, the military leadership increased pressures on the secular government to take firmer measures against political Islam, described as "the gravest threat" to the secular Republic. Civilian leaders, however, suggested that Islamic fundamentalism should be curbed through democratic means and the military should keep out of politics.

As usual in Turkey, the armed forces prevailed. Under continued pressure from the military, investigations have been stepped up into the activities of the Islamic municipalities and businesses, and more court cases have been opened against prominent Islamists, including Erbakan.

In routine retirement ceremonies at the end of August, outgoing generals warned that Islamic fundamentalism continued to pose the primary threat to the state, and the Turkish armed forces were there to safeguard the country's democratic and secular institutions. The new chief of General Staff, General Hüseyin Kıvrıkoğlu, has pursued the same line, warning Turkish society to be cautious toward those who want to install an Islamic order.

It wasn't easy to meet radical Islamists that summer of 1998. Most militants were either silent, underground, or in prison. There were a few prominent Islamist writers like Adurrahman Dilipak, who openly advocates *Sharia* and was constantly in and out of the courts for his frankness.

One of the most influential Islamists, Mustafa Karahasanoğlu, is editor in chief of *Akit*, a leading Islamic daily newspaper. An old hand at party politics, he started out in Erbakan's National Salvation Party in 1969, became a youth leader in 1973 and party secretary in 1978. Later he was director and owner of the pro-Islamic newspaper *Milli Gazete*. He is used to speaking his mind and not hiding behind diplomatic niceties.

"Our aim is to be the voice of Muslims living in this country—because most of the press is trying to stifle that voice," the newspaperman told me in a hasty interview. (He had to make one of his frequent court appearances on charges that his paper had violated some security law.)[2] *Akit* does not back a specific party, he said, "but any party that listens to us, and now that's Fazilet and BBP [the small ultranationalist Grand Union Party]."

Karahasanoğlu approved of Erbakan's goals but not his strategy. The Erbakan coalition went further than other governments "to meet the needs of the people and address injustices," he said, insisting Erbakan should not have resigned under pressure.

The former prime minister's biggest mistake was to antagonize the media by cutting off their huge government credits, Karahasanoğlu said. "Nowhere else is there such power in the press; the government is enslaved by the press," he stressed.

Another mistake, he said, was to sign the package of antifundamentalist measures, presented by the National Security Council. "*Akit* had told him not to sign but he wanted to get the military off his back," the editor noted. "Erbakan could have resisted because the majority of the people supported his government, all those poor people who pay for 51 percent of the national budget but receive only 21 percent of the wealth."

Karahasanoğlu said the anti-Islamist measures were the biggest problem facing the country today and that Fazilet "is being held hostage" by them. "We want a genuine representative government that allows freedom of thought, religious belief, and practice, where Muslims can follow their beliefs to the fullest," he said, emphasizing this was not the case now. He noted the paradox that whereas Muslims were being taken to court for their religion, Jews and Christians were not being prosecuted.

The newspaperman argued that the present secular government was not carrying out the people's will, even in foreign policy. For example, entering the Customs Union with Europe had been a mistake; the flood of European imports offset any increase in exports. Relations with Israel should be normal, he said, but they have grown "too close." Turkey was always a bridge between East and West, but for a long time now that balance has been upset as governments have concentrated on the Western connection. Erbakan tried to restore the equilibrium.

"Erbakan and Erdoğan share the same philosophy and ideology although their strategy may differ," Karahasanoğlu emphasized. "They both want the real owners of Turkey to take control."

But the Islamic movement, led by Fazilet, has clearly learned lessons from the Erbakan experience. Firebrands whose violent rhetoric was enough to get Refah closed have been excluded or hushed. Although Erbakan still hovered in the background, the new image of Fazilet was democratic moderation as the party sought mainstream status. Islamic mayors switched their discourse from religion to democracy and redoubled efforts to get things done before the next elections. Even the Islamic businessmen's association took its distance from the religious parties and embraced democratic competition.

Abdullah Gül, former minister of state in Erbakan's government and former deputy chairman of the Welfare Party, was now a member of Parliament with the new Fazilet Party. The soft-spoken forty-eight-year-old Gül with bushy mustache and academic air talked confidently of Fazilet, which had inherited most of Refah's deputies to become the leading group in Parliament. He said that in barely six months, the party had put into place a new nationwide organization with branches in every city and town.

"Their operation backfired; we are already the number one party in all the polls," Gül told me in an interview in Fazilet's parliamentary chambers. "The people see we were oppressed and they know we are honest."[3]

*Abdullah Gül, a leading reformist in the Islamic movement and a deputy from the central Anatolian city of Kayseri. He is interviewed in his office in Parliament with Atatürk's portrait above.*

In broad strokes, Gül talked about Fazilet's agenda. "This is not a religious party; we are open to all citizens, not only religious people." (In a conversation two years earlier, he had described Refah as an "Islamic-oriented party.") Now he said the party was ready to make compromises. If changes were made in the electoral law, Fazilet would be prepared to make alliances with other parties like the pro-Islamic Democrat Party.

Highlighting differences between Fazilet and the defunct Refah, Gül noted that the new party had three women on the executive board (Refah had been criticized, even within the party, for not allowing women to become members of the executive or candidates in elections) and would present women candidates in the next elections.

In foreign policy, there were even bigger changes, Gül stressed: "In the past, Refah was reluctant to join the European Union. We now want to become a full member. We realize that without integration into Europe, democratic standards of human rights cannot be achieved in this country.

"We want to increase relations with the United States and strengthen our traditional links," the Fazilet MP stressed. (U.S. relations had not been a priority of Refah, which had looked first to renew ties with Muslim countries like Iran and Libya.)

Gül explained that the United States had shown "more understanding" than Europe of Refah's problems, and the American press had been very critical of "the antidemocratic action" against Refah. He added that his party now had a better comprehension of what religious freedom means in the United States. "We want the same freedoms in Turkey, including freedom for nonbelievers. We don't want to impose our beliefs. The people are Muslim but minority rights should be respected."

Gül said his party favored "normal relations" with Israel but suggested there could be "a grassroots reaction to artificially close ties with Netanyahu's government, which appears to be blocking the peace process."

Erbakan's creation, the Developing Eight (D-8), which groups predominantly Muslim countries, has been "misunderstood," Gül insisted. "We never thought of it as an alternative to the European Union but only as a way to increase economic cooperation."

Viewed as a leader of the younger generation of Islamists, Gül also gave high priority to "the civilianization" of the administrative structure. (In the past, secularists have suggested that the armed forces should be subject to civilian authority, as in most Western democracies, but the premise has been shot down by the military.)

Trained as an economist, Gül was critical of the failure of the current secular government to reduce inflation, create jobs, and improve income distribution. Pointing out that two-thirds of the budget went to interest payments, Gül claimed that Erbakan's government had begun to solve the problem by decreasing the internal debt. Inflation had started to drop, and interest rates had come down to 70 percent from 160 percent, but were now back to 100 percent.

The Fazilet deputy took a firm stand on two key Islamic issues: the ban on headscarves at universities and the current crackdown on Islamic businessmen. Noting that the Koran stipulates that a Muslim woman should be covered in public, Gül said his party would defend the right of university students to wear headscarves. Expressing "shock" over accusations of fraud and violation of secular principles leveled against members of MÜSİAD, the pro-Islamic business and industrial association, Gül said he was convinced they would be exonerated by the courts.

Oya Akgönenç is a new face in Fazilet, and it was clear she would not be a token uncovered woman in the still largely traditional male party. I met her at Ankara's prestigious Bilkent University, where for the past five years she was an associate professor of history and a specialist in Balkan politics.[4] She has a Ph.D. in international relations from American University and taught there before taking up a senior post at the World Bank and returning to Turkey in 1985 to work on development projects.

As a social activist, she has wanted to go into Turkish politics for some time. Politically right of center, she first received a bid from former prime minister Tansu Çiller to become a candidate for her conservative True Path Party in the 1995 legislative elections. But True Path lost out to the pro-Islamic party, and Akgönenç went back to teaching until she was approached by Fazilet in July 1998.

Admitting she is uncomfortable in a *chador*—the cloak worn by pious women—Akgönenç described herself as "a devout Kemalist" (follower of Atatürk) and said Fazilet's leadership had accepted this. She was openly critical of some positions taken by Fazilet—such as its opposition to the law on domestic violence. In her first speech to Fazilet's parliamentary group, she said if they demand respect for human rights and democracy, they must practice what they preach.

"They want to change their image and are willing to take advice," Akgönenç said. She described Fazilet's leader Recai Kutan as a moderate, sensible, cautious, hands-on leader. "When you contact Recai about a problem, he will immediately assign someone to look into it."

Insisting she was not a feminist in the European or American sense, Akgönenç said she would like to change the system to improve conditions for women, particularly in education and health.

Her main ambition as a lawyer was to change the outdated legal system, in criminal, civil, and commercial law. Atatürk, she underlined, had wanted to change the system as rapidly as possible. He borrowed laws that were closest to Turkish law and made adjustments: the French civil code, Italian criminal code, German commercial law, Swiss banking and family law.

"But Turkish society has moved so fast and laws have not kept up with the times," Akgönenç stressed. "We must put our best legal minds together to get proper solutions, taking into consideration the traditions of the people."

In most public pronouncements, Fazilet chairman Kutan proved to be quite reasonable and moderate. But he committed a major political gaffe that raised some doubts as to the party's new inclusive image and could cost votes.

It was during the flare-up between Ankara and Damascus, when it looked like Turkey was ready to go to war over Syrian aid to Kurdish separatists. Like the other party leaders, Kutan briefed his parliamentary group on the situation, sharply attacking the Syrian regime. Noting that the majority of Syrians are Sunnite (like Turks), Kutan stressed that President Hafez al Assad and the present Syrian leadership is in the hands of the Nusayri minority, who, he said "have a kind of perverse Alawite thinking."

The slur enraged Turkey's Alevi community. Although most Alevis are not believed to be linked to Syrian Alawites, many Turks of Arab Alawite origin live in the south of Turkey, near Syria. Alevi associations from around Turkey issued a common statement declaring, "The real pervert is he whose speech is perverse." The head of the Alevi Cem Foundation accused Fazilet's leader of revealing his party's "secret prejudices" and urged him to resign. Charges were brought against Kutan for "divisiveness."

Kutan beat a hasty retreat, insisting that he had made no allusion to "our Alawite brothers in Turkey" but was talking about Assad's "politicized conception" of faith and his minority "repressive" rule in Syria.

The lesson of this outburst, if anybody needed it, was that Turkish Islamic opinion was highly sensitive and far from united.

For a different view of the Islamic agenda, I looked up Korkut Özal, former head of the Islamic wing of the Motherland Party, founded by his older brother, the late President Turgut Özal. Korkut Özal had quit Motherland in 1997 in protest against the closure of Koranic and religious middle schools and the anti-Erbakan campaign.

Now Özal was chairman of the renewed Democrat Party, descendant of the party founded in 1946 by Adnan Menderes (hanged after the 1960 military coup). Özal emphasized that besides democratizing the regime, Menderes opened religious schools, restored the Islamic prayer in Arabic, built thousands of mosques, and was tolerant of all faiths while preserving the secular state.

The burly, amiable Islamic leader received me in the Democrat Party's sparsely furnished new office in a new suburb of Ankara.[5] Özal said his party's main aim was "to bring to Turkey full-fledged Western democracy." Among his priorities: full observance of human rights, decentralization, grassroots democracy, and the supremacy of justice for poor and rich alike.

He explained that by grassroots democracy, he meant a presidential system like that in the United States. (President Süleyman Demirel has also suggested the adoption of a presidential system to bring the country political stability.) Under Turkey's present system, Özal stressed, the people voted for parties, not their representatives, and it was the party chairman who appointed the deputies. Of course most party leaders opposed this reform because they would lose their power if the nation voted for its representatives.

Critical of Refah's erratic performance in the past, Özal spoke favorably of Fazilet, describing the leadership as "strong and cautious." If the law were changed to allow political alliances, he would gladly join an alliance with Fazilet, whose leader Recai Kutan was a friend of fifty years.

Warning that the present military-led drive against Islamist activities could only lead to "catastrophe," Özal expressed the conviction that the armed forces were sincere in their fears of an Iranian-type revolution. "But it could never happen in Turkey," he emphasized. "People will discover the real Islam, the Ottoman interpretation, with freedom of religion."

An increasingly important player on the Turkish scene, MÜSİAD—the Independent Industrialists' and Businessmen's Association—was founded by a group of young Islamic businessmen in 1990 as a counterpart to the powerful secular-oriented Turkish Industrialists' and Businessmen's Association. MÜSİAD's declared aim was to promote commercial development "without sacrificing moral values" and increase economic links among Muslim countries. Now MÜSİAD had become a significant force, with 3,000 members and twenty-eight branch offices around the country and thirty focal points overseas, including London, Berlin, Paris, and New York City as well as Islamic centers.

Not long after the National Security Council, dominated by the military command, delivered its February 28, 1997, ultimatum to Erbakan to curb radical Islamic activities, the campaign was launched against MÜSİAD. Legal proceedings were started against two important Islamic business groups, MÜSİAD members, charged with smuggling gold and foreign currency into the country, allegedly to fund Islamist activities. Later the Turkish General Staff accused 100 "Islamist bosses" of funding some thirty radical organizations. Military sources indicated that the army had established a blacklist of Islamic companies, including leading members of MÜSİAD.

Following Erbakan's resignation and the establishment of a secular coalition government at the end of June 1997, the anti-Islamist campaign seemed to ease somewhat. But at the beginning of 1998, the courts went into action. Refah Party was shut down, Erbakan was barred from politics for five years, and several mayors were put on trial for violating secular principles. And legal actions were taken against MÜSİAD.

In mid-April, the authorities arrested twenty members of MÜSİAD on charges of diverting insurance funds to religious activists, but they were later acquitted. In May, MÜSİAD's chairman, American-educated Erol Yarar, was brought before the State Security Court in Ankara on charges of "inciting hatred" in a speech critical of restrictions on religious education. The prosecutor also asked for the closure of MÜSİAD for violating the law on associations.

Ömer Bolat, MÜSİAD's secretary-general, called the charges against Yarar and the organization baseless.[6] "If there is justice, rule of law, and basic human rights, he will be acquitted and the case against MÜSİAD dropped," Bolat said in an interview at the organization's İstanbul headquarters.

Suggesting that the aim of the court actions was to encourage members to quit MÜSİAD, Bolat said there had been a score of defections, but MÜSİAD had gained fifty-five new members in a strong show of solidarity.

Denying any organic links with the banned pro-Islamic Refah Party or its successor Fazilet, Bolat stressed that MÜSİAD members are not in politics and vote for different parties.

The MÜSİAD official said the organization was pursuing plans to hold the largest private fair ever in İstanbul in late November 1998, with the participation of 600 Turkish and 150 foreign exhibitors and 100,000 visitors from sixty countries. There would be four subfairs specializing in machinery, textiles, construction materials, and food products and packaging. He was equally optimistic about the organization's long-term aims to increase the number of members to 5,000 with forty branch offices and forty overseas focal points by the year 2000.

I was not surprised to learn later that in the anti-Islamic climate, the president of MÜSİAD had been convicted, sentenced to one year in prison, and forced to resign.

When I contacted Bolat the following spring, he informed me that the case against MÜSİAD had been dropped and that Erol Yarar's sentence had been "postponed" since his crime was not related to the State Security Courts. Yarar, who held the post of president for nine years, had indeed stepped down because he thought a change in leadership was needed and he had been neglecting his own business interests, Bolat said.

But he stressed that Yarar was still an active member of MÜSİAD as president of the Higher Consultative Council and head of the International Business Forum, a network of Muslim businessmen aimed at stimulating trade and mutual investment.

Another battleground of the Islamist-secular conflict has been the *İmam Hatip* schools. Originally intended as training institutions for religious cadres, there were now over 600 *İmam Hatip* schools providing general education and turning out 50,000 graduates a year, or 10 percent of the national student body.

Military commanders claimed that the religious schools were training grounds for an Islamist revolution. Social Democrats like Birgen Keleş, deputy from the Republican People's Party, claimed to have evidence of "brainwashing" in the schools and dormitories.

İbrahim Sölmaz, president of the *İmam Hatip* Alumni Association, blamed the local media for giving the religious schools "a false image," pointing out that the schools were controlled by the Ministry of Education, which provided their staff and curricula. "The people have shown we will never sacrifice the *İmam Hatip* and Koranic schools," he told me.[7]

This was reference to the rally at İstanbul's Sultanahmet Square in the spring of 1997, when at least half a million Turkish men, women, and children turned out in defense of religious schools.

That powerful show of Islamic strength only hardened the generals' resolve to crack down on Islamic activists. After Erbakan's ouster, the military leadership made sure that curbing *İmam Hatip* schools was the top priority of Prime Minister Mesut Yılmaz's secular government. Despite fervent opposition from Islamists and their sympathizers, Yılmaz succeeded in pushing through Parliament the eight-year compulsory education law that August, effectively terminating religious grammar schools.

At first there were angry eruptions at İstanbul's main mosques. Then protests continued at a relatively low key because the government did not actually close the *İmam Hatip* schools. Minister of Education Hikmet Uluğbay told me in the summer of 1998 that *İmam Hatip* middle schools would be phased out in a three-year program.[8] No new enrollment has been accepted to sixth grade in religious schools, but students already in the pipeline were allowed to continue their studies. The additional space has served to reduce class size in the *İmam Hatip* schools.

A member of the *İmam Hatip* Alumni Association arranged for me to visit the Kartal Anadolu *İmam Hatip* on the Asian side of the Bosphorus. The *İmam Hatip* alumnus, now an accountant with an international shipping concern, spoke bitterly about "discrimination" shown by some sectors toward religious school graduates. He himself had been rejected by four banks and the Koç Holding, which said they had no place for *İmam Hatip* graduates. "But some businesses are actually looking for *İmam Hatip* graduates as cashiers because they know we can be trusted with the till," he added with a smile.

My guides to Kartal were İbrahim, eighteen, a seventh-year student interested in economics, and Mahmut, twenty-one, a student at Galatasaray Law School, who kept in close contact with Kartal as a volunteer consultant. Both young men came from the Black Sea area but liked living in İstanbul because there was more opportunity. They did not belong to the Islamic party and in fact thought all parties were the same. Their families had sent them to the *İmam Hatip* school because religious schools were known to provide better general education and discipline than the public schools. (I knew some secularists who sent their children to *İmam Hatip* for the same reason.)

Admission to Kartal was not easy, according to my guides, who said only 180 students were accepted each year out of some 22,000 applications. Present enrollment was 1,391 students, including 253 girls. Only 5 percent were taking the theology course, they said, noting that 80 percent of the graduating class usually went on to university.

The school has been coeducational since 1992, but the girls—most of them in headscarves—had separate classes, separate recreation areas, and only shared laboratories with their male counterparts.

Kartal's students, like those in other *İmam Hatip* schools, carried a heavy academic load: all the required courses in state high schools plus advanced English and German. Religious courses included: Islamic philosophy, the Life of Mohammed, Islamic Laws, History of Religions, History of Islam, Calligraphy, Religious Music, the Meaning of the Koran.

Like most *İmam Hatip* schools, Kartal was built by public donations and staffed by the Ministry of Education. The school was opened in 1985 to educate children of Turkish workers in Europe in foreign languages and Turkish culture. Originally located in İstanbul's Beykoz suburb, it moved to Kartal in 1990.

For the most part, classrooms were sparsely furnished with blackboards and desks. Computers were reserved for the computer class. The library, dependant on contributions, had a good selection of Turkish literature. The English section was poor, although it included Freud—a surprise in an Islamic school. A modern auditorium seating 550 people was recently completed. Now the school's main ambition was a sports complex, but administrators said a mosque had to be built first.

Student life revolved around clubs in foreign languages, biology, religion, computers, science and technology, music, and cinema. I visited several clubs and met a number of bright, dedicated students who talked about their love of computers, soccer, movies, and poetry and who wanted to become lawyers, journalists, and businessmen. They appeared to be very normal young people, like Americans of the 1950s, before the invasion of the drug culture. And everyone was terribly proud of Kartal, which had won the national championship in science in 1996 and 1994 and came in second in 1995.

Other centers of Islamic influence under attack were the municipalities. Erbakan's Refah Party had won the 1994 municipal elections, taking 400 city halls, including the country's capital, Ankara, and most important city, İstanbul. By and large, the local Islamic administrations proved to be efficient and relatively clean, and many incumbents were expected to win the 1999 elections unless they were found guilty of excessive religious zeal. In the military-pushed drive against radical Islam, prosecutors were said to be investigating some 300 municipal governments and a number of governors' offices for alleged Islamist activities.

The most visible municipal leader under fire was Tayyip Erdoğan, forty-four, the charismatic mayor of İstanbul, often mentioned as a possible successor to Erbakan. In the spring of 1998, Erdoğan gained even wider popularity when he was sentenced to ten months in prison by Diyarbakır State Security Court for reciting an "inflammatory" poem.

Speaking at a rally in the southeastern town of Siirt in December 1997, Mayor Erdoğan had declared, "The mosques are our barracks; the minarets are our bayonets. The domes are our helmets. The believers are our soldiers." Ironically, this verse was taken from a poem by Ziya Gökalp, a nationalist and ideologue of Atatürks' regime.

While the court's decision was under appeal, Erdoğan campaigned for reelection on a "platform of democracy." But in late September, the Ankara High Court of Appeals upheld the conviction. This meant Erdoğan had to step down as mayor of İstanbul, go to jail, and would be banned from holding public office again. There was little room for reprieve except that final instance, the European Court of Human Rights, but that would take time.

Lashing out at "this unjust ruling," the popular mayor told his followers that he would continue the struggle and return to the political scene even more powerful than before.

"Tayyip Erdoğan has become the latest victim of a witch hunt against the Islamists in Turkey," İlnur Çevik, publisher of the *Turkish Daily News*, wrote, gloomily predicting that the establishment would now "level its wrath" against the moderate Islamist Fazilet Party, leading businesses supporting pro-Islamic views, and the pro-Islamic media.[9]

Unexpected support for the Islamist mayor came from the United States consul general to İstanbul, Carolyn Huggins. Clearly on government instructions, Huggins paid a formal visit to Erdoğan at City Hall in late September, while he was awaiting an appeal. Afterward the American official delivered a stern message to the authorities via the press, saying, "It is a serious matter when democratically elected leaders are subject to criminal prosecution by courts for statements they make as political figures. Such developments weaken confidence in Turkish democracy."

The Turkish Foreign Ministry promptly protested the incident to the embassy in Ankara. In İstanbul, a group of militants from the small left-wing Labor Party marched on the U.S. Consulate carrying a black wreath with the words "America Get Lost!"[10] A party spokesman denounced Huggins's visit as intervention in Turkey's internal affairs and called for her expulsion.

Turkish diplomats were clearly embarrassed over the affair. The charismatic mayor remained popular even in prison, and cassettes of his speeches were bestsellers in İstanbul. Erdoğan was released in July 1999, after serving only four months. Still considered the leader of the reform Islamists, he was expected to keep a low profile in hopes that his political friends could get the ban on his political activity lifted. But the authorities insisted that Erdoğan would not benefit from the forthcoming amnesty.

Another prominent Fazilet official under scrutiny is Melih Gokçek, fifty, mayor of Ankara and hardly anyone's idea of an Islamic leader. Gokçek, who has a penchant for flashy ties, completed studies in journalism at Ankara's Gazi University and began his political career with the Motherland Party. Breaking with Motherland's leader Mesut Yılmaz in 1991, Gokçek joined Refah, the party "closest to my nationalist and conservative views."[11] Elected mayor of Ankara in 1994, Gokçek, like most Refah mayors, turned to Fazilet when Refah was shut down.

From the start of his term as mayor, Gokçek has been the center of controversy. He claims he has been the target of "government inquisitions" (except for the eleven months when Erbakan was prime minister), first by Social Democrats, who had previously run Ankara, then his old Motherland Party.

"I could be in the *Guinness Book of Records,*" the mayor said, acknowledging he has received 200 court orders "for political reasons." The main allegations, which he denied, involved claims that he had offered tenders for municipal works to religious foundations and that religious courses were taught in his community training centers. Other suits involved failure to pay for sculptures, commissioned by the previous mayor. "It was pornography," Gökçek said disdainfully. He has also been in constant litigation with journalists and claimed to have won 100 libel suits.

A day spent in the mayor's wake showed that for all the controversy, he enjoyed a substantial following in Ankara. He is the kind of politician who cannot cross a street without stopping to shake hands with constituents and ask their concerns.

Gökçek's main complaint against the central government was that 50 percent of the city's income had been cut off in 1997 and 35 percent the following year to pay for the debt on big projects like the light rail system—which, he said, in other countries would be subsidized by the state.

Nevertheless he presented an impressive record of accomplishment. The light rail and subway have begun operations (construction had originated under the previous administration), and twenty-three under/overpasses have been built to ease traffic. Construction was completed on a $550 million waste treatment plant and 876 miles of sewage pipes. Natural gas users doubled to 300,000, and 10 percent of the 1.2 million people living in shantytowns were resettled. Green space doubled to 4.5 square meters per person, most roads were resurfaced, and most sidewalks repaved. Infrastructure was completed on the vast new Yenimahalle industrial district. Social actions included 50,000 free meals distributed daily, fifteen mobile health centers, and a center for the elderly.

Other achievements were six new football fields, two big parks and 200 small ones, and 200 fountains and pools. Some works seemed to me rather extravagant for a municipality strapped for cash, like the tallest fountain in the world, and multicolored and musical fountains, but I heard no complaints.

Employees are free to wear anything from miniskirts to headscarves at Ankara City Hall, the mayor said. He added that his wife did not cover her head and had not been pressured by Fazilet to do so. Like other Islamists, he feared confrontation if the authorities tried to enforce the headscarf ban at universities. "Force invites force," the mayor warned pointedly.

The mayor of Ankara admired the religious freedom he had observed during an official visit to the United States in 1997. "When I visited Washington, I had Sikh taxi drivers; anyone here wearing a turban is taken to prison. In Congress, a session opens with someone reading verses from the Bible; in the Turkish Parliament, if you touch on Islamic issues, it's a crime. In Washington, they held Prayer Day in front of the White House; here it is inconceivable and people would say we are backward to make such a suggestion. In a secular country like America, the church and state are separate; here it's the opposite—the state controls the mosque. The Religious Affairs Department personnel are government employees. The state minister in charge of religion prepares the same text to be read in all the mosques.

"If we had real democracy, our problems would be solved," Gokçek emphasized.

My overriding impression was that Fazilet's middle-of-the-road leadership, the business-minded leaders of MÜSİAD, and mayors like Erdoğan and Gokçek should be encouraged to integrate fully into the democratic process—not harassed. Would Turkey's secular society, including the armed forces, seize this opportunity to come to terms with its religious community? I wondered. If not, the next generation of Islamic leaders might want more than democratic reforms.

# 16 ~

## *Alla Turka*

Nationwide celebrations were held in the fall of 1998 to fete the seventy-fifth anniversary of the Turkish Republic and in the process galvanize secular spirits. Not to be outdone in patriotism, Islamic mayors participated enthusiastically in the national commemorations.

More festivities followed in 1999, for the 700th anniversary of the founding of the Ottoman dynasty. Some Islamists, who look back fondly to the Ottoman era when the sultan of İstanbul was the leader of all Muslims, hoped to appropriate these celebrations for their cause. But ardent secularists were not about to let Islamists co-opt one of the most glorious periods of Turkish history.

Implicitly acknowledging the deep divisions tearing the country apart, the minister of culture expressed hope that the two celebrations would "reconcile the republic and the empire." Pointing out that some people reject the Ottoman Empire while others reject the Turkish Republic, Minister İştemihan Talay said both were wrong and it was necessary to create "a climate of reconciliation."[1]

Despite apprehensions, the two anniversaries were celebrated by both sides. And if the jubilees did not introduce a new period of national healing, they did point to a common national pride in this country's remarkable past.

The moves by the young secular Republic to rehabilitate its Ottoman past are significant in light of the fact that until recently, modern Turkey had done everything it could to ignore its Ottoman, that is, Islamic, roots. There was even a tendency to refer to *our ancestors the Hittites*, blithely leaping over the Islamic and Byzantine Empires.

I remember just two decades ago, when anyone talked about culture it was Western culture. *Alla Turka* music and art with their Middle Eastern roots were held in general disdain by the secular elite. Coming from posts in the Arab world, I was surprised to find such an active Western cultural scene in Ankara and such a dearth of Middle Eastern influences. In fact, the only unabashedly Middle Eastern cultural tastes shared by the Turkish elite were in carpets and cuisine—at which Turks so excel.

There were Western symphony concerts and chamber music almost every night and frequent evenings of State Opera and Ballet, always crowded with young people. Jazz was also politically correct but performances of Turkish classical music were rare.

In literature, the situation was much more serious. Atatürk's Language Reform of 1928 had cut Turks off completely from their literary past. It was above all a reaction to the flowery literature of the Ottoman court, heavily impregnated with Persian and Arabic. This meant the creation of a new body of literature starting almost from scratch. A foreign Ottomanist told me once that Turkey has one of the richest collections of ancient handwritten manuscripts in the world—but Turks can't read them.

The exception was traditional folk literature, poems, legends, songs, and tales of the street minstrels, which were rendered in pure, simple Turkish.

Most first-generation Republican writers like novelist Halide Edip Adivar were inspired by the revolution, and their writings reflect the social and political realities of the time. Poet Nazım Hikmet started the Free Poetry movement in reaction to the Ottoman tradition of rhyme and meter. Later writers were generally influenced by European trends from social realism and existentialism to surrealism.

But all modern writers have had to tread a thin line whenever they took up the burning issues of their times: human rights abuses, Kurdish problems, Islamic fundamentalism. Any deviation from the official line could be condemned as a threat to the integrity of the state or incitement to ethnic hatred. The list of writers and journalists who have endured this test by fire is overwhelming.

The first modern Turkish writer to win wide international attention was Yaşar Kemal, of Kurdish origin, who started out collecting Anatolian folk tales. His works on village life, and particularly the 1955 novel *Memed My Hawk,* have been translated into many languages and made him a candidate for the Nobel Prize. Even Kemal, who rejected the nation's highest distinction—the title of "state artist"—has been threatened with official sanctions for his defense of a Kurdish identity.

Likewise, Orhan Pamuk, probably the most popular novelist in Turkey today and widely translated, turned down the nomination of "state artist" at the end of 1998. "For years I have been criticizing this society for its approach to the Kurdish problem, for its failure to move toward real democracy, for its violations of human rights and banning books," Pamuk said in an interview explaining his position.[2]

There are two main groups in Turkish literature today: the foreign-educated Francophiles, who are generally leftists, and the Anatolians, who depict more conservative Islamic values, according to Alev Alatlı, professor of the philosophy of aesthetics at Marmara University and a leading chronicler of Anatolian life.[3] Ms. Alatlı went to high school in Japan, graduated from Ankara's Middle East Technical University, received a master's degree from Dartmouth, and spent five years studying comparative Jewish, Christian, and Muslim theology.

She said 99 percent of her İstanbul-born students have no idea about the values of Anatolia. "I couldn't take being a foreigner in my own country," she stressed, explaining her interest in Anatolian culture.

Because Alatlı has dared to cross barriers and deal sympathetically with Islamic philosophy and the Kurdish reality, she is regarded with official suspicion. Lately she has been publicly accused of acting as an intermediary in trying to bring about a dialogue with Kurdish nationalists.

"Cultural schizophrenia is what I call it—and we're still trying to find our balance," remarked Cemal Kafadar, a social historian, commenting on the ambivalent attitude of Kemalists vis à vis their Ottoman past.[4] Author of *Between Two Worlds*, on the rise of the Ottoman state, Kafadar was on sabbatical from Harvard. We met at the National Archives in İstanbul, where he was studying the Janissary revolts.

In a few clear words, he outlined the Republic's cultural history.

It was without doubt a cultural revolution, every bit as sweeping as that in China. First of all, the Latinization of the alphabet caused a permanent break with the written past. Beyond that there was a total ban for several years on Orientalism, specifically Turkish classic mono-tonal music—even though it is known that Atatürk used to enjoy Turkish classics in private.

In the 1930s and 1940s, the Turkish Historical Society focused on pre-Islamic cultures. They didn't try to eliminate the Ottomans but just establish some balance.

By the 1950s and 1960s, it was an either or question, *Alla Turka* or *Alla Franga* (French, meaning Western).

Turkey of the 1970s was so polarized between left and right that people would be killed for reading a left- or right-wing newspaper. The leftist vocabulary was Pure Turkish; those on the right used heavy doses of Ottoman language. My own friends questioned me for studying Arabic and thought I must be an Islamist.

In the 1980s, the boundaries between the two currents became more porous.

Now it's both *Alla Franga* and *Alla Turka* and sometimes a combination of the two. People are crossing boundaries and experimenting in fusion. With the current Ottoman revival in the world, many Kemalists are saying that Turks ought to be able to read Arabic script. Some Turks are studying Arabic, not only for careers in theology but in diplomacy or business. And a score or so are even studying Ottoman history.

From this brief history, it was clear that Islam, which became so prominent on the political scene in the 1990s, has also penetrated the arts. But the secular clampdown on Islamic activities in politics and business has fortunately not spilled over to the cultural domain. Thus, the president of the Republic could preside over cultural events marking the 700th anniversary of the Ottoman Empire.

"This is the Republic's first big Ottoman commemoration—but it's not a celebration," Fikret Üçcan, deputy secretary of culture, stressed, reflecting an official sensitivity on the subject.[5] One historian, he noted, went so far as to suggest that "it was difficult to understand why the government was celebrating a regime it had replaced!" Üçcan admitted there had been some concern about stirring up nostalgia for Ottoman times, although some voices on the extreme right had complained the government should do more to honor the greatest period of Turkey's history.

"But," he added hastily, "there has been no sign of a yearning for the great old days."

The first major event was an international congress on "Learning and Education in the Ottoman World," organized in April by the Research Center for Islamic History, Art and Culture under the patronage of President Demirel. The formal opening took place at the luxurious Dolmabahçe Palace, the last imperial residence of the Ottoman sultans and Atatürk's presidential lodgings when he was in İstanbul and where he died on November 19, 1938.

In his address, Ekmeleddin İhsanoğlu, director of the Research Center, spoke of the Ottomans' rich cultural heritage, which included influences of the different peoples that made up the empire. Among the guest speakers were Prime Minister Haris Silajdzic of Bosnia and Herzegovina and Prince Hasan bin Talal of Jordan, countries formerly ruled by the Ottomans. More than 200 academics from thirty-five countries took part in the congress, and their papers were to be published by the Research Center.

Regardless of any reservations, the Turkish government organized an extravagant spectacle as an opener to the Ottoman commemorations abroad, with close cooperation from the French authorities. From May through mid-August 1999, the finest treasures of the Ottoman Topkapı Palace were put on display at the Chateau of Versailles. It was a worthy setting for the sultans' golden throne, rare jewelry and silverware, silk embroideries, porcelains, miniatures, and calligraphy. A series of concerts, also at Versailles, included the Janissaries' martial music, whirling dervishes, Turkish classical music, and Western music inspired by Turkey, like Couperin's *La Sultane*, Mozart's *L'Enlèvement au Serail*, and Rossini's *Le Turc en Italie*.

Although both secular and Islamic Turks took part in cultural events marking the two anniversaries, there is a broad gap between the way they view the arts. The secular art world still thinks in terms of Western culture and techniques as it aspires to universality, although there is a marked trend to adapt Anatolian imagery. Islamist culture, on the other hand, exalts traditional arts linked to religion—Sufi music, calligraphy, illumination, and decorative arts—and is openly hostile to Western ballet and sculpture, considered sacrilegious. These two worlds do meet in their common appreciation of folk art and music and jazz.

Asked about Ankara's cultural program, Arif Yılmaz, vice-secretary-general charged with cultural affairs at City Hall, spoke of the capital as a "cultural melting pot."[6] Migrants from all over Turkey have all brought their own folklore, he said.

I wasn't sure whether he understood my question. But then he showed me the Islamic mayor's cultural program: courses where young people were learning folk dances from the twelve regions, the *bağlama* (traditional lute), Janissary music, and Turkish classical music. He also talked of the municipal mobile theater bus that takes shadow puppets and improvised dramas to the shantytowns.

The City Hall official accompanied me to the Şafaktepe Cultural Center, where thirty women were busy at needlework and quilting, some laboring for hope chests, others for family needs. In the painting class, women were learning how to stain glass, and there was talk of setting up a cooperative to market their handicrafts abroad.

We also visited a center for street children, started in 1993 by the International Labor Organization, to get young vendors back to school, and now run by City Hall. More than 1,500 street children are enrolled in the center, which is located downtown in a multifloor parking lot. Here children have access to free health care, help with homework, and cultural activities like judo and Ping-Pong, folk music, and folk theater.

"Before Melih Gokçek, there was no popular culture in the capital; culture was only for the elite," the City Hall official claimed.

Although this was clearly political hyperbole, there may have been some justification because Fazilet's Gokçek was reelected mayor in the spring of 1999, against a popular Social Democratic former mayor.

When I asked Islamic friends about Islamic artists, they introduced me to Muhsine Akbaş, an illuminator, who runs the Kubbealtı Academy for Traditional Islamic Arts in downtown Ankara. This ebullient, head-scarved woman of forty is also the mother of a daughter working as an environmental engineer and a son studying civil engineering at Bosphorus University.

Akbaş says it took her eight years to become an illuminator, doing research at the National Library on the Koran, palace arts, and bazaar painters, then auditing courses at Marmara University.[7] In 1994, she began organizing exhibits for the Ministry of Culture and the National Library, then opened her own academy, where she teaches illumination, miniatures, *ebru* (paper marbling), and calligraphy. There has been a significant increase in orders for traditional art from the Ministry of Culture of late, she said, showing me some of her works and those of her apprentices.

"Yes there is a return to roots because that's what the people want," Akbaş said. "After so many years of denial, they are now celebrating the 700th anniversary of the Ottoman dynasty. But we have other Islamic roots going back to the Uigurs, Selcuks, and Rumi."

Uptown, at the sophisticated Nev Gallery, Ali Artun, the gallery owner, talked to me about Turkey's quest for identity.[8] "Contemporary Turkish art is a hybrid of Anatolian civilizations, including classic Ottoman, classic Turkish, and Greek. It's an amalgam of many influences both West and East," he said.

"How Western is Western?" Artun challenged, immediately citing some well-known Western Orientalists: Ingres, Delacroix, Gerome.

*Signature of Sultan Süleyman the Magnificent decorated by illuminator Muhsine Akbaş. Director of an academy for traditional arts, Ms. Akbaş says there's a revival in the ancient art of calligraphy.*

An architect by profession, Artun recounted that after the 1950s, many Turkish artists went abroad to study and work and stayed, joining the ranks of the self-exiled artists of that exciting world of international culture. Like their colleagues, Turkish artists took with them local inspiration and influences, sometimes unconsciously, but their style was modern. Among these, the late Erol Akyavaş, who lived many years in New York City, was influenced by theological myths. His works, like the Miraculous Journey of Mahomet—the *Miraj Nameh*—show a conscious reference to Eastern thought. Nejad Devrim brought to the Paris School his cultural heritage—elements of calligraphy and Byzantine symbolism.

"Our dilemma today is that we have many prominent painters who have proved themselves abroad but no proper museums for them at home and few proper collections," says Artun, who cofounded Nev galleries in Ankara and İstanbul, essentially to exhibit works of Turkish artists living overseas. He acknowledged the situation has improved with the opening of other galleries and the İstanbul Biennial, now in its sixth season.

Cultural life for Anakara's secular society is still very active, the pro-Islamic mayor notwithstanding. New exhibits open nearly every day; it seems that all the banks have their own private art galleries. The Presidential Symphony Orchestra plays classical music by Turkish and foreign composers Friday evenings and Saturday mornings, and the Bilkent Symphony Orchestra presents first-rate concerts at the Bilkent University Concert Hall outside of town. Also there's usually a full program at the State Opera and Ballet Company.

But the politics-absorbed Ankara society (population 3 million, counting the surrounding slums) cannot compete with the vibrant cultural life of İstanbul, which has four times as many inhabitants, who have more money, more time, and are more open to the world.

New art galleries are sprouting around İstanbul. Opera, ballet, and concerts at the grand Atatürk Cultural Center are almost always sold out. Banks and universities vie among themselves to provide the city with exciting cultural events. International festivals now take place all year long. "By the time the season begins, we're all festivaled out," remarked a longtime foreign resident, who wouldn't think of moving.

Few cities in the world offer such a rich and varied festival program. The İstanbul Festival was founded by the late art patron Nejat Eczacıbaşı as a month-long arts festival in 1973 on the fiftieth anniversary of the Republic. Now the İstanbul Foundation for Culture and Arts organizes four international-level festivals each year: an International Music Festival, Film Festival, Theater Festival, and Jazz Festival, plus an Art Biennial.

Like other such international events, the İstanbul festivals aim to enhance national prestige and attract tourists. But in 1997, organizers conceded a political intent: theirs was a loud and clear statement in defense of Western culture. At the time, Islamist Necmettin Erbakan was prime minister, and some of his followers had openly attacked Western arts, specifically ballet, symphonic music, and sculpture, as alien to Turkey's Islamic culture. Erbakan's Ministry of Culture even sought briefly to deviate state funds from Western-type orchestras and dance companies to support traditional Islamic arts.

By spring of 1999, the foundation's mood was more relaxed and conciliatory. Although the Music Festival focused mainly on European music, there were special programs celebrating the 700th anniversary of the Ottoman Empire. In a world premiere, Italian conductor Fabio Biondi presented his new version of Vivaldi's opera *Bajazet* that tells the story of Tartar emperor Tamerlane, who defeats the Ottoman sultan Bajazet and falls in love with his daughter. The İstanbul State Symphony Orchestra performed *The Fall of Constantinople* by Kamran İnce, currently a professor at the University of Memphis.

And for the first time, the festival offered a rich program of Turkish traditional music. The Turkish Classical Music State Chorus of İstanbul presented a concert entitled "From the Ottoman Empire to the Republic." Burhan Öcal and the İstanbul Oriental Ensemble performed his works, which bridge Turkish music and Western classics and jazz. Kudsi Ergüner, well-known Turkish *ney*, or reed, player who lives in Paris, led an international group in the performance of *Taj Mahal*, bringing together Turkish Sufi and Hindu music.

In another conciliatory gesture, the İstanbul Theatre Festival featured its first Greek-Turkish coproduction with Greek and Turkish actors. Greek director and chairman of the Theatre Olympics, Theodoros Terzopoulos presented the world premiere of his latest work, the *Heracles* trilogy, based on texts by Euripides, Sophocles, and Müller.

"Art is immune to politics," Nilgün Mirze, foundation spokeswoman, said when I noted that all official and nonofficial relations with Greece had been severed over Greek aid to the Kurdish leader Abdullah Öcalan. "We want to bring people together."[9]

As part of its mission to make İstanbul an international center of culture, the foundation initiated the project for a new cultural and congress center, due to open in late 2000, according to Mirze. The giant $78 million complex, financed by the Turkish government, is located near Ayazağa, north of the congested city center, and includes a 2,500-seat main auditorium, 950-seat multipurpose hall, 450-seat chamber music hall, and a 450-seat open-air theater, two cinemas, and meeting rooms.

At present the Atatürk Cultural Center hosts the main festival events. This huge modern structure in the heart of İstanbul is the home of the State Opera and Ballet, the Symphony Orchestra, and State Theater Company and is considered a bastion of secular Western art.

Just down the hill, the Municipal Cemal Reşit Rey Concert Hall offers a great variety of programs from opera and rock to Sufi music. Reşit Rey was founder of the İstanbul City Orchestra and a pioneer of modern Turkish music. His early compositions were heavily influenced by the French School, but later he turned to Turkish folk music, arranging monophonic songs using polyphonic techniques. From the 1950s until his death in 1985, Reşit Rey created a fusion of traditional Turkish music, Islamic mystical pieces, and Western symphonic works.

Arda Aydoğan, artistic director, recently stated that the mission of the Reşit Rey Hall was to give Turkish composers their due.[10] He stressed that despite Atatürk's efforts to found music and art schools, only twelve Turkish operas have been composed since the founding of the Republic. Turkish composers have been able to perform very little of their work, Aydoğan claimed, adding that the Turkish public has not had the chance to get to know its own classical music culture.

Besides the usual dose of Western classical and pop music, Reşit Rey's 1998–1999 program featured Turkish mystical music by the Turkish Historical Music Ensemble of İstanbul, set up by the Ministry of Culture in 1991 but partially forgotten. Also a program of traditional Turkish music featured the new Destegül Ensemble, whose declared mission is to save certain types of Dervish and Turkish music from extinction.

"Atatürk wanted an East-West synthesis. He didn't cut off Turkish roots. He wanted to open the gates to universal culture," insists Aydın Gün, at eighty-one a legendary figure in Turkey's modern music world.[11] Atatürk, Gün emphasized, sent talented Turkish musicians abroad to learn Western techniques, which when combined with Eastern elements would create universal music. One of these was Adnan Saygün, whose symphonic compositions were based on folk music and whose "Yunus Emre Oratorio" is "a synthesis of Western tonal music and Turkish melodies," Gün noted.

Gün recalls how Atatürk also "collected talented people" from Europe, in music, painting, theater, and the sciences, and brought them to help establish Turkey's modern cultural institutions. Gün himself attended the first class at the Ankara Conservatory set up in 1936 by Paul Hindemith and was assistant to Carl Ebert, pioneer of opera in Turkey. Gün sang the role of Pinkerton in *Madame Butterfly*, the first opera staged in Turkish, in 1941 and founded the State Opera in İstanbul in 1959. Besides performing in the main Western and Turkish operas, Gün was general manager of the İstanbul Festival for twenty years and has taught at the conservatory for sixty years.

But Aydın Gün is not just a man of the classics. An admirer of George Gershwin, Gün has been lobbying to get the conservatory to open a department for the study of musicals. Recently he was named artistic adviser for the Yapı Kredi Bank's extensive cultural program, which includes an important book-publishing division and an arts festival that runs all year long. Among the stars of the 1999 festival were Philip Glass, Robert Wilson, and Nathalie Cole.

Asked about a revival of traditional Turkish music, Gün confirmed there is currently a trend to develop Turkish classical, folk, and Sufi music. "When Eastern monophonic music and Western polyphonic music mix, they affect each other and something new and exciting is created."

Actually, Western composers have been turning eastward for inspiration for a long time. Coinciding with the Ottoman revival, work began on an opera-film, *Mozart in Turkey,* featuring a dramatization of *The Abduction from the Seraglio,* which takes place in the harem of Topkapı Palace. This BBC coproduction with Antelope and the İstanbul Foundation for Culture and Arts was set for cinema, television, and video release in 2000.

Among the Ottoman events, a series of concerts entitled "Alla Turka: From Mehter to Mozart," was held in the recently restored Imperial Artillery Arsenal. Haydn's "Military Symphony" and Mozart's "Turkish Concerto" demonstrate the influences of Ottoman music on Western music. The concert version of Mozart's opera *Zaide,* set in the harem of an Ottoman palace, was the highlight of this mini-festival.

More than in concerts and festivals, *Alla Turka* music is making itself heard in the streets of İstanbul and on Turkish radio and television. Although young Turks are as crazy about jazz and rock as any Europeans, what really grips them and most of their parents is Turkish pop and folk music. Turkish folk can be lively or languid, requires at least a *bağlama*—a long-necked lute—and is best heard in *bağlama* bars that have cropped up around the city. Turkish pop, usually played by a combination of traditional Turkish and Western instruments, can lean toward European pop or *Arabesk*—a form of Middle Eastern blues—generally found in *gazinos* or nightclubs, which can be big and lavish or small and seedy.

*Arabesk* was born in the late 1960s in the migrant ghettos, which were forming around the main cities in the wake of rapid development. It is a hybrid form, combining Turkish folk and art music and using traditional Turkish instruments and Western strings, in the manner of Egyptian pop. The father of *Arabesk,* Orhan Gencebay, was a Black Sea migrant, who voiced the frustrations, loneliness, and injustice of life in İstanbul's *gecekondu.*

At first *Arabesk* music was banned on the state-run radio and television as culturally incorrect, because of its "backward" Arabic influence and "negative" themes. But in the 1980s, *Arabesk* was rehabilitated by then–prime minister Turgut Özal, who openly enjoyed it and even used it for his political campaigns. Now it's difficult to escape from Turkish pop and *Arabesk,* which can be heard on several TV channels, all over the radio, in taxis and on intercity buses. The burly, charismatic *Arabesk* folk singer, İbrahim Tatlıses, who comes from the southeast and often sings in Kurdish, is the closest thing to a national hero in Turkey today.

The new awareness of Eastern, even Islamic, roots is also apparent in the visual arts. Turkish entrepreneur Sakıp Sabancı led off the Ottoman celebrations with a magnificent exhibition of Ottoman calligraphy in the United States. The exhibit, "Letters in Gold," opened at New York's Metropolitan Museum of Art in the fall of 1998, moving to the Los Angeles County Museum of Art in early 1999 and then to Harvard in the fall. Lavishly decorated fifteenth-century volumes of the Koran, imperial decrees with the sultans' monograms, and stylized prayer verses were among the pieces on tour.

At present most of the Sabancı collection is located in the industrialist's home at Emirgân, a suburb of İstanbul. Besides the calligraphy there's a good selection of Turkish painting from the beginning of the nineteenth century to the present day, sculpture and antique porcelain mainly from China and Europe.

Following the example of philanthropists in the United States and Britain, the Sabancı family has decided to transform the Equestrian Villa, as the Emirgân mansion is known, into a museum. Their aim is to share with the general public what Sakıp Sabancı calls "the finest specimens of our national heritage."

Emin Mahir Balcıoğlu, director of the future Sakıp Sabancı Museum, said the villa would be converted into a contemporary teaching museum and linked to the new Sabancı University.[12] An architect and former executive officer with the Aga Khan Trust for Culture, Balcıoğlu complained that none of the art museums in Turkey have "proper conditions." The Sabancı museum-school, scheduled to open by spring 2001, will have the latest state-of-the-art facilities, security, and air-control and a new underground gallery.

"This will be İstanbul's first permanent museum of Islamic arts," Balacıoğlu contended. Emphasizing that a museum has to be "alive," he spoke of plans for an active academic program with public seminars in addition to regular art courses. His goal is to create an international institute of art studies and museum management at Emirgân.

Across the Bosphorus, Hüsamettin Koçan, dean of fine arts at Marmara University, said the school was planning to open a museum based on its substantial collection of Turkish prints.[13] The museum, to be located in the historic Sultanahmet quarter, will also include a contemporary art gallery and an international area. A major selection of these prints went on tour of eastern Turkey by trailer truck in May 1999. It was the first time inhabitants of this troubled region could view works by many of the best-known Turkish artists of this century.

The print collection, begun in 1973 on the fiftieth anniversary of the Republic, includes artists of the "D Group," like Nurullah Berk and Bedri Rahmi Eyüboğlu, who worked as early as the 1930s to create a synthesis between traditional Turkish art and the new Western art movements. Some modern artists like Mehmet Güler and Selcuk Demirel tend to speak a universal language. Some, like Devrim Erbil, are inspired by ancient miniatures; others, like Balkan Naci İslimyeli and Güngör Iblikçi, use traditional images in abstract works.

"You can say there are two main directions in Turkish art: European and traditional, but lately the traditional school is divided between those who look to Turkish roots and those who want to create a new Islamic art," Dean Koçan explained. Koçan himself has long been interested in the Ottoman period and put on a spectacular exhibit, "The Ottoman," at Yıldız Palace in 1994, before the current Ottoman mode. Following the tradition of religious orders, who inscribed holy words on the mulberry leaf, Koçan drew miniature portraits of the Ottoman sultans on leaves mounted on canvas.

Friends in Ankara had told me I must meet Nuran Terzıoğlu, who had just opened an art gallery in İstanbul, and art patron Yasemin Tanbay, whose daughter was involved in the new modern dance scene.

With its raw brick walls and duplex layout, the Apel Gallery reminded me of New York City. And I could easily imagine the main exhibit by talented Turkish artist Suzy Hug Levy in a gallery in Soho. Her sculptures composed of swirls of brightly painted newspaper formed a dramatic display entitled "Silhouettes of İstanbul."

"There's a real awakening in the arts now," Nuran, a husky-voiced smoker, told me.[14] She has been deeply immersed in the Turkish art world for many years, running a gallery in Ankara, organizing international exhibits, and coordinating artistic activities at Bilkent University. At the end of 1998, she moved to İstanbul and opened a gallery in the heart of the Beyoğlu neighborhood.

"In the 1950s and 1960s, Turkish artists were producing impressionist and abstract art—nothing from our roots. Erol Akyavaş was the first artist to go back to Anatolian roots and a few others followed suit. But in the

1970s and 1980s, young people were going into medicine and engineering and business administration, not liberal arts. Only since the late 1980s have many students chosen the arts, and now there are excellent young people working in the field. Today there are more artists than ever and more buyers, private organizations and individuals."

Yasemin Tanbay and her industrialist husband Aydın live nearby in a discreet modern building with a marvelous view of the Bosphorus and the finest collection of Turkish art I've seen.

"We started buying paintings in the early 1960s, when people were not buying," Yasemin, wearing a silvery silk pants suit, said over tea.[15] She likes modern Turkish painting, and her husband prefers the Ottoman period.

She pointed out several of her favorites: Nuri İyem, who paints haunting village faces with Western techniques; Orhan Peker, abstract expressionist, who depicts the Anatolian steppes with great sensitivity; the *naïf* Anatolian painter Yalçın Gökçebağ; Neşe Erdok, who can create a mood of total submission through the simple act of cutting a woman's hair.

In stark contrast were the classic nineteenth-century Ottoman paintings in her husband's study, mostly landscapes inspired by Western masters. Among them, Ali Riza Bey faithfully reproduced the scenery of his beloved Üsküdar on the Asian side of the Bosphorus.

Yasemin spoke with pride of her daughter Zeynep, who graduated from Martha Graham's school of dance in New York and performed with the company. She has come back to İstanbul to go into the relatively new field of ballet—despite all the controversy around the art form in this Islamic-run city. She was currently teaching at Marmara University and planned to organize her own dance group.

Yasemin, who has visited many countries, does not know any other city with such an exciting cultural life as İstanbul. She has also traveled all over Turkey—"no mountain or village has escaped me"—and what she loves is the great variety of cultures.

Long an admirer of Turkish classical music, Yasemin has discovered Sufi music and is deeply moved by the mystical poetry of Rumi, often called simply Mevlâna—Our Master. Along with disciples from all over the world, she attends the annual celebrations in Konya from December 10 to 17 that mark the anniversary of Mevlâna's death in 1258. She has also gotten to know some dervishes and goes to their ceremonies, now sometimes held in carpet shops since some lodges have been closed.

An increasing number of Turks like Yasemin have straddled the cultural divide in their society and appreciate modern dance as well as the purifying rituals of the dervishes.

Perhaps the most exciting artistic revival taking place is the İznik tile story. İznik, located southeast of İstanbul, was once known as Nicaea, the site of two major councils of early Christianity. The city regained fame from the fifteenth to the seventeenth centuries with the production of artistic tiles, used to decorate mosques and palaces around the empire.

Then for nearly 300 years, production of those masterpieces simply stopped, and the special techniques used to make them were all but lost. The main reason given for the death of this art form was the decline in demand for such luxurious embellishments on public buildings with the decline of the Ottoman Empire. Then too, during the Turkish War for Independence, İznik, with its some 300 kilns, was burned to the ground by the retreating Greek Army. The tile masters dispersed, taking their secrets with them.

"Our biggest handicap has been the absolute lack of documentation on the special İznik process or where the original materials came from," said Dr. İşıl Akbaygil, who set up the İznik Foundation in 1993 and dreams of founding a university at İznik.[16] We met at the foundation's office-showroom at Kuruçesme, a green suburb of İstanbul on the upper Bosphorus.

Excavations at İznik by İstanbul University Department of Archaeology and Art History have provided important clues as to the types of kilns and the materials used. With support from Turkish scientific foundations, Princeton, and MIT, it is now possible to produce tiles "virtually indistinguishable from those of the sixteenth century," Dr. Akbaygil stressed.

"It is a collaboration art, communal, never individual," said Dr. Akbaygil, a professor at İstanbul University, describing the main characteristic of İznik tiles. What makes İznik tiles different from all others is that they are composed of 70 to 80 percent quartz, a semiprecious stone. This gives the tiles a special porous quality, which allows them to breathe and accounts for their longevity. The traditional İznik colors are difficult to achieve and look like semi-precious stones: lapis lazuli, turquoise, emerald green, and coral red. The opaque sheen glaze absorbs light and enhances the colors. The geometrical designs represent the universe; the inscriptions are usually taken from Islamic philosophy, and the figures are allegorical.

Most of the tiles on display are traditional patterns: the tree of life, birds and flowers, calligraphy, courtly hunting scenes. But there are also modern stylized tulips, poppies, and sailing ships. Increasingly popular are panels of *Kufic* script, handsome geometrical letters first used by the Phoenicians, which look at home in the twenty-first century.

Needless to say, İznik tiles are expensive. Even in the seventeenth century, one tile was the equivalent of the price of a sheep. Now they're selling on the Internet at $150 for a twenty-three-centimeter square tile, or $3,000 for a square meter panel.

And the clients: schools, banks, hotels, anyone who can afford these works of art. Fashion lord Giorgio Armani has ordered his name in *Kufic* script, industrialist Sakıp Sabancı wanted İznik tiles for his new mosque at Adana. The İstanbul Stock Exchange has purchased handsome panels, and the İstanbul Municipality will present a spectacular collection of İznik tiles in the stations of the soon-to-be-opened Metro.

This revival of Ottoman culture, which has been taking place in many fields, could be a sign of a new self-confidence in Turkish society, I decided. Perhaps those writers, painters, and musicians who have been seeking their roots without turning their backs to universal Western styles will lead the way toward a broader reconciliation in this divided society.

"Willy-nilly, Turkey is working out its original Turkish solution to the disparate, contending sources of creativity and identity," is the way historian Cemal Kafadar put it.

# 17 ～

## Shadow Politics

It was one of those chilling, drizzly spring Sundays when most people in the Turkish capital would rather stay home. But there they were, patiently waiting in huge lines at the opening of the polling stations. Some were driven by rumors that Islamic voters would congregate early at the polls and monopolize them in filibuster tactic. Others suspected the complicated voting procedures were a means to confuse and discourage ordinary, devout voters.

National elections had been called a year early because of corruption charges leveled against former prime minister Mesut Yılmaz and his liberal Motherland Party. Thus the parliamentary elections coincided with regularly scheduled voting for mayors and other municipal and neighborhood officials. It was a lengthy process in which voters had to go three times into the isolation booth with four separate paper ballots and choose among twenty-one political parties.

But after months of political uncertainty, a spate of deadly bombing and arson attacks, open revolt in Parliament, and dire warnings that the country was sliding into chaos, a record number of Turkish voters (86 percent of the 38 million eligible voters) flocked peacefully to the polls on April 18, 1999. And they surprised everyone.

Leading political analysts had predicted a two-way battle between acting prime minister Bülent Ecevit's staunchly secular and nationalistic Democratic Left Party and the pro-Islamic Fazilet (Virtue) Party. All polls had shown this trend early on, but were banned during the volatile campaign because the secular establishment feared they could influence the masses.

*Prime Minister Bülent Ecevit, the
social democratic politician, who heads
the nationalist coalition government,
formed after the 1999 elections.*

The experts were right about Ecevit's party riding the wave of nationalism following the capture of Kurdish guerrilla leader Abdullah Öcalan
and the subsequent violence attributed to his sympathizers. Then too,
Ecevit, "the hero of Cyprus," was seen as a leader who could stand up for
Turkey's rights before an unfriendly Europe. And the veteran socialist,
who has visibly mellowed with time, was the only mainstream leader
who has preserved his clean image as successive governments foundered
over financial scandals. (He and his wife still live in the same modest
apartment in an Ankara suburb, which I had visited prior to the 1980
coup.) The electorate gave Ecevit's party 22 percent of the vote, up eight
points from the last time in 1995, making it the first group in the Grand
National Assembly, as Parliament is called, with 138 seats out of 550.

But virtually everyone had failed to predict that the new mood of nationalism would also benefit the far-right Nationalist Action Party, which
won 18 percent of the vote, becoming the second largest group in Parliament. The party, founded by an ultranationalist army officer, Colonel Alparslan Türkeş, had taken part in right-wing government coalitions in the
1970s. Its youth organization, known as *ülkücü* (idealists), had been
deeply involved in the widespread left-right violence that provoked the

1980 military coup and the clampdown on all parties. Since then, the Nationalist Action Party (MHP) had attracted little attention, never reaching the 10 percent barrier necessary to enter Parliament and finally splitting apart at the death of its leader in 1997.

"It was all those funerals," a senior civil servant confided to me the day after the election shock. He explained that the Nationalist Action Party had been the first to help families of PKK victims and appeared like the only party that could put an end to the Kurdish conflict.

It seemed that Turkish voters were not only expressing nationalistic sentiments but turning out of desperation to an activist and "untried" party—at least in recent history, which might resolve some of the country's urgent problems.

A major surprise was the substantial loss in votes by the Islamic-leaning Fazilet Party compared to its banned predecessor Refah, which had won the last national and local elections. This time, Fazilet came in a weak third nationally with 15 percent of the vote, down six points from 1995. The party did manage to hold its ground in municipal elections, keeping the mayorships of Ankara and İstanbul and winning many new municipalities. The main message of the electorate was clear; while Islamic-oriented officials had generally provided clean and efficient local government, the parliamentarians had failed to keep their promises and only succeeded in antagonizing the military.

Another unexpected development was the miserable showing of the Republican People's Party, founded by Atatürk. This center-left party received only 8 percent of the vote, meaning that for the first time, it would not be represented in the new Parliament. (It too did better in local elections.) Voters apparently blamed the party leadership for its negative performance in the parliamentary opposition.

Just as clear was the electorate's rebuff to the two other main parties, the liberal Motherland and center-right True Path, which had been bogged down in bickering and corruption scandals and received only 13 percent and 12 percent, respectively. I had talked earlier to local Motherland politicians in outlying districts of İstanbul, and they acknowledged strong grassroots pressures against the party's compliance with anti-Islamic policies.

As for Tansu Çiller, she had played the religious card and lost. I accompanied her caravan on its final round through small towns on the periphery of Ankara. She looked as fresh and charming as ever, but her speeches were full of invectives against her archenemies, Motherland's leader

Mesut Yılmaz, and *Milliyet* and the rest of the mainstream press. The crowds were predominantly headscarved women, who cheered Çiller enthusiastically and engulfed her with flowers at every stop. But her fans disappeared as we approached the urban areas, and the last stops were canceled. After True Path's electoral disaster, coming in fourth, some party cadres revolted against Çiller's leadership, but she was not about to bow out gracefully.

The fledgling Peace Party, established to give Alevi voters a home, did so poorly that its founder and leader Ali Haydar Veziroğlu announced that the party would be disbanded and its property donated to the Ministry of Education.

Also unexpected was the relatively strong performance by HADEP, the Kurdish People's Democracy Party, which had been relentlessly harassed and even threatened with closure on the eve of the elections. For the first time, a Kurdish party succeeded in winning thirty-eight municipalities in the heavily Kurdish-populated southeast, including the main city of Diyarbakır. Nationally, however, HADEP received less than 5 percent of the vote, which meant this Kurdish voice would not be heard in the Grand National Assembly.

In another revolutionary move, Turks elected twenty-four women to Parliament, the largest number since women won the right to vote in national elections in 1934, thanks to Atatürk. In fact, there would have been even more if Atatürk's party had passed the 10 percent threshold, because it had fielded a number of strong women candidates. Also, for the first time, two of the winning representatives wore headscarves.

Although most people were puzzled by the election results and questioned what impact they would have on the country and its problems, the Turkish military were "happy," I was told by sources in their confidence. They were relieved above all that the country had voted for secular parties. In the generals' view, Ecevit was a proven nationalist and the MHP were also "good citizens" and the two could work well together.

Viewing this kaleidoscopic scene, I thought at least the secular establishment and, above all, the military would be satisfied with the weak performance of pro-Islamic Fazilet and perhaps now could relax. As I saw it, Turkish voters had soundly dismissed the "fundamentalist threat," which had obsessed secularists for the past five years. The Islamic movement had been called to account for its actions and then cut down to size, like most of the other political groups in the outgoing Parliament.

Would the authorities concede at last that the Republic was not in danger of an Islamic takeover? Would they ease their witch hunt against Islamist radicals, which had spilled over to the pious segments of the population? It must be eminently clear to all concerned, I reasoned, that there was no omnipotent foreign force impelling the Islamists to seize power, no vast hoards of illegitimate money used buy votes wholesale, no powerful malevolent force brainwashing unschooled voters, as had been alleged since the last elections.

But I was wrong. Apparently the archsecularists now believed their campaign against fundamentalism was working and must be pursued and redoubled in intensity. This was the only explanation I could give to the passions surrounding the so-called Merve Affair.

Merve Kavakçı, a thirty-one-year-old U.S.-educated computer engineer, elected deputy from İstanbul on the Fazilet ticket, said from the outset that she wore a headscarf for religious reasons and would not take it off if elected. Fazilet leaders were clearly aware of possible trouble if the headscarf-clad Merve attempted to take the oath to the secular Republic, but left the decision up to her. Back in 1995, the now extinct Refah Party had refrained from putting up any women candidates out of fear of just such a crisis.

The Nationalist Action Party's one headscarved deputy wisely volunteered to remove her headcovering in deference to parliamentary "rules." In fact, there was no law banning women from covering their heads in the Grand National Assembly; the dress code merely stipulated women should wear two-piece suits. Cleaning women and visitors occasionally appear in the corridors wearing headscarves without causing any stir. But never before had an elected deputy worn a headscarf in those hallowed halls.

No one, however, had expected the extent of the reaction to the headscarf incident. When Merve slipped into Parliament during the swearing-in ceremony, she was greeted with applause from Fazilet colleagues, enraged hoots of "Out! Out!" and banging desks from the Democrat Left, and embarrassed silence from the other benches. After forty minutes of pandemonium, recess was declared and Merve was persuaded by her party not to return to the hall.

Leading the secularists' attack, Ecevit cautioned: "This is not a place to challenge the state. Turkey is a secular republic and religion should not be mixed with politics." Later President Demirel publicly condemned the incident, calling the Fazilet deputy "an *agent provocateur*." Such strong reaction was reportedly provoked by a warning from the military-dominated National Security Council two days earlier that it would not remain silent in the face of a challenge to the secular republic.

Echoing secular indignation, the main television stations showed reruns of the chaotic scene for several days, joined by much of the media in a concerted campaign against the defiant deputy. Press reports linked Merve to radical Palestinian organizations in the United States, produced incendiary statements attributed to her, and claimed she had contacts with Libya. (Later I learned she was eleven years old when she visited her father working for a Turkish firm in Libya.) Solidarity demonstrations by veiled women in Iran were played up in the Turkish press, and it was suggested this might cause a rupture in relations between the two countries.

But the most damning charge seemed to be the fact that Merve had become an American citizen through her American husband (whom she later divorced) and had taken the American oath of allegiance without informing the Turkish authorities. For this, Merve was swiftly stripped of her Turkish nationality, making her unable to serve as an elected representative to Parliament. Investigations were also begun into the status of the Fazilet deputy from Ankara, Oya Akgönenç, who did not wear a headscarf but who had also married an American.

Clearly feeling the wind in his sails, Chief Prosecutor Vural Savaş, who had succeeded in closing down Refah the year before, called on the Constitutional Court to ban Fazilet and dismiss all its deputies on the grounds that it was the successor of Refah. Accusing the pro-Islamic party of deliberately provoking the headscarf crisis, the prosecutor called the party "a malignant tumor" and compared its deputies to "blood-sucking vampires." Popular Turkish newspapers reveled in the colorful language, but several columnists criticized such excess. The Fazilet deputy from Trabzon, Şerif Malkoç, filed a complaint against Savaş for having "insulted his honor and dignity."

For Fazilet's reaction to this virulent campaign and election defeat, I again went to see Deputy Chairman Abdullah Gül, increasingly talked about as leader of the party's younger generation since former İstanbul mayor Erdoğan had been jailed and stripped of his political rights.

Receiving me in his modest parliamentary office, Gül appeared to be his usual unflappable, amiable self.

"Some people say the 15 percent we received in general elections shows our real weight, but don't forget there were two elections and

Fazilet came out first in municipal polls with 24 percent of the vote, including Ankara and İstanbul," he began.[1]

But I focused on the national poll, asking what had hurt Fazilet most, the relentless official and media attacks? The party's moderation during the campaign? Tension within the party between the hard-line older generation and the more open younger Turks, like himself?

Gül contended that the secularists' campaign against Fazilet had on the contrary worked to its advantage. The party's losses, he said, were because of "our own mistakes," above all, the last minute move by part of the leadership to postpone the elections. This mistake was "political suicide" and as a result, the voters moved to other parties.

I quickly followed up: How important were the differences within the party? There had been rumors for months of a split within the party between unconditional followers of the banished Erbakan and reformists led by Erdoğan and Gül. But the party had made an effort to paper over disputes in the name of electoral unity.

Now Gül acknowledged that the split was "serious" and would probably come out into the open at the party congress, set for fall 1999 (it was postponed). "The traditional leadership will be changed and the party will emerge with a more modern, more rational face," he asserted.

Not once during our conversation, which lasted over an hour, did Gül criticize or even mention Erbakan's name. Yet it was clear that by "traditional leadership" he meant the Islamist leader and his group of followers still in the new party leadership.

(Actually the breakup of Fazilet began even sooner. At the end of July, Gül and a group of fellow reformists submitted their resignations from the party's executive board. Although they didn't say so, their move was generally said to be provoked by excessive intervention in party matters by former leader Erbakan. The reformists insisted they did not aim to set up their own party but hoped their ideas would prevail at the next party congress. It was not certain how much of the party supported them, but it was clear that the split in Fazilet would weaken the Islamic movement at least initially.)

Most of Gül's criticism was directed against the deputies of the Democratic Left for "orchestrating a campaign" against Merve Kavakçı. "They made her headscarf an issue declaring it was a challenge to the state," he said. "But in reality, her action was quite normal. The majority of Turkish women wear headscarves. It is part of their identity. Voters elected Merve after she campaigned in a headscarf."

As for revelations that Merve had acquired American citizenship, Gül replied indignantly that many deputies and even a cabinet minister have dual nationality. "It's not illegal. In fact, the government has urged Turks living abroad to take foreign citizenship for practical advantages and to serve as a kind of Turkish lobby in their newly adopted states. Merve didn't commit a crime and did nothing against the law and yet is called a traitor."

Gül said the chief prosecutor's case against Fazilet was "political with no legal grounds." The Merve incident was being used to demonstrate that Fazilet was against secularism, Gül said. Savaş has threatened to ban all Fazilet's deputies for backing Merve, citing as evidence a statement by Ecevit calling their support "an uprising."

"Is this democracy?" Gül asked calmly. "A secular state like that is against Atatürk's principles."

I objected that many secularists sincerely believed that the headscarf is a political symbol, a symbol of a movement to restore Islamic law. In his opinion, could *Sharia* ever be compatible with democracy? I asked, raising the question that all my secular Turkish friends have asked at one time or another.

For the first time, the Fazilet official visibly lost his patience. "I am not a scholar of religion; I'm an economist. My concern is that the economy is in a very bad state. It's an economy based on speculation and high interest rates. Production has been undermined, income distribution is getting worse, and unemployment 20 percent of the workforce and more if you count disguised unemployment.

"Fazilet is not a religious party," he said categorically, adding, "A religious party would not be good for Turkey or Islam. There's no movement here to set up a religious state. We want freedom. That's all."

For another view of the beleaguered Fazilet, I called party newcomer Oya Akgönenç, whom I'd gotten to know the year before when she was still a professor at Bilkent University. We met at her office in Parliament, and then she invited me to lunch in the representatives' dining room. As we crossed the lawn, a huge orderly crowd of men, who looked like a mix of deputies and office personnel, came toward us.

"Do you know where they are going?" Oya asked me with a smile. "To Friday prayers at the prayer room in the Grand National Assembly."[2]

Oya, who had formerly belonged to Çiller's Motherland Party, said she was very happy with Fazilet. They had given her a good position as one of three women in the fifty-member central decisionmaking committee.

Not once had she been questioned about her dress—that is, absence of headscarf.

The election campaign had been exhilarating but hard work, she said. Fazilet candidates had to be on their guard at all times against accusations that they were a continuation of Refah, which would get them shut down. "We were extremely careful; it was like a sword of Damocles hanging over us," she said, noting that the party had banned all religious slogans or talk about religion.

"We were running from behind all the time," she admitted candidly, pointing out that they had to work with a new organization in eighty provinces. Some of the former party members actually worked against them. There was no money and so the candidates had to pay for their own campaigns. For much of the media Fazilet was the choice target.

Since the armed forces were always in the background, Fazilet leaders asked for an appointment with the military leadership but were never received. Oya was particularly disappointed because she had heard that her papers on Bosnia and Kosovo had been appreciated in military quarters. "The minute I joined this party, they forgot me," she noted sadly.

The biggest blow to Fazilet was the movement by a group of Erbakan's followers who, without advising the party leadership, joined forces with disgruntled members of other parties to postpone the elections. "When we asked why, they said there was a chance to get enough support to let Erbakan come back and run as an independent from Konya," she said. "The episode cost Fazilet at least four points and was heartbreaking for many in the party, who consider Erbakan like a father, but had to tell him: with all due respect let us be a new party."

As for the Merve incident, Oya felt the ugly scene might have been avoided if things had gone according to plan. It had been decided that Merve should appear quietly—not challengingly—and take her seat just in time to take the oath with the other İstanbul deputies. "Her mistake was that she came an hour and a half early, which gave the Democratic Left MPs the chance to shout her out."

"What has followed is a medieval witch hunt," Oya continued. She stressed that there is no law against dual citizenship, but they made it look like a criminal act. It was normal for a wife to accept the nationality of her husband. Oya noted that she herself had married an American but had filed a petition to retain her Turkish nationality as well.

This seemingly organized tumult around Fazilet temporarily obscured or at least diminished the main result of the 1999 elections. The Turkish public had given a resounding vote of no confidence in the four leading parties, which had dominated the political scene since the last general elections.

Leaders from all the losing parties came under heavy fire from their militants to resign but struggled to hang on. Only Deniz Baykal, whose Republican People's Party came out as the big loser, was actually forced to quit his post as party leader. But in all the parties, a wide-scale soul-searching process had begun.

Even in the victors' camp, there was a certain *malaise* because the Democratic Left Party is run essentially by Ecevit and his wife. And he is seventy-five, in frail health, with no successor aside from Deputy Chairman Rahşan Ecevit, who has always provoked controversy. In fact, during Ecevit's delicate negotiations to form a coalition government with the runner-up Nationalist Action Party, Mrs. Ecevit dropped a bombshell that nearly scuttled the accord. Voicing what was on many people's minds, she said that in the past, the Nationalist Action Party and its ultranationalist affiliates had committed crimes and armed youths. "Have they really changed?" she asked.

The number two political group, the Nationalist Action Party (MHP), was in fact an unknown quantity for most people. None of my political or journalist friends claimed to know the party leaders or what they stood for. Having observed the party and its fascist youth gangs in the spiral of political violence two decades ago, I also wondered about its alleged transformation.

At the MHP headquarters in downtown Ankara, the mood was very upbeat with throngs of well-wishers and potential job-seekers. But senior officials were obviously wrestling with their old image problem, calling themselves "patriots—not nationalists," as in the old days.

"Turkey has changed since 1979," Şevket Bülent Yahnici, Nationalist Action spokesman told me in an interview when I noted concerns over a revival of the party's militant youth gangs.[3] The party had been transformed after Türkeş's death in 1997, he reassured, emphasizing that the youth groups have been reorganized outside the party under Youth Foundations for social and cultural activities.

"Our youth has not been involved in violent incidents for the past year and a half," Yahnici stressed. The stocky, jovial veteran politician, who remembered me from the old days, declared that the party's main approach now in both domestic and foreign affairs was "reconciliation."

In fact, the positions he expressed on various key issues appeared reasonable for the most part:

- Religion and the headscarf problem: All Turkish constitutions have proclaimed Turkey is a secular state with separation of religious and state affairs. Within this context, people should believe and practice religion as they see fit, and there should be new regulations allowing headscarves in universities.
- Fundamentalism: Only 3 or 4 percent of the population want to establish an Islamic state in this country, militants like IBDA-C.
- The Kurdish question: There must be a lasting solution to separatist terror. A difference must be made between the demands of separatists and innocent Kurds. In response to the latter, the MHP has new ideas, new economic, social, and cultural projects.
- The Repentance Law (amnesty): The MHP is sensitive about this matter because of more than 30,000 dead from terrorism (Kurdish). We must take care of the victims' families, and the courts can deal with any act of repentance.
- Death sentence: We must see what the people have to say on this subject.
- Europe: The European Union has done Turkey a great injustice (in rejecting Turkey's candidature) and has observed a double standard. All the new candidates (for EU membership) are behind Turkey in socioeconomic development.
- Cyprus: Southern Cyprus (Greek) supports anti-Turkish terrorism. As for the division of the island, there is a de facto situation; the problem has solved itself.
- Greece: We would like Greece to act more humanely toward Turks in Western Thrace. They violated the disarmament of twelve Aegean islands, but problems like the twelve-mile coastal waters and airspace can be easily solved.
- The new Turkic republics in Central Asia: We were not in power, but our former leader Alparslan Türkeş kept in touch with them. They are our relatives.

"People voted for us because we're clean; we haven't been in government for twenty years," the Nationalist Action spokesman declared. He claimed their voters were young people from the villages and urban

slums, academics, bureaucrats, businesspeople "dissatisfied with inflation, corruption, poverty, paralyzed parliament."

It was clearly déjà vu. These were much the same reasons given for the
pro-Islamic Refah Party's victory in 1995 and the same constituencies. It
seemed that a substantial bloc of protest voters had shifted from Refah to
Nationalist Action in hopes that this aggressive, well-organized, and
newly reformed party would get things done. But no one could venture
to predict how this largely unknown force would perform in power.

Predictably, President Demirel called on Ecevit to form the new government. And just as anticipated, the leader of the Democratic Left turned
first to the ultra-right-wing Nationalist Action Party to form a coalition
government. After tough negotiations, the two erstwhile enemies reached
an accord, with help from the third partner, the liberal Motherland Party.

The new government's program was first of all a message from Prime
Minister Ecevit to reassure the military leadership that the coalition
would pursue their intransigent policy of secularism, notwithstanding
some reservations expressed by his partners. The coalition pledged to
prevent any abuse of religious sentiments for political purposes and
specifically promised measures to prevent headscarves from becoming a
political symbol in state offices. It announced that the secular program for
eight-year compulsory education would continue. As a sop to appease
the "conservatives," that is, pro-Islamic members of the ruling Nationalist
Action and Motherland Parties, it was agreed that students would be permitted to attend summer Koran classes controlled by the Education Ministry, after completing five years primary school.

The government's immediate priorities included passage of a banking
amendment and the 1999 budget. Reforms of local administration, the
board of Higher Education, taxes, Social Security, and farm supports
would be sent to Parliament by the end of the year. Down the road, the
government would prepare bills to revise the Civil Code, Penal Code,
and Debt Law and work out a new strategy for privatizing state enterprises.

Responding to critics at home and abroad, Ecevit said his government
would seek to restructure the State Security Courts, amend the constitution to limit the immunity of deputies, pass a Repentance Law aimed at
ending the Kurdish rebellion, and implement regulations to fight organized crime.

It was an ambitious program, not very different from that of its predecessors. How effective the new administration would be in implementa-

tion depended largely on the cohesion of the coalition since the three parties have a solid majority of 351 seats in the 500-member Parliament.

Ecevit's main coalition partner, Devlet Bahçeli, leader of the Nationalist Action Party, is a soft-spoken economics professor who is credited with renewing the ultranationalist organization. Declaring that the new government's mission was to restore "stability and peace" in the country, Bahçeli, fifty-one, stressed coalition governments as a rule were based on conciliation and tolerance "but in practice can be a source of anxiety."

At the outset, Tansu Çiller declared that the economic situation would determine the fate of the new government and held the former Motherland/Democratic Left coalition responsible for the sorry state of things. She warned that an agreement with the IMF would harm small- and medium-size businesses and agriculture. But Çiller, who is strongly contested in her own party, was not expected to make great waves in the opposition, since she hopes to avoid a new parliamentary inquiry into her financial affairs.

Fazilet, under threat of closure, was also likely to mind its p's and q's and play the role of moderate opposition.

The main opposition to sweeping reforms is likely to come from within the governing coalition. There are major differences on the main issues. A reluctant Ecevit was ready to take necessary decisions to make structural changes needed to work out a deal with the IMF. But members of his government, even in his own party, were not convinced this would be the best way to go.

The challenges facing the government were the same as they have been at least for the past two decades. There is an urgent need to change the electoral and political party laws to avoid fragmentation; reform outdated economic structures; establish a real democracy with freedom of thought and expression; come to grips with the Kurdish problem; and civilianize the administration, that is, relegate the armed forces to military affairs.

Successive governments since the restoration of civilian rule in 1983 have recognized these problems, but none has had the political will or the way to make much progress. Özal at least tackled the daunting problems, but he died too soon.

All told, political prospects in wake of the 1999 election upheaval were not brilliant. The country appeared more polarized than ever between a severely secular establishment and largely devout masses. And now there was a new cleavage between the rise of ultranationalism both on the left and right and among Kurds at the expense of the center parties. Once more, no party could claim a clear parliamentary majority. The two leading groups in the governing coalition are diametrically opposed on many issues. The political scene is fragmented and volatile and faces the prospect of a continuation of coalition governments with their inherent contradictions, compromises, and inertia.

I was reminded of shadow theater, a lot of bluster and action but little substance. Despite this gloomy outlook, I had to admire the sheer unpredictability of the Turkish electorate. Time and again Turks have demonstrated their independence and their faith in democracy, no matter how imperfect it may be.

# 18 ⟍

## *Bridges*

The true believers, both secular and Islamic, depict alarming scenarios for Turkey as it moves into the twenty-first century.

Radical secularists see their enlightened, progressive, democratic society, implanted three-quarters of a century ago on the heights of the Anatolian plateau, under an Islamic siege. They claim Islamic extremists have infiltrated the core of the administration, including the police, educational system, and judiciary, and seek to restore the hegemony of a medieval oligarchy, through democratic elections.

In stark contrast, militant Islamists see a largely devout, poor, and voiceless mass, whose freedom of religion has been limited for many years, now suffering a new wave of repression. Their pleas for basic democratic rights have been crushed by what they consider to be an irreligious cabal, led by the all-powerful military and supported by a succession of secular governments, the justice system, and the media.

The chasm between these two Turkeys seems overwhelming.

As I moved back and forth across the boundaries between the secular and religious communities, I encountered moderates on both sides whose vision is not so dire. These gentler adversaries are to be sure plagued with doubts over each other's intentions. But they believe there is space for flexibility and accommodation. They do not belong to a coordinated movement. Nor are they very vociferous next to the *doctrinaires* of both secularism and Islamism.

My underlying optimism for Turkey's future stems from the bridges I have encountered during my travels, people trying to restore severed links in this fractured society.

As it should be, I found the most open, inquiring spirits in the universities. Nilüfer Narlı, for example, an associate professor of international relations at Marmara University, is making an important contribution to the understanding of Islamists through her first-hand surveys and reports published locally and abroad. I first met this vibrant, serious academic at a meeting of the Turkish Women's Union at İstanbul's Marmara Hotel in the spring of 1995. She had just completed a survey of 500 Islamist university students on the headscarf issue.[1] The Islamic headcovering, she said, had become a symbol of dissidence and protest against the existing regime, which a majority saw as illegitimate, corrupt, and without social justice.

In her study on Women and Islam,[2] Dr. Narlı raises the intriguing question: Why over half a century after Turkish women stepped out of the harem and cast off the veil were some of their daughters clamoring to go back to a segregated world and reviving the cult of veiling? Her answer: The mass migration to cities created large urban slums that fostered cultural alienation, economic imbalances, social rage. For the first time, many young women coming from this new periphery were getting the chance to attend universities—once the domain of the radical left but now dominated by radical Islam. There they put on the veil and underwent what she calls "an Islamic political socialization."

One of Narlı's most important works is a study on Moderate and Radical Islamism in Turkey[3] in which she presents an objective account of the influence of the main Islamic orders and societies in Turkey today. She provides little-known details about Islamic leaders like Erbakan's mentor, the late Sheik Mehmet Zahit Kotku, and Fethullah Gülen, head of the seemingly moderate order of Fethullahis but once a disciple of the Kurdish radical Said-i Nursi. Narlı concludes that the state has few options except to go along with "moderate Islam," in light of the ongoing political instability caused by Kurdish separatists and radical Islamists.

Another academic who has done pioneer work on Turkey's Islamist community is Nilüfer Göle, associate professor of sociology at Bosphorus University. She notes that as early as 1983, Muslim engineers had begun to enter the political power structure as an alternative to leftist intellectuals.[4]

"I wanted to know the other side of my society, which was totally alien to me," Dr. Göle explained, when we met at the fashionable Bebek Hotel by the Bosphorus.[5] Wearing snug jeans and a black turtleneck sweater, she was talking to a couple of French journalists and drifted easily back and forth from French to English.

Contrary to the general secular view, Göle contends that young Islamic women in Turkey put on the headscarf not out of subservience to men but as a means of self-affirmation. Ironically, she asserts these veiled women are "close to Western feminists" in that they reject injustice and body language that makes them an object. They are not opposed to modernization per se, but their struggle is against invasive, dominant Western culture.

Breaking Islamic stereotypes, these modern devout women are getting higher education, writing in Islamic journals, and working outside the home, emphasizes Göle, who has written extensively on this subject.[6] "They believe they can be strong militants in the Islamic movement, continue to work, and keep the traditional role of wife and mother."

The role of bridge in such a polarized society is never easy because sniping can come from all directions. Ergün Yener, a declared Kemalist, has taken on one of the most delicate assignments as president of Fatih University, the only school of higher learning established by a religious group. Fatih was founded in 1996 by the Turkish Health and Therapy Foundation, which is headed by the controversial Islamic leader Fethullah Gülen.

Located on the outskirts of İstanbul near a new luxury housing development, Fatih University is a spacious complex of handsome, modern brick buildings overlooking the Sea of Marmara. The school of liberal arts and sciences opened with 1,650 undergraduates and 110 graduates and has admitted another 1,000 students. Forty-three percent of the students are women, the classes are coeducational, and girls are free to wear what they want, although most prefer headscarves.

Dr. Yener, who completed graduate studies at Cornell and Chapel Hill and taught business administration for fourteen years at the University of Wisconsin, spoke to me enthusiastically of Fatih's new campus, the fourteen state-of-the-art laboratories, new engineering building, and many language courses, including Russian, Georgian, and Japanese.[7] Plans include a sports pavilion, conference hall, electronic library, and four more dormitories. Tuition is half that of other private schools like Koç's university. Most of Fatih's financing comes from hundreds of small businesses and industries.

But the educator acknowledged concerns about the situation. The recent campaign against fundamentalism had unleashed all kinds of pressures on Fatih University. The Board of Higher Education restricted Fatih's new programs, particularly in foreign languages. Some businessmen had been warned they would not be allowed to bid for government contracts if they continued to support Fatih. The major newspapers ignored the school's "secular activities," like modern recitals and lectures on Atatürk.

This mainstream hostility toward Fatih is based on "conjecture and speculation," Dr. Yener stressed. Most of the suspicion is focused on Gülen's education effort, which, besides Fatih, includes over a hundred high schools in Turkey and twice as many schools and universities abroad. Education Ministry inspectors, who keep a close watch on Gülen's establishments, have complained that things are so quiet, "something must be cooking," he said caustically. "I guess they would be happier if they found the students armed."

Although he does not claim to know Gülen well, Dr. Yener believes the religious leader is "sincere" when he preaches tolerance and dialogue. In his television appearances, Gülen has praised Atatürk and says Turks owe him a great deal. Dr. Yener pointed out that Gülen's community has backed different political parties, including True Path and Motherland, always takes "mild" positions on religious questions, and has shown willingness to compromise.

Thus far, Dr. Yener said, he has been given sufficient leeway to carry out his job. He has been free to hire secular professors—"even a freemason." But he admits he doesn't know how long this will last or whether the religious community will want more religious orientation in the school. "Even if Gülen has some ulterior motives, what he has done is to prepare a good future for the country," he concluded.

The most committed—and courageous—people trying to span the divisions in Turkish society are the human rights activists. The Human Rights Association (HRA) and the Human Rights Foundation (HRF) are focused essentially on problems arising from the Kurdish conflict. Women for Women's Human Rights deals with general legal issues and has promoted studies in migrant communities as well as in the Kurdish communities in the southeast. MAZLUMDER (Organization for Human Rights and Solidarity with the Oppressed) concentrates on religious abuses but cooperates with secular organizations. And most recently, AK-DER, a women's antidiscrimination organization, was set up by eleven women, dismissed from their jobs because of headscarves. These groups did not exist when I first covered Turkey in the 1980s, and just their presence and constant denunciations mean progress. At least now there's a voice against abuses that still persist.

For anyone concerned over the human rights situation in Turkey, it has become essential to contact the HRA, which provides the best up-to-date statistics on overall violations, be it gang killings, disappearances, torture cases, political detentions, or the closure of organizations and publications.

When I last saw Akın Birdal, former president of HRA, in the summer of 1997, he told me that despite official promises, there was no improvement in the situation.[8] The disappearances, tortures, and arbitrary arrests continued. Another peace conference had been banned. Only the evacuation of villages had ceased "because there are no more villages left," he said bitterly. Besides the usual abuses, there were new pressures on the association's branch offices in the southeast, more detentions and closures. He pointed to the case of the doctor in charge of the HRF torture treatment center at Adana, who was convicted and fined for refusing to identify 167 torture victims. Birdal himself faced eleven court cases on charges of spreading separatist propaganda and taking part in illegal peace demonstrations.

"They have to change the institutions—the constitutional and legal system," he emphasized. The calm, professorial activist referred in particular to the powerful State Security Courts, which handle cases of alleged terrorism and separatism, as well as specific laws that must be changed. These include the Anti-Terror Law permitting detention for "separatist propaganda," Article 312 of the Criminal Code on incitement to racial or ethnic enmity, Article 159 pertaining to insult to the army or the Republic, and Article 16 of the Press Law that limits freedom of expression.

Every time I interviewed Birdal, I thought it might be the last—because of his outspoken denunciations of the system. But I did not dream he would be the victim of an armed attack in broad daylight in his office. After all, he had become the leading spokesman for human rights in Turkey and was deputy president of the International Human Rights Federation.

On May 12, 1998, two strangers met briefly with Birdal at the HRA headquarters on the upper floor of an office building in Ankara's busy Kavaklıdere district. Returning shortly afterward, the assailants opened fire, hitting the human rights leader with six bullets, and then got away.

Miraculously Birdal survived and was home recovering when I visited the HRA a month later. Thirteen bullet holes were still visible on the office wall and door, but no special security measures were in evidence.

"We had expected some kind of an attack," said Nazmi Gür, secretary-general of the HRA, noting that the attack followed the widely publicized "confession" of a captured Kurdish guerrilla leader, Şemdin Sakik, who accused Birdal and the association of being in the pay of the PKK. (Later Sakik reportedly denied making the accusation.)[9]

Gür said the incident was "related to Susurluk"—code word for the state-run counterguerrillas. He stressed that nine people had been arrested, including a Gendarmerie officer, clearly indicating connections with a state organization.

From his sickbed, Birdal was unrepentant. "No illegal organization can dare to organize an assault of this caliber unless they have a government presence with or behind them," he told the *Turkish Daily News*, adding that the perpetrators wanted to give a message. "This is a threat against all human rights activity and all its members."[10]

I have dealt with Women for Women's Human Rights (WWHR) on all manner of issues from headscarves to female illiteracy, virginity tests, honor killings, and attempts to change man's role as the head of household.

Pınar İlkkaracan, coordinator of WWHR in İstanbul, who has long supported a woman's right to cover herself, was amazed that duly elected Merve Kavakçı had not been allowed to take her seat in Parliament. "One headscarved deputy is hardly a threat to the Republic," she commented, adding that Fazilet had been considerably weakened by the campaign against alleged Islamic extremism.

Every time I went to see Pınar in her office in Suadiye, a modern residential neighborhood on the Asian side of the Bosphorus, she would produce the latest research done by her group. On my last visit, her sister and cocoordinator, İpek İlkkaracan, told me of an important new study they had just completed on the tradition of bride-price in eastern Turkey. The survey shows that this is still a widespread practice—61 percent of the women respondents said their families had received payment from the groom. But contrary to claims by some sociologists that bride-price is advantageous for women, an overwhelming 80 percent of the women questioned were opposed to the custom. When asked why, 50 percent of the women answered: "It's against human rights."

For the İlkkaracans, this was an encouraging sign in Turkey's least developed region, where female literacy is a low 47 percent compared to the national average of 75 percent, and anachronistic traditions have been slow to go.

The most positive development on the human rights scene is that the government now has a cabinet minister in charge of human rights and admits reforms are necessary. In the 1980s, there had been no official agency dealing with human rights, and in fact any mention of the subject was considered tantamount to sedition.

In 1998, I had tried to see Hikmet Sami Türk, then minister of state for human rights, who had the reputation of being committed to the cause. Unfortunately the minister was leaving for the United States to meet with Secretary of State Madeleine Albright, Attorney General Janet Reno, and a host of civil rights organizations. I was told there was no one else who could articulate the government's human rights policy when the minister was absent.

This situation has changed. The following spring, I met the secretariat of the Human Rights Supreme Coordination Council, as the interministerial group charged with human rights is called. Tucked away in an anonymous downtown office building, the secretariat is composed of ten experts from the concerned ministries, who act as liaison with Turkish NGOs and international agencies. Set up by Erbakan (it's rare anyone mentions anything positive coming out of his governance), the Coordination Council was the brainchild of Onür Oymen, a former senior official in the Foreign Ministry and now head of the Social Democratic Party. The main job of the secretariat is to prepare draft laws to update and improve legislation involving human rights and organize courses on human rights for schools and the security forces.

Gürsel Demirok, who heads the secretariat, said that they had eight draft laws and various amendments ready to present to the new government.[11] Among these were a draft law to eliminate the military presence in the State Security Courts (already enacted during the Öcalan trial), a draft law to get rid of the death penalty, stiffer penalties for torture, and changes in controversial Article 8 of the Anti-Terror Law that would guarantee freedom of thought.

Under the proposed changes in Article 8, most of the journalists, the mayor of İstanbul, and other prisoners of conscience would not have gone to jail, according to the secretariat. But it was not at all certain that the National Security Council, which has the last word on such matters, was ready to take such a major step in view of the continued perceived threat from Islamists and Kurdish separatists.

The most persistent human rights question in Turkey today is the Kurdish problem. There was still no public debate on the subject because any reference to Kurds made one liable to legal action, even prison, on charges of separatism.

Nevertheless, some new openings have appeared. On the Kurdish side, the People's Democracy Party (HADEP), whose leadership has been in and out of prison for alleged links to the PKK, has moderated its rhetoric. Speaking at HADEP's convention in late 1998, former chairman Murat Bozlak declared his party was against the idea of separation and wanted to work together with other parties to find solutions to the country's grave problems.[12] But then Bozlak was jailed for separatist propaganda.

In the spring of 1997, the Turkish press publicized a new organization called TOSAV, Turkish acronym for Foundation for the Research of Societal Problems. The founders were said to be a group of Turkish and Kurdish citizens of Turkey who shared grave concerns over the so-called Eastern or Kurdish Question. I recognized the names of several academics and journalists who were trying to bridge the secular-Islamic gap as well as improve Turkish-Kurdish relations.

The president of the new group was Doğu Ergil, Ankara University professor of political science. Ergil had attracted wide attention in 1995 by publishing the first-ever report on the Kurdish problem, commissioned by the Turkish Chambers of Commerce. Although he concluded that the overwhelming majority of Kurds reject separatism and terrorism, he was indicted by the State Security Court. Eventually charges were dropped.

I met the controversial professor at an uptown hotel, where he was holding "a conflict resolution session" (closed to the press) with a score of Turks and Kurds.[13] He told me his survey of Kurdish attitudes revealed that 90 percent of the Kurds do not want independence but want to live in Turkey as Kurds. "That's why it's important to understand Kurdishness, what the protest is about, and why other people are afraid of it," he said.

Ergil argued that Turkey's Kurds "are caught in the middle," victimized by Turkish authorities and terrorized by militant Kurdish separatists. He noted that TOSAV was the first and only Turkish organization that engaged Turks and Kurds in "collaborative activities to support human rights and democracy." TOSAV has received support from the Peace Research Institute of Oslo and the European Center for Common Ground for projects like workshops, TV and radio programs, and publications.

After various meetings, TOSAV produced in the spring of 1999 "A Proposal for Further Democratization and Solving the Kurdish Problem in Turkey."[14] This candid document blames the overly centralized, restrictive, and authoritarian state structure for "the estrangement of society from the state." Emphasizing that the Kurds do not want to carve a second state out of Turkey, the document declares that what the Kurds want are legal guarantees of "the free exercise of their cultural identity." The document advocates "institutionalizing respect for all ethnic and religious values and strengthening democratic institutions," and could also serve as a blueprint for reducing tensions between the secular and religious communities. It concludes with an appeal for public support for the movement "which aims to base our national unity on the principles of pluralism, the rule of law and multiculturalism."

Ceylan Orhun is an idealist, who has been working with Kurdish and other women through ANAKÜLTÜR, a cultural organization that reaches out to rural women.[15] Firmly convinced that NGOs, not politicians, will bring change to society, Ceylan has also taken part in the recent dialogue involving a group of Greek and Turkish women called WINPEACE (Women's Initiative for Peace).

After studying international relations in the United States and graphic design and cuisine in England, Ceylan returned to İstanbul where she began writing articles from a feminist perspective. She admits she panicked after the Islamist victory in municipal elections in 1994. "I thought democracy is in danger. What can I do?" At that point, she became actively involved in the secular women's movement, but she is one of the few activists who has preserved contacts with Islamist women.

It was the "honor killing" of Sevda Gök in February 1996 that led Ceylan to create ANAKÜLTÜR and focus on women of southeastern Turkey, where this kind of family murder is still a common tradition. Sevda Gök was a sixteen-year-old girl from Şanlıurfa, in love with life, Ceylan recounted. The girl had run away from home a couple of times before, but each time the police took her home. Although a virginity test proved Sevda was still intact, an informal court made up of family members decided that she must be executed. A fourteen-year-old cousin stabbed her four times and slit her throat but as a juvenile, received only two years and seven months' prison.

Several members of Parliament, women activists, and journalists, alerted by Ceylan and her friends, attended the trial in Şanlıurfa. But none of the local women showed up. "The men wouldn't let them out," Ceylan said. "That's when I learned that women in the East don't have the right to live."

To honor Sevda Gök, ANAKÜLTÜR held its first Love Feast in Şanlıurfa on International Women's Day, March 7–10, 1997, with the presence of the state minister for women's issues. This time Ceylan carefully prepared the way, making house visits and office calls and contacting local authorities and schools. Fifty Western women from İstanbul, Ankara, and other cities and 500 local women participated in the event, which included an East-West musical exchange, traditional dances, a fashion show, and opportunity for the local women to give vent to their demands.

Several other Love Feasts have been held in southeast and central Anatolia, with the biggest success on International Women's Day 1988 in the remote town of Dargeçit, southeast of Batman. It was a bilingual celebration in Turkish and Kurdish—the first of its kind in the region. An estimated 3,000 local women attended the event, which included performances and workshops led by prominent Turkish writers and artists, local poetry readings, singing, and folk dances.

With each celebration, permanent links have been established. ANAKÜLTÜR volunteers keep in touch with the eastern women, sending them books, clothing, stationery, and, at their special request, hygienic pads. ANAKÜLTÜR has also agreed to market kilims for the Dargeçit Community Center.

Ceylan sees Anatolian women as descendants of those Mother Goddess figures of ancient Anatolia, which she points out means "full of mothers" in Turkish. Her long-term aim is to establish a Mother Goddess Museum and Women's Center. She purchased a site, a traditional mud-brick house in the village of Küçükköy, near the Neolithic ruins of Çatalhöyük, and was ready to begin sewing courses for women. But the project has been delayed because the center was virtually destroyed by a mysterious fire the spring of 1998. Undaunted, Ceylan organized another Love Feast there, this time as part of an international symposium on "Women in Prehistory, Today and Tomorrow."

Initially I questioned the utility of Love Feasts for a population deprived of basic needs like security, decent livelihood, and freedoms. But the human contact has been positive for both Easterners and Western visitors. And these visits have established a precedent in an area that has been considered out-of-bounds for so long.

"We've shown that ordinary people can go East," commented Nur Mardin, who teaches at Bosphorus University and is a member of ANAKÜLTÜR. She noted that after ANAKÜLTÜR's tour to Siirt the spring of 1999, a group of businesspeople from İstanbul went on a tour of the region.[16]

More NGOs are reaching out to the long-neglected southeast and are beginning to cooperate with each other. Women for Women's Human

*Ceylan Orhun (right, with flower in her hair) is the head of a nongovernmental organization, ANAKÜLTÜR, which is reaching out to traditional women. Her friend, Naime Küçükavcılar (with headscarf), comes from a village near Çatalhöyük.*

Rights and KA-DER—the Turkish version of Emily's List—for example, have established links with the Gaziantep Women's Platform. The Turkish Development Foundation has started various projects in the area. The Association in Support of Contemporary Living organized a seminar at Tunceli to put NGO representatives in contact with village chiefs. They have also invited village children from the east to visit İstanbul.

Although some of these initiatives may get lost in the immensity of what is euphemistically known as the southeast problem, one group is becoming a pivotal force for social development in the region. The ÇATOM (Turkish acronym for Multi-Purpose Community Centers) are part of the Southeastern Anatolia Project's (GAP) Social Action Plan, but are to gain autonomy by 2005. The ÇATOM (CHAT-tom) were set up after a 1994 study of Women's Status in the nine GAP provinces showed a serious lag in women's living standards. Problems include the early marriage age of rural women, frequent marriages of blood relatives, persistence of customs like polygamy and bride-price, continuing illiteracy, and domestic violence.

The first ÇATOM was born at Şanlıurfa at the end of 1995. In two years, time, some 5,000 women ages fourteen to fifty took part in activities at fifteen ÇATOMs, according to Aygül Fazlıoğlu, who supervises the centers from GAP's headquarters in Ankara.[17] Now there are twenty-one ÇATOM around the region, offering health, education, and income-generating programs. The number of centers is planned to triple by the year 2005, and GAP has plans to open similar centers for men.

"One secret behind the success of the ÇATOM is that we're flexible; we don't have a rigid model but ask the women what they want," Ms. Fazlıoğlu told me. She stressed that the ÇATOM were not just another government bureaucracy but collaborative efforts, involving various NGOs and international agencies and businesses (like UNICEF and Benetton), local authorities, business groups, and volunteers.

When I visited the Şanlıurfa ÇATOM, I saw twenty-seven young women busily sewing, some by hand, others by machine, on blouses, dresses, baby clothes, and bed linen. Most of the women were Kurds from the neighborhood and wore traditional colorful headscarves. The staff of six local women spoke in Kurdish as well as Turkish.

"The participants bring their own materials and decide what they want to make; we just teach them how to do it," Seçil Arslan, a social worker, said. At present the ÇATOM women sell their work by word of mouth, but now they want help in organizing a cooperative, she said.[18] A few of the girls have found jobs in the local cotton mill but most prefer to work at home or in the ÇATOM.

"Most of the older women don't know Turkish and are learning how to read and write," the social worker noted. They generally came with their children for health care services. Arslan said the ÇATOM was trying to find a bigger place so they could set up a game room for the children. She showed me a rudimentary kitchen where cooking classes are held and women are taught how to cook vegetables, not commonly available in the area before irrigation.

The ÇATOM have had no trouble with men in the area, Ms. Arslan said, countering the general notion that southeastern men adamantly oppose the advancement of women. "The ÇATOM staff make house calls first and explain what the centers are all about," she said. "Then the men are not a problem; they want their women to learn how to improve the family's living conditions."

Among the most influential voices for conciliation are those of journalists. I've known İlnur Çevik, *Turkish Daily News* editor-in-chief, since the early 1980s and found him to be an aggressive, open newsman of the American school. In recent years, he has been widely criticized by secularists as having "sold out" to the Islamists. I have closely followed his paper, and although he did present the Islamist side of the story, he criticized their blunders and excesses. He also fully reported the military point of view (so much so that some people say he is in the pay of the military) and that of secular politicians.

In our private conversations, Çevik said his paper had supported Refah because it was "a clean, reformist party."[19] But he openly attacked Refah when it backed its coalition partner against parliamentary investigations into corruption scandals.

Perhaps before anyone else, Çevik repeatedly warned the secular authorities against a generalized clampdown that could "alienate the moderate Islamic masses." When we met during the offensive against the Erbakan government in the spring of 1997, Çevik expressed concern that the secular establishment was engaged in a witch hunt against Islamists. Secularists, including the military, had made the basic mistake of putting all Muslim activists into one basket, he told me. This would have the adverse effect of uniting moderates with zealots in self-defense. If it appeared they were trying to "get" all Islamists, it could be interpreted as a campaign against Islam and this could provoke a violent reaction.

Çevik repeatedly argued against closure of Refah, but his was a lonely voice. When the party was finally closed in early 1998, Çevik wrote, "So is Refah dead and gone? Maybe the name is buried in history for good, but its ideals are far from dead. If Refah was the party of Islamic radicalism, then of course it is dead and gone. But if Refah stood for the rights of the deprived masses who are facing serious hardships because of the current economic disaster that we are going through in this country, then it is far from dead."[20]

Over the years, the primary cause Çevik defended was the need for true democratic reform. In one of his characteristically blunt editorials, he wrote: "The state forces have always feared that real freedoms and rights such as those given to citizens in Western democracies would lead to the creation of a system that would threaten the Republic. So they have been using separatism and terrorism in Turkey as an alibi and say that Turks can only be granted such freedoms and rights once the 'threat of terrorism' is eliminated. When you have a lack of democracy, you have political favoritism supported by the state, you have corruption which cannot be questioned and you have irregularities which are covered up."[21]

Fehmi Koru is a devout Muslim who studied theology and journalism and received his master's degree from Harvard's Center for Middle Eastern Studies. I first met him in 1995, when he was Ankara bureau chief for the leading Islamic daily *Zaman*. Now he is a regular columnist for the *Turkish Daily News* and the Islamic daily *Yeni Şafak* as well as political commentator for the Islamic TV Channel 7.

Koru is courageous. In the heat of the secular assault on Erbakan's government, Islamic-led businesses, and Refah's mayors, Koru wrote that "people, institutions and organizations are being witch-hunted."[22] He compared the situation to the "temporary insanity" of the Joseph McCarthy period.

The columnist views his world as a Muslim and sometimes sees news that other people ignore. For example, he wrote about three recent studies, showing that Turkey's Muslims are religious but not fanatical.[23] Koru's ability was to note an important trend by putting together these separate studies by the TESEV Foundation, the Konrad Adenauer Foundation, and ANAR, an Islamic think tank.

Despite his Islamic perspective, Koru is a keen political commentator. Analyzing the April 18, 1999, elections, he wrote that Ecevit had won not only because of Öcalan's capture, but because of his "non-quarrelsome election campaign and his honest statesman image and careless attitude towards worldly values."[24] The MHP, Koru said, was rewarded for not being in Parliament and gained from the weaknesses demonstrated by the two secular conservative parties and critical mistakes by Refah and its successor. "The closure of the RP (Refah) and the anxiety caused by expectations that the FP (Fazilet) would suffer the same fate have pushed the FP supporters towards different political alternatives," he wrote. But he cautioned against seeing the elections as a victory for the February 28 process, that is, the military-led drive against alleged Islamic extremists, noting that the Republican People's Party, a major supporter of the anti-Islamist campaign, had suffered important losses.

In the broader Turkish press, Etyen Mahcupyan, a university professor who frequently writes columns and appears on television, is widely respected as an independent thinker, someone who is trying to further understanding in this fragmented society. He has backed Islamist demands for the freedom to wear headscarves in universities and the opening of a land route for pilgrims going to Mecca. But he supported the secularists in their opposition to Erbakan's plan to build a mosque in Taksim Square, which he said "would change the nature of the city."

A Turk of Armenian origin, Mahcupyan contends that both radical secularists and radical Islamists are authoritarian, "but the Islamists will listen to other opinions whereas you can't talk to secular extremists."

We met in his wife's office in İstanbul in the spring of 1997, when Erbakan was still prime minister. "The secularist leadership feels threatened, that it has been pushed aside and has nothing to lean on but its authoritarian ideology and the military," Mahcupyan said.[25] "The Islamists are gaining from being in government. Islamic people are coming out of their houses now. They feel they're living for the first time in 70 years. They are accustomed to being ruled. Now they want to show off."

Mahcupyan was not at all worried that Turkey's Islamists would try to follow Iran's direction. Iranian Shiism emphasizes "the deeper hidden meanings of Islam," whereas most Turks are Hannefi Sunnites, whose views are "freer, more worldly, more individualistic," he said.

Like many other Turkish intellectuals, Mahcupyan was attracted in 1994 to the New Democracy Movement and its dynamic young leader Cem Boyner. The number one item on their agenda was the Kurdish question. But the party collapsed in the local elections, not winning enough votes to get into Parliament.

"We felt the old regime could not go on, that changes were taking place everywhere in South Africa and the Eastern bloc, but we didn't realize how difficult it was to change things in Turkey," Mahcupyan admitted. Pointing out that current polls said 35 percent of the public didn't like any of the constituted parties, Mahcupyan said what was necessary was to create a new political entity that could cover secular and Islamic concerns.

"Everyone is waiting for a new leader," he concluded.

Initially I believed that President Demirel could be the conciliator needed to help this secular state come to terms with its Islamic grass roots. He had acted judiciously in a potentially explosive situation, calling on Erbakan, as leader of the largest party in Parliament, to form the government in 1996. Of course he had the disastrous example of Algeria, which has been engulfed in civil war since 1992, when Islamists had similarly won the election but were barred by the military from taking office.

In an interview in the Presidential Palace, Demirel made it clear that he did not favor any kind of compromise with the Islamists, and Prime Minister Erbakan was expected to toe the secular line.[26] "This is a secular country, if somebody is using Islam and its influence for political purposes it is wrong," he told me. "The basic principles of the Turkish Republic are set out in the constitution, which stipulates that the Turkish Republic is a democratic, secular, and social legal state. This cannot be amended, nor can an amendment even be proposed."

Subsequently Demirel has done little to curb the relentless drive against Refah and other Islamic circles. Nor, as far as I know, has he stood up to the military and other radical secularists or cautioned them against an anti-Islamist campaign that verges on religious persecution.

For a time, I thought former prime minister Yılmaz and his deputy prime minister Bülent Ecevit were ready to lead a movement of reconciliation with the Islamic sector of the population. It was spring of 1998, when the military had stepped up pressures on the secular government to implement the "antifundamentalist" measures.

Former prime minister Yılmaz went further to openly defy the military, declaring that it was the government's task to fight fundamentalism and there was no need for a military watchdog. The Turkish press suggested that Yılmaz's show of independence was out of electoral considerations rather than conviction.

The chief of General Staff issued a firm statement to the effect that the constitution gave the armed forces the obligation to defend the Republic against all kinds of threats. He contended that not only the armed forces but the Turkish nation has agreed that "the reactionary ideology which aims to found 'a state based on *Sharia* poses the gravest threat to the democratic, secular, social welfare state. . . .'"

Backing down from his brave stand, Yılmaz endorsed the military position. He also moved rapidly to produce a comprehensive package of anti-fundamentalist legislation, including a reversal of his flexible position on the headscarf issue.

I had known Ecevit as a fighter for democracy since the 1980 military coup. This mild-mannered, genteel poet had been fighting against military interventions since the first coup in 1960 and was jailed three times for his struggle against the military regime. Now he was publicly admonishing the military over their fundamentalism scare. He also defended Fethullah Gülen against charges of radicalism, emphasizing that Gülen's schools in Azerbaijan and other countries in the area had saved them from falling under Iranian influence.[27]

When the military brought new pressures on the government to crack down on fundamentalism, Ecevit again spoke out. "Fundamentalism can be prevented not by restricting democracy but by expanding democracy," Ecevit declared, adding that the real way to fight fundamentalism is to fight poverty, corruption, and injustice.[28]

But then the armed forces issued a firm warning to the government that there should be no letup in the fight against fundamentalism. Ecevit agreed and dropped the issue. It was clear he felt he could not challenge the military at that time.

Now as prime minister, Ecevit seems to be even more cautious. Clearly in response to a warning from the military, Ecevit and his party drew the line on headscarves over the Merve Affair. Yet when security services launched a new crusade against Fethullah Gülen, Ecevit once again defended the religious educator.

Ecevit has put together what was generally said to be a serious and competent cabinet on the basis of a no-nonsense program. One popular nomination was that of Saadettin Tantan as minister of interior (whom I had met earlier as the dynamic mayor of İstanbul's Fatih district).

My friend Sedat Ergin, Ankara bureau chief of the leading daily *Hürriyet,* stressed that former police chief Tantan was known for his integrity. "This is the time to clean up the mafia extensions in bureaucracy, politics, and the business world," Ergin wrote. "And Tantan is the kind of person who would not hesitate to do that."[29]

Ecevit's Democratic Left–Ultra Nationalist–Conservative coalition, with 351 deputies out of 550, easily won a vote of confidence on its program, which listed among its priorities reforms in the banking and tax laws, social security system, and local administration. The program also called for restructuring State Security Courts, limiting immunity of deputies and cabinet members, and an intensive struggle against terrorism and gangs.

Clearly bowing to military exigencies, the new government emphasized its determination to prevent the use of religious feelings for political purposes. It actually said that measures would be taken to prevent headscarves from becoming a political symbol in state offices. Although Ecevit and his coalition partners have all expressed flexibility on religious garb in the past, they were apparently not ready to confront the military on the issue.

If Ecevit succeeds in consolidating his government, restoring political stability, and undertaking essential economic restructuring, then he just may be in a position to introduce real democratic reforms. This is the intent of his recent declarations.

Thus far, no political leader has had the forcefulness to say if Turkey is a democracy, there must be freedom of expression—for everyone, including Islamists and ethnic Kurds. No politician has shown the determination to say to the militant secularists: Stop, Turkey cannot exclude from public life an important segment of the population on religious grounds. No civilian leader has persuaded the military commanders that Europe cannot accept Turkey as a full-fledged member as long as generals are in command of civil authority.

And no Islamic leader has demonstrated the will, courage, and ability to convince the secular society that Islamists are not intent on destroying Atatürk's Republic.

# 19 ⌐

---

## Conclusion:
## What Next?

---

For a long time, followers of Atatürk thought he had solved the problem of political Islam when he mapped out the direction for the secular, indivisible, westernized Turkish Republic. The Turkish elite has fully embraced Western mores and appears as much at home in London or New York as İstanbul. Turkey is an active member of NATO and various European organizations and is convinced it would have joined the European Union by now were it not for its historic rival Greece.

But it is increasingly clear that Atatürk's revolution has not penetrated as far and wide as many Turks and foreign observers assumed. The public outcry over Islamic dress and schools demonstrates that a significant part of the population is pious or believes that religious practices should be respected. Furthermore, the Islamists' persistent pursuit of influence and the occasional outbursts of violence are indications that the worldwide Islamic revival has found fertile terrain among religious activists and the inhabitants of disadvantaged rural areas and urban slums in Turkey.

Although it ebbs and flows, a struggle is taking place between two very different concepts of life. In the name of democracy, the military and their civilian allies forced the resignation of an elected Islamist-led government and have launched an all-out offensive against anything that smacks of militant Islam. In the process, basic democratic norms have been violated, which has spawned deep resentment within the country and led to strains with Turkey's democratic partners.

On the other hand, an Islamist movement is making use of democratic institutions to try to establish a more Islamic society. Turkey's Islamists promise that should they come to power, the rights of the nonreligious community would be guaranteed. But secularists are skeptical, pointing to profoundly undemocratic Islamist regimes like Afghanistan, Pakistan, Iran, and Sudan.

At present, archsecularists are in control and working to consolidate Atatürk's laic republic. They are determined to cut down all individuals or organizations that show any inclination toward political Islam, even at the risk of sacrificing Turkey's democratic credentials with their Western friends.

Islamists, encouraged by their brief period in government, are seeking ways to return to power. Leaders of the Islamic movement have been careful to control their own hotheads and portray each new assault as an infringement of their democratic rights.

While these two rival forces pursue their power struggle, precious time, energy, and talent are wasted. None of the country's major problems has been resolved: the Kurdish question, tremendous income disparities, basic human rights, political instability, hostile relations with neighbors, and above all, the deep divisions among Turks.

Contrary to most predictions, early elections in April 1999 brought to power two nationalist parties, leaving the pro-Islamic Fazilet in third place. This did not necessarily signify a decline in the Islamic movement, since Fazilet came in first in municipal elections. Rather, it signaled a radicalization among religious voters. Concerned over the attempts to close Fazilet down and frustrated with its moderation, voters turned to the Nationalist Action Party, which had more forcefully supported the headscarf movement and opposed the closure of religious schools. This was no victory for the anti-Islamic forces but a warning that the public would resist attempts to circumscribe Islamic practices.

From my personal observations, the two extremes—those who want to establish Islamic law and those who are determined to stamp out any manifestation of political Islam—are still a minority.

Within recent years, I have seen some progress toward a respectful coexistence between Western modernism and Islamic piety, although it has been overshadowed by militants on both sides.

The new generation of Islamic Turks whom I have come to know are generally forward-looking, hardworking, capable people who want modern education for their children and do not eschew Western technology. Even the most devout headscarved young women want to complete their studies and find jobs as well as raise a family. They are people like İnci and Murat Mercan, deeply religious and committed to defend their beliefs, but tolerant of others' convictions. They are modern, moderate, patriotic, critical of hard-line Islamists, and strongly opposed to Kurdish separatism.

I first met İnci, who works for a municipal think tank in Ankara, during the headscarf crisis at the universities, and we have had lengthy conversations on several occasions since. İnci wears a headscarf, but her mother, sister, and sister-in-law do not, and she will let her eight-year-old daughter decide whether to cover herself. For İnci, the headscarf is not a political symbol but a symbol of freedom of religion.

"If ever a pro-Islamic party won the majority in Turkey, it would not impose religious dress," İnci insisted at our last meeting over Sunday brunch at the popular Turkish Daily News Café in Ankara.[1] "The Iranians are wrong to impose the *chador* and what the Taliban are doing in Afghanistan—keeping girls out of school and the workplace—cannot be called Islam," she emphasized.

Her husband, Murat, who teaches at Bilkent's Business School and is an adviser to Fazilet's reformist leader Gül, conceded that the party had suffered significant losses in the 1999 legislative elections, and a change in leadership and policies was "inevitable." He was worried about the revival of a xenophobic nationalism with the rise of the Nationalist Action Party, but his main concern was the growing Kurdish underclass in ghettoes around Adana and other cities.

"What I fear is a conflict between the two militant nationalisms, Kurdish and Turkic," he said. None of his Islamic-minded friends favors Öcalan or the PKK but they fear that if the death sentence is implemented, the Kurds could create serious problems that would split the country.

"Historically we used to live together with shared religion and common goals," he said. "Religion used to be the main value but we lost that commonality. We have put a lot of pressure on the Kurds. Only enhanced democracy can cure these divisions and restore common values and aspirations."

Secularists—particularly women—are still worried about Islamic radicalism and the prospect of an Iranian-type revolution. Any kind of Islamist gesture will trigger panic, like headscarved Merve Kavakçı's much-publicized entrance into Parliament. And so it was not surprising that more than 500 prominent women representing forty organizations rushed to Atatürk's Mausoleum once again to protest headscarves.

*İnci and Murat Mercan, moderate, modern, and pious, in front of Karum, popular shopping center in Ankara, festively decorated with the national flag and Atatürk's portrait for Children's Day.*

But most secularists I know were uncomfortable about the Merve Affair. While they generally agreed that Merve had pushed the limits in appearing in Islamic garb in the national Parliament, some considered her a hapless tool in the hands of the wily Erbakan. Many thought she had been given undue attention by secular politicians and media, who had unintentionally turned her into a martyr.

An artist friend, Aişe Zadil, who belongs to several secular-led organizations including ANAKÜLTÜR, was critical of the Merve protests as "overreaction." She was afraid that demonstrations like the 500 Women's March would only provoke headscarf militants to organize marches of their own. And since any headscarf protest would be quashed, the devout women would be seen as victims by many Turks and world opinion.

Aişe feels that rather than marching to Atatürk, secular NGOs should concentrate their energies on the positive activities that they have undertaken, like education, job placement, and help against family violence. "It's a long-term investment but this just may be one of the reasons for the drop in the Islamic Party's vote," she suggested.

Another secular friend, Nur Mardin, who teaches marketing research and statistics at Bosphorus University, believes that as a legislator, Merve had to obey the rules—whether they are right or wrong. "If she thought they were wrong she should take her place in Parliament and try to change them."[2]

Nur is open and naturally tolerant, the kind of person who will reach out to Islamists and try to understand them. I remember she was uneasy when the pro-Islamic Refah came to power in 1995 because she didn't know what were their intentions. But she expressed open admiration for the dedication and hard work of the party cadres. She was always comprehensive of any headscarved students (before the ban) and has participated in university symposia to improve contacts with Islamic women.

As a member of ANAKÜLTÜR, she worked on an exhibit of Kurdish women's handicrafts from the ÇATOM in the southeast and helped market their work in İstanbul. She thinks these relations can be expanded.

Now—like my Islamic friends the Mercans—Nur is worried about the Nationalist Action Party. "I don't trust the MHP's present tolerant face; I can't forget the group's fascist origin. They're not open and won't take to social reform."

A recent survey on "Political Islam in Turkey" confirms my own impressions of the continued religiosity of Turkish society, after three-quarters of a century of firm secular rule. But it also shows the openness of religious Turks. The study concludes that although the general population is religious, only an insignificant minority wants to establish an Islamic state. I obtained details from coauthor Binnaz Toprak, president of the Department of Political Science and International Relations at Bosphorus University.[3] The study was based on a national sample of 3,054 respondents and commissioned by the respected independent Turkish Economic and Social Studies Foundation (TESEV).

Professor Toprak noted an overwhelming 97 percent said their religion was Islam, whereas only 2.16 percent said they were nonbelievers. But only 35.5 percent identified themselves as Muslim; 53.9 percent said Turk or citizen of Turkey, and 4.3 percent said Muslim and Turk.

The observance of religious practices is widespread: 92.2 percent said they fast during the holy month of Ramadan; 62.4 percent of the men attend Friday prayers at the mosque (women are not expected to attend); 46 percent said they perform the *namaz* or prayers five times a day.

But the majority, or 67.2 percent, didn't want religion to interfere with state affairs, politics, or public life. Although 21.2 percent said they would support an Islamic state based on *Sharia,* only 10.7 percent favored changing the present civil code, which stipulates one wife, to the Islamic law that allows four wives. Only 14 percent wanted to change the civil divorce law, and 13.9 percent would change the inheritance law and adopt Islamic laws, which favor men.

Probably the most significant message of the study was tolerance: 89.2 percent said those of other religions could be good people, and 53.1 percent said atheists could be good. People should still be considered Muslims, even if they do not pray, according to 85.6 percent; or if they do not fast, according to 82 percent; or if they drink alcohol, according to 66.6 percent.

On the burning headscarf issue, 76.7 percent of the respondents said university students should be free to cover their heads, and 74.7 percent said civil servants should be able to wear headscarves. A significant 83.5 percent were not bothered by people wearing headscarves, and 66.3 percent were not offended by miniskirts.

This is hardly the portrait of a country engulfed by Islamic fundamentalism; nor is it a country cowed by secular fundamentalism. It is, however, scientific proof that despite increasingly aggressive secular policies, the broader Muslim community is still there and will have to be recognized sooner or later. These Muslims have been enriched by Atatürk's progressive, nationalistic heritage, yet seek to preserve Islamic moral values.

It is also strong evidence that Turkey is not Iran and that an Iranian-type revolution is unlikely. To be sure, there are similarities between these two former great empires, Muslim countries that fell into decline in the nineteenth century and suffered the encroachment of foreign powers. In the twentieth century, the elite of both countries wholeheartedly embraced Western civilization, including the emancipation of women, and tried to forge their own new secular nationalism to counter what was seen as retrograde Islamic, Arabic influences. Both the modern Turkish Republic and Iranian monarchy achieved rapid economic growth but failed to satisfy the needs of their peoples. Similarly the secular establishments of the two countries underestimated the resilience of Islam.

But beyond these analogies, the specifics are very different. There is no *shah* in Turkey, no supreme ruler who holds all political power. Turkey is not a police state with a detested, omnipresent secret police keeping tabs on all dissent. Although income disparities are great, Turkey is not an oil state, whose wealth is in the hands of the ruling elite.

There is the obvious difference: The majority of Turks belong to the orthodox Sunni branch of Islam, whereas most Iranians are Shiites who dispute the Sunni version of the succession to the prophet Mohammed. (This is no guarantee against militant fundamentalism; Afghanistan's radical Taliban are Sunnis.) More important, in Turkey's social structure, there is no influential clergy that must confer legitimacy on the country's leadership. Above all there is no Khomeini in the wings, no powerful populist cleric to challenge the secular authority from self-exile with a constant barrage of sermons, statements, and decrees.

Furthermore, unlike Iran, for over half a century Turkey has developed democratic institutions, which, although flawed, provide hope and channels for change. There are real political parties and generally free elections, a judiciary that often corrects political actions, a powerful, vocal press, independent labor unions and management associations, and a broad array of nongovernmental organizations, including human rights groups that dare to denounce official abuses.

Contrary to Iran, Turkey's armed forces have always played an important political role in defense of the state. Turkish military leaders command broad respect at home and are not generally viewed as the tool of a repressive regime, although in recent years, many Kurds and Islamists would disagree.

In an insightful column in the *New York Times*, Philip Taubman describes Turkey as "a military democracy," a contradiction in terms, of course.[4] "Elections are fair, the press is relatively free and the rule of law prevails to a point, as long as the generals permit," Taubman wrote. "When they believe Turkey's national security or its secular traditions are threatened, either by Kurdish separatism in the Southeast or by domestic Islamic politics, no freedom is safe."

Emphasizing that the generals "underestimate" the common sense of their countrymen and the durability of the secular tradition, Taubman continued: "This society is not ready to embrace Islamic fundamentalism or toss aside its Western Conventions." He concluded that the generals should view the Islamist party as "an outlet for legitimate concerns that will only intensify if suppressed."

I firmly believe that for all their good intentions, the military have weakened Turkish democracy by their regular interventions and constant supervision. They should show their faith in Atatürk's revolution. A large segment of the Turkish population—probably the majority—has clung stubbornly to tradition and religious beliefs. But these devout citizens have also been imbued with Atatürk's strong sense of nationalism, desire for progress, and admiration for Western values. Harsh imposition of secular rule may have stirred widespread resentment, but this can be corrected by more flexibility. Turks do not want to go backward. Even the most radical Islamists do not envy regimes in Iran or Pakistan or Saudi Arabia.

Turkey's Islamists have demonstrated they are willing to engage in party politics, they are capable of compromise, and can turn the other cheek in the face of arbitrary sanctions. The younger generation of Islamic politicians has expressed a commitment to democracy and publicly welcomed women into the party leadership. They have acknowledged that the language of extremism got them nowhere. Even militants claim they subscribe to "the Ottoman tradition" of guarantees for the rights of non-Muslims and nonpracticing Muslims. They have recognized that the Islamic world is not an alternative to Europe, that when their rights have been abused, it was Western democratic leaders and organizations, not Muslim brothers, who offered solidarity.

Secularists, on the other hand, have shown through multiple civic groups like the Anatolian Modern Education Foundation and some public institutions like the Southeast Anatolian Project that they can reach out to the Islamic community while respecting their beliefs and customs. Granted, for some secularists the spirit is more competitive than conciliatory, but the results are positive.

Leaders of the business community have urged democratic reforms and more social justice as the way to confront the Islamic movement and continued Kurdish unrest. Politicians have openly called for an end to human rights abuses by security forces and investigations into the web of complicity between the state and criminal gangs spawned by the Kurdish war. Even the armed forces have come to the conclusion that military action alone cannot resolve the Kurdish problem, but social and economic reforms are needed.

The last elections brought a little-publicized opportunity to the Kurdish scene with the election for the first time of a number of Kurdish mayors. "A process of tolerance and compromise has begun in Turkey," the new mayor of Van, Şahabettin Özaslaner, told the press. "We can criticize the regulations and the Constitution of the state, just like the other political parties. We can seek modifications if we find them anti-democratic; however I will be loyal to the existing Constitution and regulations and carry out my duties."[5]

These positive developments do not mean that Turkey is ready for dialogue with either Islamists or Kurdish nationalists.

On the contrary, Bülent Ecevit's secular-nationalist government was barely in place when another virulent campaign against Islamic activists was launched. This time the target was the gentle Fethullah Gülen, the religious leader, who has eschewed political Islam in favor of developing education. The campaign reeked of artificiality and seemed aimed to build Gülen up as a kind of scheming Khomeini to better cut him down.

This new anti-Islamic witch hunt coincided with attempts to clean up the police and administration by the new minister of interior, Saadettin Tantan. Clamping down on illegal wire-tapping, Tantan sent Ankara's director general of security on mandatory leave and suspended eleven police officers from their duties. The police, who were caught monitoring telephones at the Presidential Palace and other government and military offices, justified their actions as part of investigations into clandestine activities of Gülen's religious order.

Subsequently, various secret reports and cassettes leaked to the media depicted Gülen and his followers as a major threat to the secular state. One intelligence report described the broad reach of Gülen's empire, which was said to include 238 high schools and six universities in fifty-four foreign countries; 292 high schools and a university in Turkey; and 500 companies, 200 foundations, a TV channel, and a daily newspaper.[6] This network was portrayed as a sinister force spreading like a cancer through the vital organs of the state and the country's youth. Specifically Gülen was accused of bringing up some 3,000 of his students as suicide commandos to prepare for the Islamic revolution. Even worse, he was denounced for allegedly encouraging his sympathizers to infiltrate military and police schools.[7] The leaked documents, which also contained blasphemous attacks on Islam, were purportedly the work of Ankara police intelligence, national intelligence, and military intelligence services.

Some respected voices in the mainstream press questioned the libelous campaign. *Sabah*'s Necati Doğru wrote: "All these years Fethullah 'Hoca' Gülen has been the religious crutches of the state. Now all of a sudden he is being accused of trying to seize control of the state administrative and judicial organs.[8]

"What has changed to bring about this new attitude?" Doğru asked, raising suspicions as to the motives of this new campaign. "Are certain circles trying to hit some other people while they are ostensibly directing their fire at Gülen? For example, are they trying to punish President Süleyman Demirel and Prime Minister Bülent Ecevit for having condoned the Gülen movement to become entrenched?"

Although some press reports revived old stories of Gülen's being on Saudi Arabia's payroll, others suggested that he was being used by the United States in its strategy to counter German, Iranian, and Chinese influences in Central Asia.

Gülen, in the United States for medical treatment, firmly denied that he had ever thought of taking over the state. In remarks to his daily newspaper *Zaman*, he noted that in the past he had been cleared of similar charges by the courts. He then delivered a pointed warning: "In Turkey, almost every Muslim risks becoming indignant because of the attacks which are made against Islam in the name of reactionaryism."[9]

When the incendiary reports first began to circulate, Prime Minister Ecevit, who has firmly defended Gülen's education mission, reportedly declared he was unconvinced by the allegations.

Only three weeks later, after the religious leader had been thoroughly dragged through the mud by the main television news shows and newspapers, the military distanced itself from the controversy. The National Security Council and the General Staff issued statements denying that they had anything to do with any of the reports or videocassettes that had been publicized by the media.

Nevertheless, after its regular monthly meeting in late June, the National Security Council issued a firm communiqué stressing that "the measures taken against anti-secularism would be enhanced and the state would make no concessions against reactionary groups and adversaries of the regime."[10] It was reported that the government did not challenge the allegations against Gülen made by the military leaders at the meeting.

*Turkish Daily News* editor İlnur Çevik denounced the "smear campaign" against Gülen and said it was part of a power struggle within the state apparatus. Clearly out of patience with yet another anti-Islamic offensive, Çevik wrote his sharpest editorial yet under the headline "Do We Really Need an Elected Parliament?"[11]

Every month the civilian and military leaders of Turkey get together at a meeting of the all-powerful National Security Council (MGK) and make a series of decisions which are then presented to the public as "recommendations" to the government. In essence these are direct orders of the MGK to the government and whenever a prime minister drags his feet in implementing the "recommendations," he either gets into trouble or is reprimanded by the power centers in Turkey.

We have seen this before with banned Prime Minister Necmettin Erbakan and former Prime Minister Mesut Yılmaz. We now see today that Prime Minister Bülent Ecevit is also being put on the spot. . . .

The extraordinary situation in Turkey has the characteristics of a post-coup period while certain freedoms are restricted. People are being accused and even persecuted in an arbitrary manner. . . .

Let us end all this confusion. If we are to have a coup and a military administration, let us have it. Then we will know the rules of the game, and we will all act accordingly. . . .

If we are to have a democratic parliamentary system then let us have that. But let us stop trying to impose an authoritarian system on Turkey while we pretend that we are a parliamentary democracy. Let the MGK be an advisory body and not the sole authority that takes vital decisions and demands their implementation.

But there was no visible letup in the campaign against pro-Islamic quarters that spring of 1999. Despite Fazilet's moderation and attempts to distance itself from a religious agenda, the chief prosecutor pressed ahead with legal action to close the party down for being a "replica" of Refah and all the other outlawed pro-Islamic parties.

The Council of State also moved to put an end to the inflammatory headscarf controversy. Turkey's highest administrative court ruled at the end of May that university students could not wear headscarves in schools, just as civil servants could not wear headscarves in their workplaces. Putting the stamp of approval on this decision from the highest authority in the Republic, Chief of General Staff General Hüseyin Kıvrıkoğlu was reported saying that the headscarf affair was over.

But of course the fallout continued. The Education Ministry embarked on a summer housecleaning. In Ankara alone, it was reported that some 600 teachers were being dismissed, 500 accused of involvement in fundamentalist activities and 100 for allegedly engaging in propaganda for the PKK. At the same time, three women journalists announced they had been denied press cards by the state Press Commission—merely for wearing headscarves.

The Öcalan affair put the Kurdish problem at the top of Turkey's agenda. Officially there was no change in policy: Öcalan and his Kurdistan Workers Party (PKK) are terrorists with whom one doesn't negotiate. But there are indications that the government is seeking a way out of the Kurdish imbroglio.

The facts of the case have been widely reported in Turkey and abroad. The Turkish military, who had delivered devastating blows against PKK guerrillas in southeastern Turkey and northern Iraq, decided in the fall of 1998 to strike against the Kurdish leader in his longtime sanctuary in the Syrian capital.

The Turkish General Staff announced it would hold military maneuvers close to the Syrian border. At the same time, retired military officers, political voices, and the media warned Damascus that if it did not expel Öcalan and the PKK, the Turkish army would move in a matter of hours. In a gesture of mediation, Egyptian president Hosni Mubarak flew to Ankara and was told by President Demirel that the case was serious.

"The Syrians threw Öcalan out even before the Turkish maneuvers began and so Turkey cancelled the exercise," Sedat Ergin, Ankara bureau chief for the leading daily *Hürriyet,* told me.[12]

Then began Öcalan's futile shuttle around Europe in search of political asylum. But no European country, not even Russia, Italy, or Greece, which had openly supported the PKK, was willing to harbor the Kurdish guerrilla leader, apparently out of fear of Turkish wrath. The best Athens could do was to provide the PKK chief with shelter at its embassy in Nairobi, while trying to find a country that would take him.

Nairobi, bristling with American intelligence since the August 7, 1998, terrorist bombing of the U.S. embassy, was clearly a Greek gaffe. On February 16, 1999, Öcalan was snatched from a Greek escort by a Turkish intelligence team, with help from the Nairobi police, and flown back to Turkey.

Prime Minister Ecevit's announcement the following day was characteristically modest, giving credit to the Turkish Intelligence Organization and the Turkish General Staff for the operation. The brunt of his message was addressed to Öcalan's young supporters, urging them to take advantage of the Act of Repentance now before Parliament.

"While you were made accessories to murder for years, while you were living in misery in mountain caves, the person you thought was your leader was living in luxury in posh mansions," Ecevit said. "You are now at dead end. Surrender yourselves to the justice of the state."[13]

Washington, which considers Öcalan a terrorist, denied direct involvement in his capture, but was widely believed to have provided crucial intelligence. While Turks celebrated what was called a historic victory, Kurdish exiles held violent protest demonstrations across Europe.

There were few surprises at Öcalan's month-long trial before a State Security Court on the prison island of İmralı in the Sea of Marmara, south of İstanbul. Press coverage was limited for security considerations, but foreign diplomats and twelve parliamentarians from the Council of Europe were permitted to attend although they were not given observer status.

From the outset, the Kurdish guerrilla leader accepted responsibility for the fifteen-year insurgency in which some 40,000 people have been killed and apologized to families of the victims. The thrust of his defense was that the court should spare his life so he could work to end the senseless conflict.

What would happen if he died? Öcalan reportedly asked the court. Answering his own question, he warned that the PKK would send out thousands of fighters and hundreds of thousands of people would die. Then he made his offer. If the judges gave him and the PKK a chance, he could get the fighters down from the mountains within three months. Unmoved by his change of heart, the court convicted Öcalan of treason and on June 29, sentenced him to death.

While awaiting the conclusion of the appeals process, Öcalan has continued to play a conciliatory role. From his cell, he called on his forces to cease fire and pull out of Turkey by September 1, 1999, and urged the Turkish authorities to recognize the Kurdish people as a minority with cultural rights. In response, the PKK leadership declared in early August 1999 that it would comply with Öcalan's bid to withdraw and announced plans to convert their guerrilla movement into a political organization.

"Political struggle is seen as necessary to make way for a democratic development instead of an armed struggle which is not seen as vital anymore," Osman Öcalan, a PKK leader and brother of the jailed chief, said in an interview to the Kurdish daily *Özgür Politika*.[14]

One positive by-product of the trial was Parliament's agreement to a constitutional amendment removing military judges from State Security Courts. The European Court of Human Rights had complained in the past that the presence of a military judge was a violation of a fair and objective trial. This move to "civilianize" the special courts was clearly intended to ward off such criticism of the Öcalan trial, but it was also seen as a significant precedent.

*Turkish Daily News* columnist Fehmi Koru seized the occasion to ask: "Do We Really Need State Security Courts?" Pointing out that the State Security Courts were a leftover from the 1980 military coup, Koru stressed that in democratic countries there is no need for special courts.[15]

*Kurdish guerrilla leader Abdullah Öcalan, head of the Kurdistan Workers Party (PKK), before a State Security Court on İmralı prison island. He was sentenced to death on June 29, 1999, for treason in the conflict that has taken nearly 40,000 lives since 1984.*

Another quite unexpected consequence of the Öcalan arrest was Turkey's rapprochement with Greece. Prime Minister Ecevit had called the Greek role in the Öcalan affair "unforgivable," and the Turkish government had brought out a devastating report on "Greece and PKK Terrorism." It appeared relations between the two NATO allies were compromised once and for all. Then out of the blue, Greek foreign minister George Papandreou, clearly unhappy over the Nairobi fiasco, suggested he would like to visit Ankara and resume communications. After an exchange of amiable letters, the Greek minister and his Turkish counterpart, İsmail Cem, met in New York the beginning of July. Although they did not broach substantive issues like Cyprus and the Aegean, the Greeks said they were prepared to cooperate with Turkey in the fight against terrorism. This was interpreted in Ankara as a sign that Athens would withdraw its support from the Kurdish guerrilla movement.

But the Öcalan problem was far from over. The appeals process was expected to drag on for months. If the death sentence were confirmed by a Turkish court, it must also be approved by Parliament and the president of the Republic. At the same time, defense lawyers said they would take their appeal to the European Court of Human Rights in Strasbourg, which could mean at least another year of deliberation.

In the meantime, Turkey has already come under a barrage of contradictory pressures at home and abroad. Domestic public opinion and much of the media has been euphoric since Öcalan's capture and demanded the swift execution of the man they call "the baby killer."

Even before the sentence, Deputy Prime Minister Devlet Bahçeli, who heads the second-largest group in Parliament, the Nationalist Action Party, did not mince words. "Yes, I think that Abdullah Öcalan should be executed," Bahçeli told the daily *Star*. "If this country wants tranquility, this act against the state must be punished."[16]

Only a few isolated voices have said no to capital punishment for the Kurdish guerrilla leader. Declaring that he is personally against the death penalty, Hasan Cemal, a respected political columnist of *Milliyet*, wrote that "it would be more in line with national interests not to execute" the PKK chief.[17]

Hüsnü Öndül, the new head of the Human Rights Association, declared that the organization was categorically against the death penalty in principle and has campaigned for the abolishment of capital punishment in Turkey's legal system since 1987.

"There are no problems between the country's Kurdish and Turkish citizens," he declared, but warned there could be trouble if Öcalan were executed.[18]

My colleague Mehmet Ali Kışlalı, who is familiar with military thinking, did not believe the death sentence would be carried out, not unless Turkish pride were seriously put under pressure by the Western world.

After a fifteen-year moratorium on executions in Turkey, the death penalty was again on the table. Besides Öcalan, there are currently forty-seven people on death row. In the early 1980s, Turkish public opinion had been so revolted by the executions—mainly of university students—under the military regime, that Parliament has simply disregarded all death sentences since 1984.

Abroad, in a rare show of unity, Europeans—politicians and press—urged Turkey to commute Öcalan's death sentence. Some diplomatically urged Turkey to pursue its present humanitarian policy. Others dangled the carrot of possible admission to the European Union, which has abolished the death penalty. But what was uppermost on European minds was the reaction of the Kurdish diaspora—half a million Kurds in Germany alone.

Öcalan's capture had been followed by violent displays of Kurdish anger throughout Europe and in Turkey. The response to his conviction was more muted: some assaults on Turkish installations in Europe and isolated attacks in Turkey, but these were accompanied by threats of a new wave of violence if Öcalan were put to death.

Some influential voices have looked beyond the trial to what has been called a window of opportunity, resulting from the capture of the Kurdish guerrilla leader. They imply that Turkey should take advantage of its position of strength and the disarray of the Kurdish forces to work out a political solution to the Kurdish question.

Among these, Şükrü Elekdağ, former Turkish ambassador to Washington, wrote in *Milliyet:* "Turkey's ability to put to good use the historic opportunity it is faced with and to take substantial steps towards a solution, will depend on Turkey's not ignoring the realities. And the essential condition for that is recognition of the Kurdish identity."[19]

Seizing the initiative, the opposition Fazilet Party urged the prime minister to declare the southeast a disaster area. A Fazilet report noted there are 24 million people living in poverty in the region and another 13 million at the hunger level. It called for urgent measures, including setting up mobile soup kitchens, the distribution of Social Cooperation and Solidarity funds to residents, and the cancellation of regional municipalities' debts.

State Department spokesman James Rubin was reported as saying that the United States does not believe there is a "purely military solution" to Kurdish issues in Turkey. He described the arrest of Öcalan as "an opportunity for Turkey to seek a dialogue with its citizens of Kurdish origin and to strengthen the rule of law and protection for all human rights for all its citizens."[20]

It is clear whatever the fate of Öcalan, the Kurdish question will not go away. Reporting from Diyarbakır in May, *New York Times* correspondent Stephen Kinzer observed "growing support for Kurdish nationalism," despite the capture of Öcalan and heavy PKK losses on the ground.[21] He quoted the new People's Democracy Party (HADEP) mayor, Feridun Çelik, as saying: "We won [the local elections] because we talked about identity, about the fact that there is a Kurdish population in this country that cannot be ignored."

But HADEP'S chairman Murat Bozlak was jailed for calling Öcalan "a party leader," and although he has been released, he was forced to resign. And there's still a court suit pending against HADEP, accused of maintaining "organic links" with the PKK. A public prosecutor declared he would bring action to remove all of the HADEP mayors, whose election, he claimed, constituted "terrorist takeovers" of local administration.

Turkey has yet to demonstrate it is prepared to accept European standards on human rights. Journalists, writers, politicians, and human rights activists are still going to jail for crimes of thought and expression.

On the eve of the April 1999 elections, Human Rights Watch in New York issued a grim study on the "Violations of Free Expression in Turkey," including the harassment, even murder, of journalists, Islamists, and Kurds.[22] The rights group called for the repeal of all laws violating international human rights standards, starting with the preamble of the constitution. This states: "No protection shall be given to thoughts or opinions that run counter to Turkish National interests, the fundamental principle of the existence of the indivisibility of the Turkish state and territory, the historical and moral values of Turkishness, or the nationalism, principles, reforms, and modernism of Atatürk."

In Ankara, the Human Rights Association declared: "All fundamental freedoms and rights were infringed systematically during 1998."[23] Its annual report stated that 270 people were killed by unidentified assailants or extrajudicial executions (so much for the moratorium on the death penalty!); 42,991 people were detained and 3,659 jailed; torture remained widespread and systematic; 133 intellectuals, journalists, and writers were in prison; 300 HADEP members, including chairman Murat Bozlak were still in jail (his release was reported later); and 2,500 cases were brought against Turkey before the European Court of Human Rights. In a separate report, the association said that for the week of February 16, 1999, after Öcalan's capture, 3,369 people were arrested—mainly in Diyarbakır and İstanbul.

The country's leading human rights activist, Akın Birdal, resigned as president of the Human Rights Association and went to jail in early June to serve a one-year sentence for "inciting the people to hatred by dividing them along religious, linguistic and racial lines" in a speech on World Peace Day, September 1, 1996. He was replaced by a little-known Ankara lawyer, Hüsnü Öndül.

The two most urgently needed reforms are an end to restrictions on freedom of expression and an end to torture, according to Jonathan Sugden, Human Rights Watch representative for Turkey. He noted there were hundreds of laws and regulations limiting freedom of expression, even though long ago Turkey committed itself to the European Convention of Human Rights, including Article Ten, which safeguards freedom of expression. In connection with the Anti-Terror Law, he said, "incommunicado detention is still the rule in Turkey, and that is the single most powerful factor contributing to torture."[24]

When the political horizon seems particularly bleak in Turkey, something generally happens to reverse the situation—or at least shake things up.

That summer of 1999, Turkish authorities banned a book, which was the first personal account by Turkish army veterans of the fifteen-year-old war against Kurdish guerrillas. *Mehmet's Book* (the nickname of Turkish army recruits) contains interviews with forty-two soldiers, who paint a devastating picture of the war, the slaying of Kurdish civilians, the profiteering, and the traumas suffered by the soldiers.

Published in April, the book received favorable reviews and sold 15,000 copies in the first two months—bestseller status in Turkey—before it was banned on June 23 for insulting the army. The author and human rights advocate, Nadire Mater, risks one to six years' prison under Article 159 of the penal code.

"In the fifteen years we have been living with this conflict, everyone has had a chance to speak out except the young men who are doing the fighting," Ms. Mater, fifty, told the press bitterly. "Now they are telling their stories. For letting them do it, I'm accused of insulting the military."[25]

Yet almost at the same time, Mehmet Ali İrtemçelik, state minister for human rights, gave a candid and lengthy interview on reforms planned in the area of human rights legislation. His statement was published in the *Turkish Daily News*, clearly meant for foreign consumption.

Declaring that the government was aware of the "shortcomings" in human rights, İrtemçelik put most of the blame on "PKK terrorism, which is sponsored by foreign powers" but also mentioned the violent events that led to the military coups of 1971 and 1980.[26]

Now, the minister said, Turkey had achieved "great success" against PKK terrorism and dealt it "a major blow" with the capture of Öcalan. In light of these events, the new administration, which has stronger parliamentary support than any government since 1961, was "giving priority to human rights issues."

He described in detail four bills before the new Parliament: increased punishment for people using torture, protection and compensation for witnesses, facilitating the investigation of civil servants accused of criminal acts, and linking interest on state debts to the consumer price index.

In a significant gesture, President Demirel formally received a group of the newly elected Kurdish mayors in midsummer 1999. The HADEP mayors reportedly spoke of their local problems and also called for a general amnesty and the abolishment of the death penalty. Demirel for his part spoke in general terms, emphasizing that the Republic had been founded by people from the East and the West acting together. Although nothing new was said on either side, the meeting was in itself an implicit recognition of HADEP as a Kurdish voice and a possible opening to a peaceful solution to the seemingly insoluble Kurdish problem.

At the same time, the governing parties negotiated a compromise accord with the opposition Fazilet, enabling passage of a constitutional amendment that would allow international arbitration (as stipulated by the International Monetary Fund). In return, the coalition agreed to the opposition's demand for changes in the law on political parties, which could save Fazilet from being shut down and permit banned Islamist leader Necmettin Erbakan to return to politics as an independent.

These reforms would clearly not begin to satisfy internal or external critics of Turkey's human rights record. But the reasoning behind them was an important signal: The government now feels militarily and politically strong enough in its struggle against the PKK insurgency to initiate long-delayed reforms in the country's antiquated legal system involving human rights.

Important encouragement to the government's moves to improve the human rights situation has come from a senior American official, Assistant Secretary Harold Hongju Koh, who visited southeastern Turkey the summer of 1999 and met with a broad range of people in the area. Koh praised Ecevit's commitment to human rights as a top priority and the steps taken to improve the situation and urged the vigorous implementation of the new measures.

His conclusion: "Any enduring solution [to the Kurdish problem] must lie in the expansion of democracy, and in bold and imaginative political participation for all of Turkey's citizens and to promote broader freedom of expression on the Southeast."[27]

Some foreign human rights observers have pointed out that Ecevit and his MHP partners had enough nationalist credentials to avoid accusations of being soft on terrorism. These observers, including myself, feel this augurs well for an eventual nonimplementation of the death penalty in the Öcalan case. But aware of the volatility of the situation and knowing the

Turks and their visceral reaction to outside pressures, I would not stake any big bets on clemency.

With its glaring contradictions, Turkey does not fit into any mold, neither West nor East. The Europeans have spurned Turkey ostensibly for its continued violations of democratic standards, particularly the abusive treatment of the Kurds. Even Turkey's closest ally, the United States, in its annual human rights report, sharply takes Ankara to task for serious human rights abuses.

Yet because of its Western proclivities, its active membership in NATO, and above all the vigorous new alliance with Israel, Turkey has antagonized most of its neighbors and other Muslim countries.

Turkish society must come to grips with the very basic issues: who they are and where they want to go. This means it is essential for Turkey to recognize its multiple identity. The sophisticated Westernized elite must be assured the freedom to pursue its lifestyle, just as those who wish to should be free to live their Muslim identity.

A solution to the corrosive Kurdish problem can probably be reached through an end to violence on both sides and official recognition of Kurdish cultural rights. Turks from the Balkans and the Caucasus, like those of Alevi and Arab origin, should also be free to express their own personalities.

What is imperative is fair, far-sighted, imaginative leadership, with secularists and religiously oriented people working together to find solutions to their common problems. The generals must return to their military duties and give civilians a chance to rule. The laws of the land must be revised to ensure real freedom of democratic expression.

Abdullah Gül, a leader of the Islamic reformists, proposed an American-type bill of rights for Turkey, and I think he means it.

A respected secular voice, the presiding judge of the Constitutional Court, Ahmet Necdet Sezer, has called on the newly elected Parliament to amend all laws restricting freedom of expression. Declaring that freedom of expression is the basis of a democratic society, the chief justice specifically criticized the Anti-Terrorism Law and other laws that punish personal beliefs. Only criminal actions and acts inciting to crime should be penalized, he stipulated.

"Turkey is obliged to make the necessary changes in its laws to adapt to the international norms on human rights," Judge Sezer asserted.[28] He noted that most of these laws restricting personal freedoms had been passed shortly after the 1980 military coup and were still in force.

"The Voice of Reason," hailed several leading Turkish newspapers.

Hope surged around the country and among Turkey watchers abroad. Maybe Turkey was ready after all to commit itself to real democracy?

Although the modern Republic of Turkey is young, barely seventy-five years old, it has matured rapidly and has acquired new self-confidence. If the new governing coalition provides the long-yearned-for political stability, the country is now in a position to enact far-reaching political and social reforms and promote greater economic equality.

My conviction is that despite all the uncertainties, Turkey will find its own Third Way, an accommodation between secularists and Islamists, ethnic Kurds and Turks of other origins, within the framework of the democratic system. The integration of a vibrant Islamic movement under a fully democratic Republic of Turkey would be a powerful and positive experience for the Islamic world.

A genuinely democratic Turkey would assume its rightful place as the center of a vast region stretching from the Balkans to the far reaches of Central Asia. It would be an even more valuable partner for the United States, a strong candidate for membership in the European Union, and a model for Muslim nations everywhere.

# Epilogue: Quake

The terrible earthquake that struck the industrial heartland of western Turkey the summer of 1999, taking an estimated 20,000 lives, has shaken the very foundations of the state.

A major victim of the quake was public trust. The immense devastation lay bare the corruption, greed, and negligence not only of builders and developers but also local and central authorities, who ignored, condoned, or connived with a rotten system.

Just as serious was the failure of authorities at every level to provide a rapid and effective response to the disaster, the absence of emergency planning, and lack of direction and coordination.

The seismic shocks also dramatically brought to the surface the deep fissures in Turkish society. Some secular officials actually obstructed desperately needed aid from Islamic-based organizations—on the grounds that it was politically motivated.

Out of an acute sensitivity to civilian prerogatives, the government rejected an offer by the military to take over the rescue and relief operations. The armed forces set up their own crisis center, but probably could have been more effective if they had been in control.

Despite public protest and pressures in the wake of the quake, Bülent Ecevit's nationalistic coalition enjoys a comfortable majority in Parliament and is not likely to go away in the near future. Since its inception in May 1999, the government has engaged in a barrage of legislative activity. Some acts appear to be piecemeal, image-related gestures; others could have long-term positive effects, but fall short of the sweeping reforms people demand.

Hovering in the background, the powerful armed forces have remained steadfastly intransigent in their struggle against what they continue to see as the main threats to the Republic: Islamic extremism and Kurdish separatism. They have demanded tougher measures against Islamists and dismissed PKK peace overtures as a ploy to save the life of Kurdish guerrilla leader Öcalan, waiting on death row.

Yet amid the rubble of this national tragedy have sprung seeds of hope. It's as though the seismic shocks have wiped the political slate clean. Various voices are demanding a fresh start. For the first time in modern history, certain taboos were shattered. People have begun to criticize the sacrosanct state and even the inviolable armed forces. There are calls for more official accountability, greater freedom of expression and thought, even a profound revision of the military-inspired constitution. Private citizens have learned they must rely on themselves and each other, not a distant, centralized bureaucracy.

Turks have also found that they are not alone. Long accustomed to the role of outsider, they were deeply moved by the overwhelming display of international solidarity. Assistance and sympathy came not only from European and American allies but even usually hostile neighbors like Greece, Armenia, Iraq, and Iran.

Admittedly the massive August 17 earthquake, measuring 7.4 on the Richter scale, would have proved challenging for any country. The epicenter was in the densely populated İzmit region on the Sea of Marmara, but the shock was felt as far as Ankara, 220 miles away, and completely disrupted communications, cutting the capital off from the quake zone for two days.

But the dimensions of the catastrophe were so great that it was clear that things had gone terribly wrong all along the line. Errors started with a general disregard of scientific warnings, faulty urban planning, shoddy construction, and absence of emergency plans. These faults were compounded by the tardy, haphazard, inadequate official rescue and relief effort.

No one knows for sure how many people died in the quake because there was such a state of chaos that initially victims were buried without official death notices and some people were believed to be interred in the bulldozed ruins. But both Turkish and foreign journalists who rushed to the scene were generally critical of the sluggish and disorganized response of the authorities and action to impede private, particularly Islamic, assistance.

Scientists had predicted "a large event" south of the industrial port of İzmit for two decades, but the government appeared to have no contingency plan, according to Metin Munir, a Turkish Cypriot friend and colleague. People were shocked to learn that corruption—even more than the tremors—was the cause of so much ruin, Munir reported to the *Economist's* Economic Intelligence Unit. He pointed out:

> Successive governments and municipalities, which are responsible for supervising construction practices, pocketed bribes encouraging land speculation and turning a blind eye to sloppy building practices. Half of all buildings in Turkey are built in violation of construction regulations and are prone to collapse in an earthquake. According to the Architects Chamber of Turkey in - İstanbul, where more than seven million people live, this ratio is 65 percent.[1]

One of the most devastating reports came from Fehmi Koru, *Turkish Daily News* columnist, who had been vacationing in the area when the quake struck. In his article, "The Day After: Yalova in Ruins," he wrote:

> One thing is evident: there is no civil society in Turkey to assume responsibility in times of need. No volunteers, no stockpiled necessities, no trained dogs. Nothing whatsoever in a country, which bestowed the idea of endowment *(Vaqf)* to the world, people historically united around vocational lodges as a full-fledged civil society and even fighting fires was a voluntary activity; this is shameful. I for one, would direct my accusing finger at those in authority who never trust their own people, who feel forever uneasy when they see the people mobilizing as responsible civilians to take their fates in their own hands and who consistently forbid them to organize into either religious or non-religious groups. For the last three years, all the associations, foundations and endowments have been under close scrutiny and inspection by the state. . . . Those in authority use the power of the state relentlessly; but when the time comes to show the strength of the state for the benefit of the people, the state is nowhere to be seen.[2]

Hasan Cemal, a senior columnist for the influential daily *Milliyet*, commented: "This is the first time I've seen such a strong wave of anger directed at the state, at the politicians." For the first three days, he added, people in the quake region complained that they were abandoned to their fate and criticized builders, the state, and local administrations.

Instead of heeding the widespread criticism of official shortcomings, officials lashed out at the media. The state regulatory agency for radio and television closed down one critical channel for a week. The minister of health blamed the media for provoking public ire. There was talk of a blacklist of foreign reporters. Prime Minister Ecevit, usually sensitive to the press, accused the media of "demoralizing coverage."

When official agencies failed to provide a timely response to people's needs, a number of nongovernmental organizations moved into the vacuum, demonstrating resourcefulness and effectiveness. Volunteers rallied from all over the country. Even the Kurdish mayors in the southeast sent food, medicine, and doctors. Leading the civilian relief effort were various Islamic-based foundations, businesses, and municipalities. They sent in rescue and cleanup teams, soup kitchens, and mobile hospitals.

*Milliyet* called it a "civilian uprising" and said the people had become aware of their own power. The most prominent rescue team was a private group of students and mountain climbers called AKUT, the Rescue and Research Association. A secular group, AKUT won widespread public praise but was accused of providing help "just for show" by the minister of health.

Erol Çakir, the secular governor of İstanbul, accused Fazilet Party and other pro-Islamic groups who had rushed to the scene of trying to use the earthquake "to further their own interests."[3] It was widely reported that on his orders, the police raided the main Islamic human rights organizations, Mazlumder and the Foundation for Human Rights, and their bank accounts were frozen. Other authorities rejected urgently needed earthmoving equipment and confiscated 3,000 tents because they bore the logo of Kombassan, a major Islamic holding company.

A few radical Islamists suggested that the quake was "divine retribution" for the authorities' anti-Islamic drive. But generally the Islamic reaction to this new show of official mistrust was muted.Yilmaz Ensaroğlu, head of Mazlumder, responded calmly: "If the state authorities can trust the NGO's and properly direct them, the problems would be solved more efficiently. But if the state doesn't trust its own people, how can it expect people to trust the state?"[4]

My Islamic friend Aynur Demirel told me: "We are as a nation all depressed. Whatever comes from Allah, we accept, but it is hard to accept things coming from elsewhere." (A few days after the quake, Aynur left Turkey for Hungary, where she enrolled in the Albert Szent Medical University. She had lost two years' schooling in the Headscarf War and has given up hope that the ban will be relaxed any time soon.)

A notable absence in the early days of the emergency was the armed forces. The military had suffered a devastating blow with the destruction of the naval command center at Gölcük, just a few miles north of the epicenter, the loss of 500 lives, and communications failure. But public opinion could not understand why the army—known as the best-organized institution in the country—had not taken charge of the rescue and relief effort early on.

Stung by the unusual criticism, General Hüseyin Kıvrıkoğlu, commander-in-chief of the armed forces, told journalists: "The Government decided that it could handle the quake by giving further authority to itself and to governors." Rejecting accusations that the military had been slow to join the rescue operations, General Kıvrıkoğlu castigated "fundamentalist circles" for spreading the word that God was punishing the military. He seized this opportunity to declare that the army would continue its drive against Islamic fundamentalism and separatism "for a thousand years if necessary."[5]

Agreeing that some Islamists had made "senseless accusations," İlnur Çevik stressed, however, that moderate Islamic volunteers were making important contributions to the relief effort. Then expressing public frustration, Çevik wrote that "the military has much explaining to do. . . . The people want to learn why Turkey's communications, which were allegedly designed to withstand a nuclear war, failed so badly. They want to know why the Turkish naval command headquarters was built on top of a serious fault line. They want to know why many people did not see units around the earthquake zone in the first few days of the quake. They also want to learn why the military does not have specialized disaster rescue units and a field hospital such as the one the Israelis put at our disposal."[6]

Prime Minister Ecevit's main coalition partner, Devlet Bahçeli, confirmed that the government had decided there was no need to impose a state of emergency and it was necessary to prove the civilian authorities were capable of dealing with emergencies.

This civilian sensitivity was understandable—in light of the four military interventions over the past four decades. The trouble was that the government didn't have any kind of Federal Emergency Management Agency prepared to deal with national catastrophes. This was one occasion when the army should have intervened.

The Turkish Red Crescent, the agency appointed by the government to oversee the relief effort, failed miserably by most accounts. The main charge leveled against the organization, known as Kızılay in Turkish, was that it had spent most of its funds on flashy new headquarters in Ankara instead of disaster relief equipment. Refugees were especially irate over the miniscule leaky tents, some dating back to World War II. Following widespread complaints, Dr. Kemal Demir, the head of Kızılay, resigned seven weeks after the quake, claiming he had been the object of "unfair" criticism, and turned his position over to a friend. Finally, the government dismissed all the executives of Kızılay and put it under a court-appointed trustee.

It was the minister of health, Osman Durmuş, who drew the most public fire for his misguided comments. At a time when Turks were desperately crying out for help, the ultranationalist minister claimed Turkey had no need for medicines or foreign doctors, spurned aid from an American hospital ship, rejected Armenian help, and warned Turks not to accept Greek blood. Fortunately, other official voices prevailed, and the Turkish people gratefully welcomed foreign aid. But the blundering minister remained in his post.

There were silver linings to this grim scene.

First of all, the government appeared resolute in remedying the scandals in the building industry. A few days after the quake, Interior Minister Saadettin Tantan declared that all the contractors of the collapsed buildings would be investigated and receive severe sentences if found guilty of neglect. Then the public works minister drafted legislation stipulating that all construction sites must be inspected and subject to stricter controls.

For its part, the public showed it was in no mood to countenance official misdoing. A fortnight after the quake, the coalition government rammed through Parliament an amnesty law that would have freed 26,500 prisoners, including murderers, swindlers, gang members, and even contractors but not political prisoners. After widespread protests in the media and thousands of letters, faxes, and phone calls from ordinary citizens, President Demirel hastily vetoed the bill and sent it back to Parliament.

Another positive result of the quake was the marked improvement in Turkey's relations with its neighbors—particularly with Greece. The Greek Special Disaster Unit EMAK was one of the first and most effective rescue teams to arrive at İzmit. When Athens was hit by a lesser quake a week later, Turkey's emergency group AKUT rushed to the scene.

The dramatic rapprochement between Turkey and Greece since the capture of the Kurdish leader Abdullah Öcalan has accelerated. Greek foreign minister George Papandreou not only approved European Union aid to Turkey but said his government would not block Turkey's application for membership in the EU. A Greek naval vessel visited a Turkish port for the first time in years. Diplomats from the two countries met to discuss improvement in trade, cultural, and tourism relations. Even soccer teams from the two countries met in friendly competition.

*Milliyet's* veteran columnist Sami Kohen wrote: "The post-quake period is opening up new horizons for Turkey in foreign affairs."[7]

One far-reaching consequence of the shock and aftershocks appears to be a change in Turkish mentality. Old taboos have been swept away, and with them, the mystique of the state. Nongovernmental organizations, the media, and even some leaders clamored for democratic reform.

Seizing the mood for change, the PKK began withdrawing its guerrillas ahead of the September 1 deadline set by Öcalan. Without any reciprocal gesture from Turkey, the movement announced the end of the armed struggle and declared it was entering the political process.[8]

The Turkish Armed Forces received the news with skepticism. General Kıvrıkoğlu said the PKK had announced unilateral cease-fires before but nothing had come of them. Confirming that some guerrillas had left the country, the general said the PKK usually moved across the border to set up winter camp. Once again, the military reiterated its demand that the guerrillas surrender and lay down their arms.

In a rare meeting with journalists, General Kıvrıkoğlu said that Öcalan's fate now lay with the politicians—not the military. The chief of General Staff stressed that the PKK had altered its aims, announcing it no longer sought autonomy but would be satisfied with cultural rights. Finally the general noted that Kurds already enjoyed some cultural rights like Kurdish newspapers and music.

None of this was new, but the fact that it was said publicly by Turkey's top military commander sent a wave of euphoria through the media and Kurdish circles. Subsequently, the chief of staff's office felt it necessary to dampen spirits with a clarification, that indeed, there was no new opening, no softening on the Kurdish issue. But the seeds of change had been planted.

The most resounding political tremor came from Turkey's highest judge, Sami Selcuk, head of the Court of Appeals. Speaking at a ceremony to open the judicial year, the chief justice declared that the constitution, produced by the military regime in 1982, limited democratic freedoms and must be rewritten.

"Turkey should not enter the new millennium with a constitution whose legitimacy is almost zero," Selcuk said, noting that the charter was not the work of a government chosen by the free will of the people.[9] He said the constitution restricted the freedoms of citizens rather than restricting the powers of the state.

A number of public figures and the popular press applauded Selcuk's words. Recalling that TÜSİAD had demanded sweeping democratic reforms two years earlier, a leader of the industrialists' group, Bülent Eczacıbaşı told the press: "We are way behind in matters of freedom of thought and expression."

Prime Minister Bülent Ecevit called Judge Selcuk's speech "extremely important" and promised to work to change the constitution.

As many Turks sought to reconstitute their lives out of the rubble that fall of 1999, all eyes were fixed on Washington. Turkish expectations were so high in connection with the first official visit of a Turkish prime minister to the United States in over twenty years that nothing short of a miracle would have given satisfaction. In the aftermath of the earthquake, Secretary Albright and other American officials had expressed strong sympathy, and President Clinton had said: "We must do all we can to help and we will."

Turks, who estimated losses from the earthquake in the neighborhood of $18 billion, clearly expected their closest ally to cover a substantial part of the tally. Turkish officials actually indicated they hoped Washington would provide around $5 billion in loan guarantees plus forgiveness of military debts, which amount to $6 billion.

In an apparent effort to sweeten the atmosphere in Washington, Ankara announced several measures in human rights just before Ecevit's departure. A ceremony was held at the Justice Ministry marking the completion of a two-year revision of the Statute on Trial Procedures. Minister Hikmet Sami Türk called it a "legal revolution" that reflected progressive legal developments around the world.

Then the jailed human rights leader Akın Birdal was set free "for health reasons." Earlier thirty-two journalists and writers were released from prison on condition they not repeat their "crimes" in a three-year period.

But as is often the case in Turkey, positive developments were accompanied by various steps backward. Shortly after the amnesty for writers and journalists, author Nadire Mater was charged with "insulting the armed forces" and faced a possible six years in prison for her book of interviews with Turkish soldiers who had taken part in the fight against Kurdish guerrillas.

A few days prior to the prime minister's departure for the United States, rioting erupted in the overcrowded prisons, apparently triggered by delays in the amnesty bill. In İstanbul's Bayrampa şa prison, seven inmates were killed in what was described as a dispute between rival gangs. In Ankara's Central Prison, gendarmes and prison guards stormed a cell with unruly leftist prisoners, killing ten of them on the very day Ecevit left for the United States. In retaliation, prisoners seized seventy guards in various prisons, holding them hostage for five days. İstanbul police detained a hundred people protesting against the prison "massacre," raided the office of the Human Rights Association, and arrested one of the leaders, who later complained of mistreatment.

At the same time, in case anybody in Washington or anywhere else might think Turkey was ready to show flexibility on the Kurdish issue, the Turkish General Staff firmly rejected the PKK's proposals for a negotiated settlement and called for an unconditional surrender of the guerrillas. From death row Öcalan ordered a group of his followers to comply, in a sign of goodwill. Dismissing Öcalan and the PKK's peace offers as "propaganda," the military command stated: "The Turkish armed forces are determined to continue the battle until the last terrorist has been neutralized."

Later, while Ecevit was still in the United States, a group of eight PKK guerrillas, led by the organization's former representative in Europe, Ali Sapan, did surrender to the Turkish Army at Şemdinli near the Iraqi border. They said they were answering Öcalan's order and applied for leniency under the new Repentance Law. Pointedly ignoring the new peace offering, the Turkish Army announced that thousands of troops, backed by helicopter gunships, had carried out another incursion into northern Iraq in pursuit of PKK terrorists.

In Washington, as Clinton and Ecevit and their entourages were exchanging views in the Oval Office, two small but fervent groups were sending out contradictory messages in front of the White House. Close to the fence, about fifty people marched in a circle, waving Turkish and American flags and placards saying: "Turkey-U.S. Partnership," "Öcalan in Jail; Peace Prevail," "Welcome to the U.S. Prime Minister Ecevit."

Nearby but separated by a barricade and an important security force, a slightly larger group chanted "Free Öcalan! Free Leyla Zana!" and brandished placards saying "Give Peace a Chance!" This was the livelier rally, with Kurdish songs and dances and various speakers, including Sanar Yurdatapan, a Turkish human rights activist, and Eugene Rossides, a leader of the American Hellenic Institute.

Najmaldin Karim, a member of the Washington Kurdish Institute and organizer of the demonstration, expressed the hope that Prime Minister Ecevit would hear their calls for peace. "If we cannot hear Kurdish songs, Kurdish language, literature, culture . . . what sort of peace is it?"

After the speeches, Kani Xulam, a founder of the American Kurdish Information Network, told me: "We thought the Turkish military were ready to change their policy—but now we're not so sure. Our hope is in Turkish public opinion, that the change of air will become a wind."

Shortly after his talks with President Clinton, the Turkish prime minister addressed a crowded meeting hosted by the Washington Institute for Near East Studies in the Willard Hotel. Looking sober and frail, Ecevit highlighted the positive, thanking the American people for their solidarity in "the biggest calamity we have witnessed."

Emphasizing his country's progress toward democracy, he said Turkey has shown that "Islam can be compatible with secularism and democracy." There were still shortcomings, he added, but Turks were "increasingly sensitive to human rights."

The Turkish leader listed some of his government's legislative achievements in its first three months: naming civilian judges to State Security Courts, enacting laws against criminal gangs and for repentance (Kurdish rebels), liberalizing the Political Parties Law, and passing banking and social security reforms and a law enabling international arbitration.

Ecevit also noted improved foreign relations, saying: "A few years ago, we were surrounded by hostile nations; now it's the opposite, with friendly countries all over . . . even with Greece relations seem to be improving." Acknowledging that the European Union remained closed, he stressed that Turkey would not give up its legal right to belong. "I'm sure sooner or later the European Union will knock on Turkey's door and ask us to join."

The talks with President Clinton went "very well in a friendly atmosphere," Ecevit reported, noting "new vistas of cooperation." But he stressed that economic and trade relations between the two countries were "much below their potential." Even tourism was unsatisfactory—Americans represent only 5 percent of total tourists in Turkey. And although Turkey's military cooperation extends far beyond NATO—to

Bosnia, Kosovo, and northern Iraq—the United States has stopped all financial support to the Turkish military. "This is a contradiction in terms, which we hope will be corrected," he stressed.

Among the positive aspects of the meeting, the Turkish prime minister noted President Clinton's recognition that Turkey had paid a heavy price for its cooperation in the Gulf War; the U.S. government's commitment to the Baku-Ceyhan pipeline through Turkey; and agreement on the Cyprus issue that "there's no going back to the situation before 1974." (For Turks this implies no return to the time when the Turkish Cypriot community was subordinate to the Greek Cypriot community.)

But the only concrete results of the talks were a slight increase in the quota for Turkish textiles and the signing of a joint trade and investment agreement. There was no American commitment for earthquake reconstruction aid, no specific loan guarantees or investments nor any writeoff of the military debt, no expected financial support from the International Monetary Fund and World Bank.

The Washington Institute's Turkish expert, Alan Makovsky, explained why despite "the warm atmospherics," there was no major earthquake-related aid package. He said the Clinton administration had planned to make loan guarantees the centerpiece of Ecevit's visit but, after consulting Congress, came up with less than $1 billion. Turkey apparently decided that the amount offered was not worth possible congressional demands for concessions on Cyprus and other matters, Makovsky concluded.[10]

Both American and Turkish officials stressed there would be a second round to the talks, when President Clinton paid an official to Ankara in mid-November, before attending the summit meeting of the Organization for Security and Cooperation in Europe in İstanbul.

On the very day of Ecevit's talks with Clinton, Turkish newspapers published ominous reports on the prime minister's health, provoked by his recent lapses of memory. Prior to the April elections, Ecevit had issued a statement denying rumors that he was seriously ill. Now *Sabah*'s Zülfü Livaneli cited speculation by unnamed doctors that Ecevit's movements suggested the possibility of Parkinson's or Alzheimer's disease. "Ecevit must immediately undergo a medical examination at a reliable medical institution and the results must be made public," Livaneli wrote.[11] Responding to the new wave of rumors, Ecevit's doctor, Professor Mehmet Haberal, declared the prime minister had no health problems but was showing signs of "fatigue."[12] Turkish official sources said at times Ecevit's movements seemed to have slowed down but his extemporaneous responses to journalists' questions were as alert as ever.

Back in Turkey, the general atmosphere was overcast with only a few bright clearings. Ecevit's health remained a concern because he was the leader keeping together the coalition, which has given a sense of stability, despite the serious criticisms leveled against the state. Even Ecevit's critics acknowledge he is the best hope to lead the country to democracy.

Meanwhile, Ecevit's government was coming under pressure from all sides. The International Monetary Fund and the World Bank delayed signing a standby agreement because they were waiting to see if the government would take the necessary austerity measures in the year 2000 budget—which it did—and begin to implement them. This meant above all reducing inflation from around 65 percent to 25 percent.

There were reports that the government was unable to pay subsidies owed to farmers because all available funds were going to the earthquake regions. Yet reconstruction was slow because of bureaucracy and lack of funds. Also since relief efforts had been concentrated under the discredited Red Crescent, private contributions were not coming in.

Officials wondered aloud where the money was going to come from. There was more talk of an earthquake tax—no matter how unpopular it would be. There were even suggestions in the press that the armed forces might temporarily postpone for a time new purchases under the modernization program ($5 billion a year for the next twenty-five years). It was also suggested that devout Muslims might postpone the costly (in foreign currency) trip to Mecca for a year.

Pointing to the dire condition of the earthquake survivors, the pro-Islamic opposition Fazilet Party called for the government's resignation, but found little support, basically because of the general feeling of shared responsibility for the tragedy.

Disregarding official moves to improve the country's human rights image and the liberalization of the Political Parties Law, Turkey's chief prosecutor presented his case for closing down the Fazilet Party. Charging that it was a continuation of Refah Party, banned the year before, the prosecutor cited as evidence a secretly taped conversation of former Refah leader Necmettin Erbakan, who was portrayed as running Fazilet.

Nor was there any letup in the strains between the military and Islamists. Ankara State Security Court initiated investigations into a religious recital at Kocatepe Mosque in which Mehmet Kutlular, head of the powerful Nurcu brotherhood, allegedly linked the earthquake to the military drive against Islamic circles.

Concerned over the increased tension with the armed forces, Mehmet Nuri Yılmaz, head of the official religious directorate, sent a message to be read out in all 76,000 mosques around the country that said: "No one should try to wear out the military by using the Aug. 17 quake as a pretext. Let no one take a hostile stance towards the military. Doing damage to the army would be the biggest harm a person can do to this country."[13]

Meanwhile, the government came under important new pressures to respond positively to the Kurdish peace offensive. Belatedly, Italy announced the decision to grant Öcalan political asylum. Although the move would have no practical impact, it could reinforce European opposition to Turkey's carrying out the death sentence.

Then a group of fifty international writers and artists, led by Turkey's best-known novelist, Yaşar Kemal, and including Nobel Prize winners Günter Grass, Jose Saramago, Nadine Gordimer, and Elie Wiesel, called on Turkey to grant language and cultural rights to its some 12 million Kurds. "While dressing the wounds caused by the catastrophic earthquake, please also dress this social wound that has been bleeding for more than seventy years," the writers urged.[14]

There were also various Greek-Turkish peace initiatives. Municipal leaders, members of chambers of commerce, and journalists from the two countries met at the Aegean resort of Kuşadası to discuss ways to promote peace. In İstanbul, a Friendship Concert was organized on behalf of the earthquake victims by Turkish musician-journalist Zülfü Livaneli and Greek composer Mikis Theodorakis.

Belatedly, the government launched its own human rights offensive to prepare for the European Union's Helsinki Summit at year's end, which was to decide whether Turkey would finally be admitted as a candidate for membership. For the first time ever, State Minister Mehmet Ali İrtemçelik called a meeting of the main human rights specialists and groups, including the pro-Islamic Mazlumder and the pro-Kurdish Human Rights Association, to determine what measures must be taken to improve the situation.

Then it happened. Surprising most Turks and Turkey watchers, the European Commission, executive body of the European Union, recommended that Turkey should be considered "a full candidate for membership." The Turkish Foreign Ministry had expected the commission's positive verdict, but didn't want to raise the country's hopes if it were to be let down like the Luxembourg summit two years before.

There was of course the fine print. Turkey was to be in a class of its own, not part of the group of five East and Central European candidates, which were already lined up to begin negotiations for entry. In fact, it was specified that negotiations would not begin with Ankara until human rights and civil rights in Turkey were brought up to Western standards. There was also a preaccession strategy, involving "enhanced dialogue" between Turkey and the EU on human rights, foreign policy and security, harmonization of legislation, and coordination of EU financial assistance. And of course the commission's recommendations had to be approved by the European leaders at Helsinki.

Regardless, the country breathed a huge sigh of relief. This time was clearly different. There were no negative reactions to the commission's proposals in EU member countries. At the conclusion of a presummit meeting at Tampere, Finland, French president Jacques Chirac and German chancellor Gerhard Schroeder announced that all the members had expressed views in favor of Turkey.

Prime Minister Ecevit called the commission's report "encouraging" but cautioned that it was necessary to wait for the final outcome of the European Union summit. The still-cautious Foreign Ministry said if the recommendations were approved at Helsinki, "a new era" would be opened in Turkey's relations with Europe. Pro-Islamic opposition leader Recai Kutan declared that all the parties in Parliament had reached a consensus regarding Turkey's bid for EU membership.

The Turkish press was generally enthusiastic, but many columnists pointed out that Turkey would need to make major changes to qualify even as a candidate. *Hürriyet*'s Oktay Ekşi wrote: "Turkey must prepare itself for the EU. It cannot drag its feet anymore about democratization. It must attach more importance to human rights and to the prevention of torture. It cannot drag its feet about the judicial reform the country needs. Also freedom of expression must be ensured."[15]

An editorial in the popular daily *Radikal* went further: "The growing possibility of Turkey being formally given candidate status will force it to find solutions to a number of complex problems, including the Kurdish problem and the need for economic reforms."[16]

As Turkey finally seemed headed in the right direction, one of those dark incidents occurred that posed a direct threat to the moves toward democracy and national reconciliation. On October 21, 1999, my friend Ahmet Taner Kışlalı, a mild-mannered professor and columnist for the progressive daily *Cumhuriyet* and a leader of the Atatürk Thought Association, was murdered by a powerful plastic bomb placed in front of the windshield of his car.

The immediate suspects were shadowy Islamic extremist groups seeking to silence this passionate secular voice. Officials even suggested an Iranian hand in the murder, and a number of Iranian suspects were detained then released. But several newspapers cautioned this might be another "mystery killing" (euphemism for death squad activity), like the 1993 unsolved car-bomb murder of human rights activist and investigative journalist Uğur Mumcu.

Prime Minister Ecevit, a personal friend of Kışlalı, went to the hospital where his mangled body lay and pledged to do everything in his power to bring about justice. President Demirel visited *Cumhuriyet*'s office to present his condolences. All the main political parties, including pro-Islamic Fazilet, denounced the vicious deed.

Kışlalı's funeral at Ankara's huge Kocatepe Mosque turned into a political rally attended by 3,000 military officers and thousands of supporters of left-wing political parties. The crowd cheered the army, shouted slogans against the government, and chanted "Turkey is and will remain secular!"

Some analysts warned that Kışlalı's assassination could be a provocation, aimed at pitting secularists against even moderate Islamists. The murder did indeed play into the hands of those militant secularists who have been pressing the government to enact tougher anti-Islamic legislation. It provided the opportunity for Vural Savaş, chief prosecutor of the Court of Appeals, to attack Parliament and call for sweeping restrictive measures against religious activism. A few prominent secularists denounced Savaş's antidemocratic diatribe. The minister in charge of human rights, Mehmet Ali İrtemçelik, declared the chief prosecutor's proposals "unacceptable," and on the contrary, Turkey must raise its democratic standards.

But in what looked like a secular backlash, there were persistent reports that the government was putting together a package of strict "antireactionary" measures, that is, against political Islam. Also the National Security Council intensified its fight against "antisecularism," bringing new pressures on religious foundations, private schools, and Islamic-owned businesses as well as television and radio stations. Meanwhile, the chief prosecutor seemed more determined than ever to close down the moderate Fazilet Party. (In a new demonstration of moderation, a Fazilet delegation visited Washington and met with officials. The party leader, Recai Kutan, publicly came out in support of the Anglo-Saxon "concept of secularism," emphasizing: "There is no danger of Shariah Law in Turkey.")[17]

Compounding the gloom, on November 12 a major new earthquake struck a sparsely populated farming area around Düzce, just east of the region devastated by the August quake. This time government and military rescue teams lost no time and provided efficient relief. The death toll was kept down to about 400.

Toward the end of the year, several things happened that completely changed the national mood.

In mid-November, President Clinton arrived for a five-day official visit and took the country by storm, appearing as champion of the downtrodden and the repressed, meeting with human rights advocates and democratic reformers as well as earthquake victims. During a special parliamentary session, the American president made a ringing endorsement of the "democratic revolution" that is under way and referred to Turkey as "a strategic partner." This time the friendly words were backed up with concrete help: a million-dollar low-interest loan from the United States Export-Import Bank for earthquake victims plus a strong endorsement for the International Monetary Fund standby accord (a $4.5 billion loan and $500 million earthquake aid), signed in Washington a few days later. It was to be followed by pledges of $3 billion from the World Bank, and possibly more.

Coinciding with Clinton's visit, a meeting of the Organization for Security and Cooperation in Europe brought sixty other heads of state and government to İstanbul. For Turkey, it was important that the last OSCE summit of the century take place at İstanbul, which gave its name to the document mapping out plans for the future security of Europe. Above all, Turks had the chance to demonstrate their capacity to stage a major international event and attract tourists back to İstanbul, after the crippling earthquakes.

In a side event to the OSCE summit, President Clinton presided over the ceremonial signing of the long-suffering Baku-Ceyhan pipeline project by the leaders of Turkey, Georgia, Azerbaijan, and Kazakhstan. The $2.4 billion project involves building an oil pipeline through Azerbaijan, Georgia, and Turkey and would ease the Caspian countries' dependence on Russia. The intergovernment accord was unequivocal but not conclusive because the oil companies, led by a British-American group, were yet to be convinced there are enough oil reserves in the area to make the project viable.

Finally, on December 10, 1999, the European Union leaders, meeting at Helsinki, announced that Turkey had been accepted as a candidate for membership, along with Bulgaria, Slovakia, Latvia, Lithuania, Malta, and Romania.

Greece had at last lifted its veto. Foreign Minister George Papandreou declared in the *International Herald Tribune:* "Greece believes if Turkey is

willing to submit to the rigors of the process of candidacy, which apply
equally to all candidate countries, then it should be accepted into the European Union."[18]

Initially Turkish officials balked over the EU's final document, which
seemed to pose special conditions on Turkey's candidacy. Javier Solana,
the European Council's head of Foreign Affairs and Security, flew to
Ankara to assuage the Turks, assuring them that they must comply only
with the Copenhagen Criteria, like all other candidates. The Helsinki declaration had indeed expressed the hope that Turkey would resolve its territorial disputes with Greece prior to 2004 or take the matter to the International Court of Justice, but no deadline was set, Solana stressed. The
European emissary noted that the summit had declared that a political
settlement of the Cyprus issue would facilitate matters, but it was not a
precondition for Turkish accession negotiations. Finally, according to
Turkish diplomatic sources, Solana persuaded the Turkish leadership that
this was "a historical chance" and that it was important "to be on the inside" of the enlarged European entity.

Ignoring any doubts, the İstanbul stock market soared to a record high.
Much of the foreign and local press highlighted the significance of the
event. An editorial in the *New York Times* said: "The European Union's offer to accept Turkey as a future member is one of those developments that
mark a historic step beyond restrictive old rivalries and power align-
ments."[19] The mainstream daily *Hürriyet* exulted: "For the first time the
European Union has given a Muslim country candidate status."[20] *Milliyet's* usually sober Hasan Cemal wrote: "Turkey is stepping into the new
century with a boost to its morale. It is nominating itself for the first
league of the world nations."[21] Both pro-Islamic and Kurdish newspapers
praised European acceptance as a move toward democracy. Only the far-
right nationalist daily *Ortadoğu* emphasized the difficulties, saying, "We
will have a difficult time with the EU. . . . Full membership will cost
Turkey dearly."[22]

İlnur Çevik hailed the candidacy as "the dawn of a new era," but raised
two key questions: Would the conservative establishment be willing to
bow to pressures from international human rights groups and European
politicians? And would the Turkish military "be able to stomach European demands to lessen its influence on the way the country is run?"[23]

As an early test of the government's democratic intentions, thousands
of Islamists and their supporters poured into the streets around the country and formed a human chain to protest against the headscarf ban. Riot

police broke up the demonstrations and detained 400 protesters, but reportedly acted with more restraint than usual.

The military made it clear that, Europe notwithstanding, there would be no letup in the campaign against Islamic extremism. At year's end, Chief of Staff General Hüseyin Kıvrıkoğlu declared: "The Turkish Armed Forces . . . are resolved and determined to stand against all threats against the Turkish Republic, including militant Islam."[24] His statement was read at a ceremony honoring an officer who had been killed in a 1930 Islamic uprising.

Regardless of European opinion and the earthquakes, the Armed Forces have shown they are not about to make a retreat. The Defense Ministry's budget for 2000 was set at a hefty $7.61 billion, or 8.8 percent of the overall budget, almost as high as 1999's $7.88 billion. The *Turkish Daily News* reported that following August's earthquake, the Turkish General Staff held a series of meetings to reconsider priorities, such as battle tanks, attack helicopters, unmanned aerial, surface-to-air missiles, and an antitactical ballistic missile system. "But security concerns and the necessity for the military to prepare itself for the wars of the 21st century with costly advanced electronic equipment have overcome economic considerations."[25]

In the glow of the Helsinki summit, however, it seemed nothing was out of bounds from now on. Some newspapers questioned the need for a military-dominated National Security Council (known by its Turkish initials MGK) and suggested that the all-powerful military must assume a new role in a European Turkey.

Preaching caution, İlnur Çevik agreed that an overhaul of the National Security Council was needed but warned against rushing things as far as the military are concerned. "It is clear that Turkey is ruled on delicate balances. It is also a fact that the military does play a dominating role in our state system, which is not the case in the EU countries. . . . It is true that Turkey needs to adapt to the way of doing things in the EU. It has to change its rules and regulations as well as its legislation. Meanwhile, it has to change the mentalities of so many people who have been used to living in a system where the state is the supreme power and the citizens are the subjects."[26]

On the delicate Kurdish issue, a number of voices suggested that, with the decrease in violent incidents, the controversial state of emergency in the southeast could be terminated and the Village Guard system dismantled. And there were moves to set up a new Kurdish-led liberal political party.

It was Foreign Minister İsmail Cem who opened the debate on Kurdish cultural rights, declaring on television that everyone in Turkey should have the right to broadcast in his own mother tongue. The Turkish Bar Association followed up saying that all ethnic citizens should be given the freedom to use their own culture and language. Not to be outdone, Mesut Yılmaz, leader of the coalition's junior partner, told a rally of his Motherland Party in Diyarbakır that Kurds as well as Turks "deserved democracy," emphasizing: "The road to the E.U. passes through Diyarbakır."[27]

As a reminder that Turkey is not yet Europe, President Demirel promptly slapped down advocates of Kurdish cultural rights, declaring "Turkish is the only language that can be used for education, training and TV broadcasting." In an interview published in *Milliyet*, the president stressed that demands for collective cultural rights would only "encourage tribalism and acts of separatist violence."[28]

Dashing hopes of a post-Helsinki relaxation on the Kurdish front, the new year opened with police raids on offices of the pro-Kurdish HADEP party and pro-Kurdish unions in Diyarbakır and four other southeastern towns. A dozen party leaders were arrested, and books, documents, and journals were seized. And breaking the PKK's declared truce, a renegade faction attacked an army helicopter as it was landing near Tunceli and killed six soldiers.

It is, however, the Öcalan case that stirs the most heated passions and presents the most dangerous pitfalls as Turkey gingerly picks its way through the obstacles that line the road to Europe. Europeans have made it perfectly clear that if the Kurdish leader is executed, it will be a death warrant for Turkey's EU aspirations. All fifteen countries of the EU have abolished the death penalty.

The problem is that the vocal majority of Turks in and outside Parliament favor execution of the man held responsible for the death of some 40,000 people since 1984. And the politicians are well aware of this fact. The Nationalist Action Party and other conservatives have demanded that the Öcalan file be sent promptly to Parliament, which is almost certain to ratify the death sentence.

President Demirel and Prime Minister Ecevit both repeatedly urged the public to put Turkey's national interests before personal feelings and wait for the European Court of Human Rights in Strasbourg to consider Öcalan's appeal. But Turks are an emotional people.

The debate was so heated within the ruling coalition, it appeared the Nationalist Action Party would walk out, forcing a government crisis.

Prime Minister Ecevit finally prevailed with aid from intelligence services, who warned that executing Öcalan would undoubtedly result in a new flareup of terrorism around the country, and the Kurdish leader would become a martyr.

On January 12, 2000, Ecevit announced that action on the Öcalan death sentence would be deferred until the European Court presents its conclusion . . . which could take another two years. Then to placate his ultra-nationalist partners and the voters, Ecevit emphasized: "If the rebel organization and its supporters attempt to use this process against the high interests of the state, then the process of delaying will be halted and the process of execution will be started immediately."[29] The Turkish government's freeze on the death sentence won wide applause abroad, particularly from Europeans who saw this as a concrete move to abide by European standards.

But at home, the delay did not go down well. There were angry protest demonstrations and calls for the government to resign. The two main parties in the ruling coalition had come to power because of their tough nationalist positions—and now it looked as though they were bowing to outside pressures. The opposition parties, which viewed the death sentence as a popular issue, were expected to keep up pressure on the government.

Revelations of an abominable new scandal involving the Islamic extremist group Hizbullah could reinforce hard-liners, who argue that Turkey is not ready for democracy. During a raid on a luxury villa in İstanbul's Beykoz District on January 17, 2000, a Hizbullah leader was killed and information obtained leading to the discovery of secret graves in İstanbul and other urban communities. Some sixty mutilated corpses have been found, but police are looking for hundreds of bodies of persons who "disappeared" in the past two years. The victims are believed to be mostly moderate Islamic businessmen and members of a Kurdish group, affiliated with the Nurcu religious order, who opposed both Hizbullah and the PKK. One woman's body has been identified as Konca Kuris, an Islamic feminist writer, known for her flexible interpretation of Islam.

"What is sad is that there are reports that this terrible terrorist organization was encouraged by some state officials who wanted to create a Muslim Kurdish group that would counter the Marxist Kurdistan Workers Party (PKK) terrorists," İlnur Çevik wrote, urging Turks to "band together and fight radicalism and extremism."[30]

The Office of the General Staff rejected reports that the armed forces used or tolerated Hizbullah's activities against Kurdish nationalists, and

President Demirel denied allegations that the state secretly supported Hizbullah. "There may be forces belonging to the state acting illegally," Demirel was quoted by the Anatolian News Agency as saying. "But they are committing a crime and the first duty of the state is to eliminate them."

Turkey's entry into Europe is not going to be an easy process for the European Union or Turkey, and it will take time. It is not at all certain that Europeans can put aside the negative stereotypes of the Muslim Turks, which really date from the Crusades. Nor is it sure that Atatürk's followers are ready to give up national sovereignty to the degree required.

Prime Minister Ecevit has set an ambitious target: resolution of democracy and human rights problems in one year and economic problems in three years.[31] Turkish analysts are thinking in terms of a decade at least for the country to adapt its legislation and practices to European standards. There will be more steps forward and back, but it is important for the future of democracy and human rights in Turkey that the doors remain open and dialogue continue.

The European opening comes at a propitious time when Turkey has seen a groundswell of civic consciousness and demands for democratic reform and renewal of outdated government institutions. Europe, with U.S. backing, can provide powerful incentives and guidance as Turkey moves ahead on its chosen path to become a modern democracy. This necessarily implies a clear division of powers (with less influence for the military—who have apparently agreed), respect for the civic rights of all citizens, including the right to dissent, and willingness to resolve problems with neighbors through dialogue.

The earthquake made it all much easier by turning European public opinion around. The image of Turks has changed from cruel oppressors of Kurds and headscarved girls to brave victims of a heartless nature, unscrupulous builders, and inefficient bureaucrats. For their part, Turks now have a clearer view of the world around them, which is not inherently hostile, but can even be sympathetic and supportive.

# Notes

## Chapter 1

1. Interview with Mehmet Ali Şahin, 1995.
2. Interview with Abdurrahman Dilipak, 1995.
3. Conversation with Professor Binnaz Toprak, May 12, 1997.
4. Interview with Dr. Turkan Saylan, May 14, 1997.
5. Conversations with Yasemin Pirinçcioğlu, spring 1995.

## Chapter 2

1. Conversations with Gülter Kolankaya, 1996, 1997.
2. Lord Kinross (Patrick Balfour), *Atatürk* (New York: William Morrow and Company, 1965), pp. 550–567.
3. Conversations with Zekiye Gülsen, June 1997.
4. Interview with Turgut Özal, November 1983.
5. Conversation with Feride Acar, June 23, 1987.
6. Conversation with Ayşen Ergin, June 26, 1998.
7. Conversation with İhsan Çetin, June 15, 1997.
8. Conversations with Cennet Köse, June 1997.
9. Şerif Mardin, "Projects on Methodology: Some Thoughts on Modern Turkish Social Science," *Rethinking Modernity and National Identity in Turkey* (Seattle and London: University of Washington Press, 1997), pp. 70–71.
10. Stephen Kinzer, "Atatürk the Icon," *New York Times*, October 3, 1997.
11. Necla Arat, "The Enlightenment and Women in Turkey," *Ataturk: From the Past to the Future* (İstanbul: ÇYDD, June 1996), pp. 28–36.
12. Emin Çölaşan, "What is Ataturk?" (İstanbul ÇYDD, June 1996), pp. 54–57.
13. "Persons of the Century," *Time,* January 12, 1998.
14. Conversations with Ahmet Taner Kışlalı, June 1997, April 1999.

## Chapter 3

1. Tutkun Akbaş, "Where is the Refah Party Going?" (İstanbul: Center for Inter-cultural Dialogue and Cooperation, July 1997), pp. 92–94.

2. Mehmet Ali Birand, *The General's Coup in Turkey* (London: Brassey' Defence Publishers, 1987), p. 169.

3. Richard L. Tapper, ed., *Islam in Modern Turkey* (New York: St. Martin's Press, 1994), pp. 10–11.

4. Akbaş, "Where is the Refah Party Going?" pp. 92–98.

5. Pınar İlkkaracan, *Women's Movement(s) in Turkey* (İstanbul: Women for Women's Human Rights, May 1996), p. 27.

6. Interview with Mayor Tayyip Erdoğan, 1995.

7. Interview with Abdullah Gül, May 21, 1996.

8. Fehmi Koru, "Democracy and Islam: The Turkish Experiment," *Muslim Politics Report*, Council on Foreign Relations (September/October 1996).

9. Alan Makovsky, "Erbakan's Turkey: An Early Assessment," rapporteur's summary, *The Washington Institute's Policy Forum*, Washington, D.C. (July 18, 1996).

10. Sabri Sayarı, "Turkey's Islamist Challenge," *Middle East Quarterly* (September 1996).


## Chapter 4

1. Bernard Lewis, *The Emergence of Modern Turkey* (London: Oxford University Press, 1961), pp. 398–419.

2. Nilüfer Narlı, "Moderate Against Radical Islamicism in Turkey," *Zeitschrift für Türkeistudien* (Essen, Germany: Essen University, January 1996), pp. 42–45.

3. James Wilde, unpublished interview with Fethullah Gülen for "Turkey on the Brink," *Time*, January 12, 1998.

4. "Miliatary Weeds Out Islamists," *Turkish Daily News*, June 17, 1998.

5. "The Fethullah Gülen Report," *Cumhuriyet*, June 8, 1999.

6. "Bugging Scandal Creates Rift at Police," *Turkish Daily News*, June 9, 1999.

7. "Religious Personnel Shortage Continues," Anatolia New Agency, *Turkish Daily News*, October 8, 1998.

8. Interview with Mehmet Nuri Yılmaz, May 27, 1996.

9. Interview with Professor Hayrettin Karaman, May 22, 1997.

10. Interview with Yaşar Nuri Öztürk, July 14, 1998.

11. Interview with Ekmeleddin İhsanoğlu, July 1, 1997.

12. Interview with Reha Çamuroğlu, May 9, 1997.

## Chapter 5

1. Metin Heper, "Islam and Democracy," *Middle East Journal* (Winter 1997), pp. 42–44.

2. Nilüfer Narlı, "Moderate Against Radical Islamicism in Turkey" *Zeitschrift für Türkeistudien* (Essen, Germany: Essen University, January 1996), pp. 42–45.

3. "Hizbullah Threat Grows," Turkish Daily News, November 11, 1997.

4. "Seminar Hears of Fight Against Terror," *Turkish Daily News*, July 1, 1998.

5. Ibid.

6. Narlı, "Moderate Against Radical Islamicism in Turkey."

7. "Kamikaze Attack Islamist-Style," *Turkish Probe*, November 8, 1998.

8. "Mezarçı," *Hürriyet*, June 15, 1997.

9. "Yılmaz," *Turkish Daily News*, May 31,1997.

10. "Çelik," *Yeni Yüzyıl*, May 9, 1997.

11. "RP Leader Rejects 'Radicalism' Charge," *Turkish Daily News*, November 20, 1997.

## Chapter 6

1. Everett C. Blake and Anna G. Edmonds, *Biblical Sites in Turkey* (İstanbul: Sev Matbaacılık ve Yayıncılık A.S., 1997), pp. 149–154.

2. Mark Rose and Özgen Acar, "Turkey's War on the Illicit Antiquities Trade," *Archaeology*, March/April 1995, pp. 45–56.

3. Özgen Acar and Melik Kaylan, "The Turkish Connection," *Connoisseur*, October 1990, pp. 130–137.

4. Özgen Acar and Melik Kaylan, "The Hoard of the Century," *Connoisseur*, July 1988, pp. 74–83.

5. Conversation with Özgen Acar, May 12, 1999.

6. Conversations with Toni Cross, 1995–1999.

7. Conversations with İlhan Temuzoy, 1996, 1997.

8. Freya Stark, *Turkey: A Sketch of Turkish History* (London: Thames and Hudson, 1971), pp. 47–48.

9. Conversation with Ahmet Ağa, 1983.

10. Interview with James B. Irwin, 1983.

11. Interview with Kenneth Sams, June 22, 1997.

12. Stark, *Turkey*, p. 169.

13. Interview with Kenan T. Erim, 1983.

14. George E. Bean, *Turkey's Southern Shore* (New York: Frederick A. Praeger, 1968), pp. 67–77.

15. Seton Lloyd, *Ancient Turkey: A Traveller's History of Anatolia* (London: British Museum Publications, 1989), pp. 94–109.

16. Bernard Lewis, *The Emergence of Modern Turkey* (London: Oxford University Press, 1961), p. 13.

17. Lloyd, *Ancient Turkey*, p. 231.

## Chapter 7

1. Mehmet Ali Kışlalı, Güneydoğu: Düşük Yoğunluklu Çatişma [Southeast—Low Intensity Conflict] (Ankara: Umit Yayinçilik, 1996).

2. Interview with Kadri Bilen, May 30, 1996.

3. Interview with Sara Ara, May 30, 1996.

4. Interview with Abdullah Akın, 1996.

5. Henri J. Barkey and Graham E. Fuller, *Turkey's Kurdish Question*, Carnegie Corporation of New York (Maryland: Rowman and Littlefield, 1998), p. 180.

## Chapter 8

1. Evliya Efendi, *Narrative of Travels in Europe, Asia and Africa*, translated by Ritter Joseph von Hammer (London: Printed for the Oriental Translation Fund of Great Britain and Ireland, 1834–1850).

2. Conversations with Mete Göktuğ, June 1998, April, May 1999.

3. Whitaker Almanack, 1981, London.

4. Interview with Susan Tarablus, May 21, 1997.

5. Ibid.

6. Greek Embassy sources, Ankara, April 22, 1999.

7. Conversation with Leyla Üstel, June 13, 1997.

8. Audience with Ecumenical Patriarch Bartholomew I, May 31, 1997.

9. Sources at the Ecumenical Patriarchate, May 31, 1997.

10. Interview with Ara Koçunyan, May 19, 1997.

11. Conversation with Andrew Hoard, June 14, 1998.

12. Conversation with Ken Erickson, June 19, 1998.

## Chapter 9

1. A. Yusuf Ali, *The Holy Koran*, translation and commentary (New York: Hafner Publishing Company, 1946), vol. 2, Sura 24, verse 31.

2. Interview with Aysel Ekşi, July 9, 1998.

3. Interview with Necla Arat, May 16, 1997.

4. Interview with Gültan Das, June 19, 1998.

5. Interview with Feride Acar, June 13, 1998.

6. Interview with Ayşen Ergin, June 26, 1998.

7. Conversation with Sinem Köymen, June 20, 1998.

8. Conversations with Aynur Demirel, July 6, 8, 1998.

9. Conversations with Hayrünnisa Gül, June 23, 24, 1998.

10. Conversations with Ayşe Yılmaz, June 23, 1998.

11. Conversations with Sema Özdemir, June 23, 24, 1998.

12. Interviews with İnci Mercan, June 16, 23, 24, 1998.

13. Interview with Selime Sancar, June 7, 1997.

14. Ibid., June 5, 1998.

15. Interview with Pınar İlkkaracan, June 4, 1998.

16. Pınar İlkkaracan, "Exploring the Context of Women's Sexuality in Eastern Turkey," *Reproductive Health Matters*, vol. 6, no. 12 (November 1998).

## Chapter 10

1. Interview with Şirin Tekeli, May 6, 1997.

2. Interview with Birgen Keleş, June 18, 1997.

3. Conversation with Gülter Kolankaya, April 17, 1997.

4. Tekeli.

5. Conversation with İlnur Çevik, May 20, 1996.

6. Interview with Feride Acar, June 23, 1997.

## Chapter 11

1. Interview with Halide Pek, May 24, 1997.

2. Interview with Fatih mayor Saadettin Tantan, June 30, 1997.

3. Bülent Tanör, "Democratization" (İstanbul: TÜSİAD, January 1997).

4. Conference on Media and Democracy, May 10, 1997.

5. Interview with Ayseli Göksoy, June 25, 1997.

6. Interview with Feride Acar, June 23, 1997.

7. Interview with Ayla Hatırlı, June 24, 1998.

8. Interview with Rıdvan Budak, June 25, 1997.

9. Interview with Gencay Gürün, June 28, 1997.

10. Interview with Yekta Güngör Özden, June 23, 1998.

## Chapter 12

1. Excerpts from the Constitution of the Republic of Turkey, *Violations of Free Expression in Turkey* (New York: Human Rights Watch, 1999), p. 111.

2. Kemal Kirişci and Gareth M. Winrow, *The Kurdish Question and Turkey* (London and Portland: Frank Cass, 1997), pp. ix–x.

3. Conversation with Gülter Kolankaya, June 21, 1997.

4. Interview with General Kemal Yavuz, July 10, 1998.

## Chapter 13

1. Samuel Huntington, "The Clash of Civilizations," *Foreign Affairs* (Summer 1993), pp. 22–49.

2. "National Security Council Declaration," *Turkish Daily News*, March 10, 1997.

3. İlnur Çevik, ". . . And Turkey Again Loses Bid to Host the Olympics," *Turkish Daily News*, March 8, 1997.

4. "Ecevit: Never Give Up the Objective of EU Membership," *Turkish Daily News*, December 20, 1997.

5. "Turkish Wrongs and Rights," *New York Times*, December 18, 1997.

6. Interview with Farouk Lolloğlu, June 21, 1998.

7. Interview with Cem Kozlu, June 2, 1997.

8. Interview with Hasan Subaşı, June 13, 1998.

9. Hugh Pope, "Crossroads City," *Wall Street Journal*, March 27, 1997.

10. Kozlu.

11. "Central Asian and Caucasus Petroleum and Natural Gas Pipelines," *The Arı Group* (İstanbul: 1998).

12. Interview with President Süleyman Demirel, May 23, 1996.

## Chapter 14

1. "The 7 Wonders of the Modern World," *Infrastructure Finance Magazine* (Summer 1993).

2. "Eight Modern Wonders Abuilding," *Time*, January 24, 1994.

3. Stephen Kinzer, "Restoring the Fertile Crescent to Its Former Glory," *New York Times*, May 29, 1997.

4. Interview with Servet Mutlu, June 18, 1998.

5. Interview with Mustafa Aydoğdu, June 30, 1998.

6. Interview with Ahmet Lami Çavusoğlu, June 30, 1998.

7. Interview with John Chalfant, May 23, 1997.

8. Catalog, Central Turkey College (Constantinople, 1901).

9. Interview with Dr. Barclay M. Shepard, July 2, 1998.

10. Alice Shepard Riggs, *Shepard of Aintab* (New York: Interchurch Press, 1931), pp. 183–198.

11. Interview with Sevim Türkân Öztahtacı, July 2, 1998.

12. Conversation with Nihal Tütüncüler and Emine Durak, July 1, 1998.

13. Interview with Mayor Celal Doğan, June 29, 1998.
14. Interview with Kurşat Göncü, June 29, 1998.
15. Interview with Emel Tavşancıl, July 2, 1998.
16. Interview with Ali Öztahtacı, July 3, 1998.
17. Interview with Aykut Tuzcu, June 29, 1998.

## Chapter 15

1. Anatolia News Agency, "NATO officials meet banned Islamist leader Erbakan," published in *Turkish Daily News*, February 26, 1998.
2. Interview with Mustafa Karahasanoğlu, July 14, 1998.
3. Interview with Abdullah Gül, June 11, 1998.
4. Conversations with Oya Akgönenç, June 10, 15, 1998.
5. Interview with Korkut Özal, June 10, 1998.
6. Interview with Ömer Bolat, July 9, 1998.
7. Interview with İbrahim Sölmaz, May 21, 1997.
8. Interview with Hikmet Uluğbay, June 16, 1998.
9. İlnur, Çevik, "The Establishment Continues to Hit Back," *Turkish Daily News*, September 24, 1998.
10. Anatolia News Agency, "Black Wreath presented to US Consulate in İstanbul," published in *Turkish Daily News*, October 1, 1998.
11. Interview with Mayor Melih Gokçek, June 25, 1998.

## Chapter 16

1. "Turkish Republic and Ottoman Empire to Be Reconciled Through Anniversaries," *Turkish Daily News*, January 9, 1998.
2. Stephen Kinzer, "A Novelist Sees Dishonor in an Honor from the State," *New York Times*, December 15, 1998.
3. Conversation with Alev Alatlı, April 30, 1999.
4. Interview with Cemal Kafadar, May 6, 1999.
5. Interview with Fikret Üçcan, deputy secretary of culture, May 14, 1999.
6. Interview with Arif Yılmaz, vice-secretary-general, Ankara City Hall, May 10, 1999.
7. Interview with Muhsine Akbaş, illuminator, May 12, 1999.
8. Interview with Ali Artun, director, Nev Gallery, Ankara, April 21, 1999.
9. Interview with Nilgün Mirze, spokesperson for the İstanbul Foundation for Culture and Arts, May 3, 1999.
10. Arda Aydoğan, general artistic director, Cemal Reşit Rey Concert Hall, 1998–1999 program.
11. Interview with Aydın Gün, artistic adviser, Yapı Kredi cultural program.

12. Interview with Emin Mahir Balcıoğlu, director of the Sakıp Sabancı Museum, May 7, 1999.

13. Interview with Prof. Hüsamettin Koçan, dean of the Faculty of Fine Arts at Marmara University, May 5, 1999.

14. Conversation with Nuran Terzıoğlu, head of the Apel Gallery, April 30, 1999.

15. Conversation with Yasemin Tanbay, April 27, 1999.

16. Interview with Dr. Işıl Akbaygil, founder of the İznik Foundation, April 29, 1999.

## Chapter 17

1. Interview with Abdullah Gül, May 12, 1999.

2. Interview with Oya Akgönenç, May 14, 1999.

3. Interview with Şevket Bülent Yahnici, May 13, 1999.

## Chapter 18

1. Nilüfer Narlı, "Islamist Movement, University Students and Politics in Turkey," unpublished report for The Ford Foundation (1995).

2. Nilüfer Narlı, "Women and Islam: Female Participation in the Islamicist Movement in Turkey," *Turkish Review of Middle East Studies* (1996–1997).

3. Nilüfer Narlı, "Moderate Against Radical Islamicism in Turkey," *Zeitschrift für Türkeistudien* (Essen: Essen University, January 1996), pp. 35–59.

4. Nilüfer Göle, "Engineers: 'Technocratic Democracy,'" in Metin Heper, Ayşe Öncü, Heinz Kramer, eds., *Turkey and the West* (London/New York: Tauris and Co., 1993).

5. Conversation with Nilüfer Göle, 1995.

6. Nilüfer Göle, "The Quest for the Islamic Self Within the Contest of Modernity," in Sibel Bozdoğan and Reşat Kasaba, eds., *Rethinking Modernity and National Identity in Turkey* (Seattle and London: University of Washington Press, 1997).

7. Interview with Ergün Yener, June 2, 1998.

8. Interview with Akın Birdal, June 19, 1997.

9. Interview with Nazmi Gür, June 22, 1998.

10. "Akın Birdal Tells TDN: 'I will continue on my path,'" *Turkish Daily News,* June 22, 1998.

11. Interview with Gürsel Demirok and members of the Secretariat of the Human Rights Supreme Coordination Council, April 22, 1999.

12. Mustafa Erdoğan, "A New Period for HADEP," *Turkish Probe,* November 8, 1998.

13. Interview with Doğu Ergil, June 18, 1997.

14. "Document of Mutual Understanding" (Ankara: Foundation for the Research of Societal Problems, March 1999).

15. Conversations with Ceylan Orhun, May 1997, June 1998, April 1999.

16. Conversation with Nur Mardin, April 30, 1999.

17. Interview with Aygül Fazlıoğlu, June 18, 1998.

18. Interview with Seçil Arslan, June 30, 1998.

19. Conversations with İlnur Çevik, June 16, 17, 1997.

20. İlnur Çevik, "They Have Finally Closed Refah, or Have They," *Turkish Daily News*, February 23, 1998.

21. İlnur Çevik, "Fundamental Defects at the Heart of Pessimism," *Turkish Daily News*, February 11, 1998.

22. Fehmi Koru, "Blindness," *Zaman*, June 19, 1997.

23. Fehmi Koru, "Public Speaks Loudly but Will the Politicians Listen?" *Turkish Daily News*, April 14–15, 1999.

24. Fehmi Koru, "The Day After: An Assessment," *Turkish Daily News*, April 20, 1999.

25. Conversation with Etyen Mahcupyan, May 29, 1997.

26. Interview with President Süleyman Demirel, May 23, 1996.

27. "Ecevit Claims an Artificial Crisis is Being Fabricated," *Turkish Daily News*, March 14, 1998.

28. Fatih Çekirge, "Ecevit's Strongly Worded Message," *Sabah*, March 13, 1998.

29. Sedat Ergin, "The New Government," *Hürriyet*, May 30, 1999.

**Chapter 19**

1. Conversation with İnci and Murat Mercan, April 23, 1999.

2. Conversation with Nur Mardin, April 29, 1999.

3. Interview with Binnaz Toprak, April 28, 1999.

4. Philip Taubman, "A Fateful Miscalculation in Turkey," *New York Times*, November 9, 1997.

5. "New Van Mayor Özaslaner: I Will Be Loyal to the Constitution and the Law," *Turkish Daily News*, April 28, 1999.

6. "The Fethullah Gülen file" *Star*, June 20, 1999.

7. "BCG Report Says Army Is Fethullahcis' Real Target," *Sabah*, June 23, 1999.

8. Necati Doğru, "Gülen" *Sabah*, June 23, 1999.

9. "Gülen: The Law Judges Deeds Not Intentions," *Zaman*, June 23, 1999.

10. "MGK Vows Enhanced Struggle Against Anti-Secularists," *Turkish Daily News*, June 24, 1999.

11. İlnur Çevik, "Do we Really Need an Elected Parliament?" *Turkish Daily News*, June 26, 1999.

12. Conversation with Sedat Ergin, April 18, 1999.

13. Bülent Ecevit, Ministry of Foreign Affairs, Information Department, February 17, 1999.

14. "Turkish Kurd Rebels Want Political Role," *Reuters*, August 9, 1999.

15. Fehmi Koru, "Do We Really Need State Security Courts?" *Turkish Daily News*, June 5, 1999.

16. "Bahçeli: Apo Should be Executed," *Star*, June 9, 1999.

17. Hasan Cemal, "Execution or No Execution," *Milliyet*, June 27, 1999.

18. Esra Erduran, "Öndül: We're Totally Against Capital Punishment," *Turkish Daily News*, July 27, 1999.

19. Şükrü Elekdağ, column, *Milliyet*, June 14, 1999.

20. Harun Kazaz, "US: The Öcalan Trial was Conducted in an Orderly Manner," *Turkish Daily News*, July 1, 1999.

21. Stephen Kinzer, "Nationalism Is Mood in Turkey's Kurdish Enclaves," *New York Times*, May 11, 1999.

22. "Turkey Violates Rights of Free Expression," Human Rights Watch, New York, April 15, 1999.

23. "Human Rights Situation in Turkey," Human Rights Association, January 5, 1999.

24. Jonathan Sugden, statement to the author, August 2, 1999.

25. "Recruits War Reminiscences Draw Censorship," Agence France Presse, July 15, 1999.

26. Yusuf Kanli and Esra Erduran, "Exclusive Interview with State Minister Ali İrtemçelik," *Turkish Daily News*, July 26, 1999.

27. Assistant Secretary for Democracy, Human Rights and Labor, Harold Koh, at a press conference at the U.S. Embassy in Ankara, August 5, 1999.

28. Ahmet Necdet Sezer, speech before Constitutional Court, April 26, 1999.

## Epilogue

1. Metin Munir, "Economy Expected to Rebound Substantially," *Economist* Group's Economic Intelligence Unit, September 1999.

2. Fehmi Koru, "Yalova: The Day After," *Turkish Daily News*, August 19, 1999.

3. Lee Hockstader, "Turkish Quake Has Political Aftershocks," *Washington Post*, August 27, 1999.

4. Yılmaz Ensaroğlu interview, *Turkish Daily News*, August 30, 1999.

5. Sedat Ergin, "Chief of the General Staff's Statement," *Hürriyet*, September 5, 1999.

6. İlnur Çevik, editorial, *Turkish Daily News*, September 6, 1999.

7. Sami Kohen, column, *Milliyet*, September 9, 1999.

8. Washington Kurdish Institute, online news service, September 3, 1999.

9. Chief Judge Sami Selcuk, speaking at the Court of Appeals, September 6, 1999.

10. Alan Makovsky, in a comment by e-mail, October 5, 1999.

11. Zülfü Livaneli, "The Prime Minister's Health," *Sabah*, September 29, 1999.

12. Yavuz Donat, "Ecevit's Doctor Speaks Up," *Sabah*, September 29, 1999.

13. Yavuz Donat, "The Friday Sermon," *Sabah*, October 13, 1999.

14. Joint Communiqué by Authors and Artists, *Turkish Daily News*, October 12, 1999.

15. Oktay Ekşi, "Light at the End of the Tunnel," *Hürriyet*, October 15, 1999.

16. "EU Path Thorny," *Radikal*, October 15, 1999.

17. "FP Delegation in Washington," *Turkish Daily News*, November 1, 1999.

18. George Papandreou, "Greece Wants Turkey to Make the Grade," *International Herald Tribune*, December 10, 1999.

19. "Turkey and Europe," *New York Times*, December 14, 1999.

20. "The Turkey Wind," *Hürriyet*, December 12, 1999.

21. Hasan Cemal, "Optimism," *Milliyet*, December 12, 1999.

22. "Turkey Will Pay Dearly," *Ortadoğu*, December 13, 1999.

23. İlnur Çevik, "We All Have to Learn to Live with Brussels," *Turkish Daily News*, December 13, 1999.

24. "Kıvrıkoğlu Discusses 'Armed Forces Matters' with Ecevit and Özkan," *Turkish Daily News*, December 25, 1999.

25. Lale Sariibraminoğlu, "Turkish Defense Industry Busy in January 2000," January 5, 2000.

26. İlnur Çevik, "Debate about the MGK is Too Premature," *Turkish Daily News*, December 15, 1999.

27. "Yılmaz: Road to EU Passes through Diyarbakır," *Turkish Daily News*, December 17, 1999.

28. Şükrü Elekdağ, "Interview with President Demirel," *Milliyet*, December 27, 1999.

29. "Öcalan Execution Put on Hold," Associated Press and other agencies, January 12, 2000.

30. İlnur Çevik, "Time to Identify and Eliminate the Radicals," *Turkish Daily News*, January 21, 2000.

31. "The First Task is Human Rights," *Milliyet*, January 2, 2000.

# Selected Bibliography

Abadan-Unat, Nermin. "The Modernization of Turkish Women." *Middle East Journal* 32 (1978): 291–306.

Ahmad, Feroz. *The Making of Modern Turkey.* New York: Routledge, 1993.

_____. *The Turkish Experiment in Democracy, 1950–1975.* Boulder: Westview Press, 1977.

Akbaş, Tutkun. "Where Is the Refah Party Going?" İstanbul: Center for Intercultural Dialogue and Cooperation (July 1997): 92–98.

Ali, Abdullah Yusuf. *The Holy Qur-an.* Cambridge, Mass.: Murray Printing Company, 1946.

Arat, Zehra F., ed. *Deconstructing Images of the Turkish Woman.* New York: Saint Martin's Press, 1998.

Barkey, Henri J. *Turkey's Kurdish Question.* Lanham, Md.: Rowman and Littlefield, 1997.

Bean, George E. *Aegean Turkey.* North Pomfret, Vt.: David and Charles, 1989.

_____. *Turkey's Southern Shore.* New York: Frederick A. Praeger, 1968.

Beck, Lois, and Nikki Keddie. *Women in the Muslim World.* Cambridge and London: Harvard University Press, 1978.

Berkes, Niyazi. *Development of Secularism in Turkey.* New York: Routledge, 1998.

Birand, Mehmet Ali. *The General's Coup in Turkey.* London: Brassey's Defence Publishers, 1987.

Borowiec, Andrew. *The Mediterranean Feud.* New York: Praeger, 1983.

Davison, Roderic H. *Turkey: A Short History.* Concord, Mass.: Paul and Company, 1998.

Eickelman, Dale F., and James Piscatori. *Muslim Politics.* Princeton: Princeton University Press, 1996.

Evliya Efendi. *Narrative of Travels in Europe, Asia and Africa.* Translated by Ritter Joseph von Hammer. London: Oriental Translation Fund of Great Britain and Ireland, 1834–1850.

Fuller, Graham E., and Ian O. Lesser. *Turkey's New Geopolitics from the Balkans to W. China.* Boulder: Westview Press, 1993.

Göle, Nilüfer. "Engineers: 'Technocratic Democracy.'" In *Turkey and the West,* ed. Metin Heper, Ayşe Öncü, and Heinz Kramer. London and New York: Tauris and Co., 1993.

_____. "The Quest for Islamic Self Within the Contest of Modernity." In *Rethinking Modernity and National Identity in Turkey,* ed. Sibel Bozdoğan and Reşat Kasaba. Seattle and London: University of Washington Press, 1997.

Hale, William. *Turkish Politics and the Military.* New York: Routledge, 1994.

Halman, Talat Sait, ed. *Contemporary Turkish Literature.* Rutherford, N.J.: Fairleigh Dickinson University Press, 1982.

Harris, George. *Turkey: Coping with Crisis.* Boulder: Westview Press, 1985.

Heper, Metin. "Islam and Democracy," *Middle East Journal* (Winter 1997).

Hunter, Shireen T. *Iran After Khomeini.* Center for Strategic and International Studies. New York: Praeger, 1992.

İlkkaracan, Pınar. *Women's Movement(s) in Turkey.* İstanbul: Women for Women's Human Rights (May 1996).

Kedourie, Sylvia. *Turkey Before & After Atatürk: Internal & External Affairs.* Portland, Oreg.: International Specialized Book Services, 1998.

Kedourie, Sylvia, ed. *Turkey: Identity, Democracy, Politics.* Portland, Oreg.: International Specialized Book Services, 1998.

Kinross, Lord (Patrick Balfour). *Atatürk: The Rebirth of a Nation.* London and New York: William Morrow and Company, 1965.

Kirişci, Kemal, and Gareth M. Winrow. *The Kurdish Question and Turkey.* London and Portland, Oreg.: Frank Cass, 1997.

Kışlalı, Mehmet Ali. *Güneydoğu: Düsük Yogunluklu Çatişma* (Southeast—Low Intensity Conflict). Ankara: Umit Yayinçilik, 1996.

Koru, Fehmi. "Democracy and Islam: The Turkish Experiment." *Muslim Politics Report.* New York: Council on Foreign Relations (September/October 1996).

Kuniholm, Bruce R. *United States & Turkey.* New York: Macmillan Library Reference, 1998.

Landau, Jacob M., ed. *Atatürk and the Modernization of Turkey.* Boulder: Westview Press, 1984.

_____. *Radical Politics in Modern Turkey.* Leiden: E. J. Brill, 1974.

Lapidus, Ira M. *A History of Islamic Societies.* Cambridge, Mass.: Cambridge University Press, 1988.

Lewis, Bernard. *The Emergence of Modern Turkey.* London: Oxford University Press, 1961.

Lloyd, Seton. *Ancient Turkey: A Traveler's History of Anatolia.* Berkeley: University of California Press, 1989.

Lybyer, Albert Howe. *The Travels of Evliya Effendi.* Journal of the American Oriental Society. New Haven: Yale University Press (September 1917).

Mackey, Sandra. *The Iranians.* New York: Penguin Books USA, 1996.

Mango, Andrew. *Turkey: The Challenge of a New Role.* Westport, Conn.: Greenwood, 1994.

_____. Atatürk: *The Founder of Modern Turkey,* London: John Murray, 1999.

Mardin, Şerif. "Projects as Methodology." In *Rethinking Modernity and National Identity in Turkey,* ed. by Sibel Bozdoğan and Reşat Kasaba. Seattle and London: University of Washington Press, 1997.

_____. "Religion in Modern Turkey." *International Social Science Journal* 29 (1977): 279–297.

Meiselas, Susan. *Kurdistan in the Shadow of History.* New York: Random House, 1997.

Metz, Helen Chapin, ed. *Turkey: A Country Study,* 5th ed. Area Handbook Series (Department of the Army). Washington, D.C.: Federal Research Division, Library of Congress, 1996.

Narlı, Nılüfer. "Islamist Movement, University Students and Politics in Turkey." Report for Ford Foundation. New York, 1995.

_____. "Moderate Against Radical Islamicism in Turkey." Zeitschrift für Türkeisstüdien. Essen, Germany: Essen University Press, January 1996.

_____. "Women and Islam: Female Participation in the Islamicist Movement in Turkey." *Turkish Review of Middle East Studies* (1996/1997).

Özdalga, Elisabeth. *The Veiling Issue, Official Secularism & Popular Islam in Modern Turkey.* Concord, Mass.: Paul and Company, 1998.

Palmer, Alan. *The Decline and Fall of the Ottoman Empire.* New York: M. Evans and Company, 1992.

Pamuk, Orhan. *The Black Book.* San Diego: Harvest Books, 1996.

_____. *The New Life.* New York: Farrar, Straus and Giroux, 1997.

Pope, Nicole, and Hugh Pope. *Turkey Unveiled.* London: John Murray, 1997.

Poulton, Hugh. *Top Hat, Grey Wolf and Crescent.* New York: New York University Press, 1997.

Randal, Jonathan C. *After Such Knowledge, What Forgiveness?* New York: Farrar, Straus and Giroux, 1997.

Renda, Günsel, and C. Max Kortepeter, eds. *The Transformation of Turkish Culture— The Atatürk Legacy.* Princeton: Kingston Press Inc., 1986.

Riggs, Alice Shepard. *Shepard of Aintab.* New York: Interchurch Press, 1931.

Rubinstein, Alvin Z., and Oles M. Smolansky. *Regional Power Rivalries in the New Eurasia.* Armonk, N.Y.: M. E. Sharpe, 1995.

Rustow, Dankwart A. *Turkey, America's Forgotten Ally.* New York: Council on Foreign Relations, 1987.

Sayarı, Sabri. "Turkey's Islamist Challenge." *Middle East Quarterly* 3, no. 3 (September 1996): 35–43.

Settle, Mary Lee. *Turkish Reflections*. New York: Simon and Schuster, 1991.

Stark, Freya, and Fulvio Roiter. *Gateways and Caravans*. New York: Macmillan, 1971.

Sumner-Boyd, Hilary, and John Freely. *Strolling Through İstanbul*. İstanbul: Redhouse Press, 1989.

Tachau, Frank. *The Politics of Authority, Democracy and Development*. New York: Praeger, 1984.

Tapper, Richard L., ed. *Islam in Modern Turkey: Religion, Politics and Literature in a Secular State*. New York: Saint Martin's Press, 1994.

Toprak, Binnaz. *Islam and Political Development in Turkey*. Leiden: E. J. Brill, 1981.

Zürcher, Erik J. *Modern Turkey*. United Kingdom: I. B. Tauris, 1995.

# Index